PRAISE FOR *OVER THE TOP AND BACK*

"This book is bound to be of great interest to pop music fans, especially those who remember Jones's glory days, when women threw their panties at this *über*male superstar. The honesty and openness with which Jones shares his life and career make it a must-read."
—*Library Journal*, starred review

"In attitude and anecdote, his engaging and illuminating book backs him up. . . . A remarkable memoir by a remarkable artist."
—*Kirkus Reviews*, starred review

"Tom Jones really has had the most astonishing life, one which he recounts here with verve, energy, and a vivid eye for detail—this is a hugely enjoyable read." —*Daily Mail* (UK)

"In Jones's new autobiography . . . the singer recounts some other excesses of his glory days, and of the leaner years and more modest venues that followed before his resurgence in recent decades. But the lasting image is that of Jones, now seventy-five, as a family man who has been married to the same woman . . . for fifty-eight years." —*USA Today*

"Packed with the kind of showbiz tales you don't get anymore . . . Jones is a charming, matey voice and the book is a terrific, star-studded journey through the world of entertainment. Even after meeting some of the greats, such as Elvis . . . and Sinatra, . . . Jones still retains an innocence and freshness that is rare." —*Daily Express* (UK)

"*Over the Top and Back* is a great read and funny. It charts his youth in the coal-mining town of Pontypridd. It captures his Welshness."
—*Sunday Telegraph* (UK)

"This lively, thoughtful, and entertaining account does justice to a remarkable life and career." —*Sunday Express* (UK)

"The book lays bare a career that has spanned sixty years, Tom revisits his past and tells tales from his journey from wartime Pontypridd to LA and beyond. He reveals the ups and downs of his remarkable life, from his early heyday to his subsequent fallow years to his later period of artistic renaissance." —*Wales on Sunday* (UK)

"A book that gets to Jones's core." —*The Daily Mirror* (UK)

Over the Top and Back

TOM JONES

THE AUTOBIOGRAPHY

BLUE RIDER PRESS   *New York*

blue
rider
press

An imprint of Penguin Random House LLC
375 Hudson Street
New York, New York 10014

Blue Rider Press hardcover edition: November 2015
Blue Rider Press paperback edition: November 2016
Blue Rider Press paperback ISBN: 978-0-399-57636-2

Printed in the United States of America
1   3   5   7   9   10   8   6   4   2

BOOK DESIGN BY MICHELLE McMILLIAN

*Penguin is committed to publishing works of quality and integrity.
In that spirit, we are proud to offer this book to our readers;
however, the story, the experiences, and the words
are the author's alone.*

CONTENTS

Over the Top and Back

In performance in 1974.

INTRODUCTION

Let's not begin at the beginning. Let's start somewhere near the bottom.

Early 1983, say. Early 1983 finds me sitting in a drab-colored dressing room in Framingham, Massachusetts, twenty-two miles west of Boston. Once this strip of Route 9 was pig farms and the occasional gas station. Now it's known as the Golden Mile—Marshalls' Mall, a Holiday Inn, a Howard Johnson's, a procession of neon signs along the roadside. "Framingham's little touch of Vegas," they call it.

And here I am on this Golden Mile, which isn't particularly golden, if we're being honest, nor actually a mile. Here I am backstage at the Chateau de Ville Dinner Theater, Framingham's premier "function room," home to weddings and sales conference parties and the annual Natick High prom—and tonight, home to Tom Jones, international singing superstar and globe-girdling sex symbol, who must remember not to go too far downstage in this venue or the spotlight at the back of the room won't be able to reach him through the ornamental chandelier.

Here I am in the eighties in the dressing room of a drive-up dinner theater in the American suburbs. Bright lights round the mirror. Stage clothes in zippered covers hanging from a rail. Sandwiches and fruit under plastic wrap on a Formica table. Vase of flowers trying to make up for the lack of windows.

Two shows per night, to a predominantly white, middle-aged crowd, seated at tables, eating chicken or premium-plate surf-and-turf. Seven thirty until 8:30; shower and change; then 10:00 to 11:00, plus encores. Thank you. Thank you so much. Good night. And afterward a car back to Boston, moving fast to get there before the good restaurants shut. And then a meal and some drinks—quite a lot of drinks—and eventually a hotel bed.

I'm here again tomorrow.

After which the caravan will move on to more of the same. One hundred and thirty-four nights like these in 1983 alone: the Circle Star Theater, San Carlos, California; the Holiday Star Theater, Merrillville, Indiana; Pine Knob Music Theater, Clarkston, Michigan. Tom Jones: Live in Concert. Singing the songs that made him famous: "It's Not Unusual," "What's New Pussycat?," "Green, Green Grass of Home," "Delilah," "She's a Lady." Stringing them together in a show-closing medley, because that's what you do in the dinner theaters. Also doing Kool and the Gang's "Ladies Night"; maybe "Don't Cry for Me Argentina"— bringing it up to date, or thereabouts.

It's 1983, and I haven't had a hit for twelve years. Twelve years! Not just singers but entire musical movements have come and gone in that time: prog rock, glam rock, disco, punk rock, post-punk, new romanticism . . . The earth has shifted under popular music at least six times without noticeably impacting upon me or even causing me to break step or slightly change direction.

Who's selling records, as a singer, in 1983? Who do you have to be? Luther Vandross? Lionel Richie? I'm neither of these people. I'm Tom Jones.

Not that anybody in the audience in Framingham will seem to mind. They love me here. I'll only have to walk on, and the place will go up. And then I'll sing, and it will really go up. And, yes, no doubt there will be some underpants. Because that's become a ritual. Not peeled off and flung there and then, as in the beginning. But most likely brought in specially and lobbed into my hands or laid on the stage at my feet in tribute, because . . . well, because that's what you do at a Tom Jones show, isn't it? Same thing every night. And I'm not complaining, either. Paid to sing. Paid to make singing my life. Paid handsomely for it, too. And brought underpants, albeit now in a kind of low-key, heritage way, with an eye on the upholding of a time-honored tradition. There are far worse jobs. Proper jobs. I know because I've done some of them. There is no hardship here. Trust me, the meal after the Framingham show will be a good one. We will dine high, back in Boston: brandy, cigars, champagne. And then maybe on to a nightclub for more of the same. Don't cry for me Argentina, is right. Don't cry for me, anybody at all.

At the same time, though, here I am in the dressing-room mirror. Spangled bolero jacket. Slashed white shirt. Substantial silver neckchain. Dark slacks fitting snug to the waist. Belt buckle the size of a manhole cover. Cuban heels. "Framingham's little touch of Vegas."

Twelve years without a hit. This wasn't exactly the plan. Assuming there was a plan. Which, coming to think of it, there wasn't.

But does anyone really plan these things? You can't, can you? You can only do your best to scramble aboard a plane that's taking off and then see what happens. And in 1983 the path of my flight looks roughly like this: in the beginning, blasted almost vertically into fame's skies, higher than I even dared to imagine; but since then, cruising. Worse than that: cruising and gradually losing height—but slowly, gently, over the course of more than a decade, so that you don't notice how close the ground has got until one day (say, in a dressing room, between shows, in a dinner theater in suburban Massachusetts) you turn your head and look down.

Two questions, then, in the Chateau de Ville Dinner Theater, Framingham, Massachusetts, in 1983. And two questions for this book.

Firstly, how did I get here?

And secondly, now that I'm here, how do I get out?

The Ed Sullivan Show, *1965*.

I Had No Idea

New York City, 1965. I am on the set of *The Ed Sullivan Show*, standing alone on a white wooden cube under hot studio lights, waiting for my cue. It's eight o'clock on a Sunday night in the golden age of pop and the dying days of black-and-white television. I am twenty-four years old and I am about to break America inside two minutes.

I seem to have no nerves—unless you count an eagerness to get going, to get *at* it, a buzz of anticipation. But there's no fear. Self-doubt doesn't really apply at this point. Singing, as my twenty-four-year-old self knows it—as my childhood self seemed always to know it—is something that happens when I open my mouth and let it go. Singing I know I can do. Hasn't everybody around me always said so? There is no other position in life in which I am so absolutely and unshakably sure of myself.

And here's Ed Sullivan, off to the side. "Now, ladies and gentlemen, we kick off the show with . . ." There's a huge pause here. Or it feels huge to me—seems to creep on forever. What's he doing? Has he forgotten? No. He's just ramping up the anticipation. ". . . Tom Jones!"

Then there's applause and, above it, a burst of screaming. The band kicks in, and the camera sweeps in with it. Sweeps in on me: dark suit, jacket carefully buttoned, trousers tight and straight-legged. White shirt with massive collar. Chelsea boots from Anello & Davide, just like the Beatles. Hair long at the back, by the standards of the day, and therefore just a little dangerous. A topping of lightly lacquered curls. Big sideburns.

The set is a small landscape of white boxes of various sizes. As I sing, I must follow a course, carefully charted beforehand by the director, stepping down from one box and up onto another—which raises the possibility of putting a foot wrong and, in front of a couple of hundred people in the studio and 15 million Americans watching at home, going down in a pile of splintered plywood. But those are the risks, and I am young and burning with ambition and more than willing to take them.

Also I know these boxes and these moves pretty well by now. I have been put through no less than a week of rehearsals—run-through after run-through in a vast downtown warehouse, a space so big that, during breaks, me and the members of a band called Ruby and the Romantics, who are also on the show, fall to chucking about this new plastic thing called a Frisbee. Before I leave, I will find a store that sells Frisbees and take one home to Wales for Mark, my eight-year-old son.

The stuff about Elvis Presley on *The Ed Sullivan Show* in the fifties— shot from above the hips at the host's insistence, according to the legend, to prevent the lower parts of his anatomy inflaming America beyond repair—is just so much myth. Sullivan let America see all of Elvis, just as he will, in turn, let America see all of Tom Jones. Still, these are without question formal and anxious times in the world of broadcast entertainment, and only a few months previous to this Sullivan had fallen out with Mick Jagger from the notorious British beat combo the Rolling Stones over his refusal to wear a jacket. I, meanwhile, have been formally warned during rehearsals, by a producer with a clipboard, to keep my hips in check or face immediate and irrevocable censorship. It's Sunday, is the stern message. This is a family show, and pop music is a potentially corruptive sexual force, the limits of whose dark effects we don't yet entirely understand. So, easy on the grinding.

And I'm not here to buck the system. I'm not here to ruin America—or not much, no more than America is willing to be ruined. I restrict myself to some big right-handed finger clicks, some swinging arms and a small selection of handclaps at various heights. I obediently fight back the instincts of a performing lifetime and omit to grind.

The song I sing is the one that has catapulted me to stardom in Britain and Europe and spun my life around. It's the song that has brought me out here to America—put me on a plane for only the second time in my life, seen me collected from the airport in a big black town car, driven to the Gorham Hotel and installed, along with a vast basket of fruit, in one of a pair of ridiculously luxurious suites on the top floor. The other suite, I get a kick out of being told, is assigned to Sammy Davis Jr.

It's the song that has carried me to New York, where I will lie in bed with the windows thrown open so that I can hear the distinctive honking of the taxis in the streets way below, a soundtrack familiar to me from the movies and now made real.

And it's the song that will now duly make me a star in America, with the help of the Ed Sullivan house band, pulsing away at its snagging beat—"bom be-dom, bom be-dom, bom de-dom . . ."—a song I have known since it was just a couple of chords, an idea for a title and a hummed melody line, my manager, Gordon Mills, prodding at it on the piano in his flat in Notting Hill Gate in London.

"It's not unusual hmm hmm hmmm . . ."

A song I had to plead with Gordon Mills to let me have because I knew the moment I heard it that it was the one—the right song, the song with the power to change everything about my life, the song that was going to take me where I wanted to be.

It's the song I recorded as long ago as November 1964, only to have to wait agonizingly while the record company held back its release to the following year, not wanting to risk losing it in the Christmas rush.

Leaving me to go home to a row house in south Wales for Christmas with my wife and our son and my mother and father, none of whose Christmases, on account of the song, would ever be quite the same again.

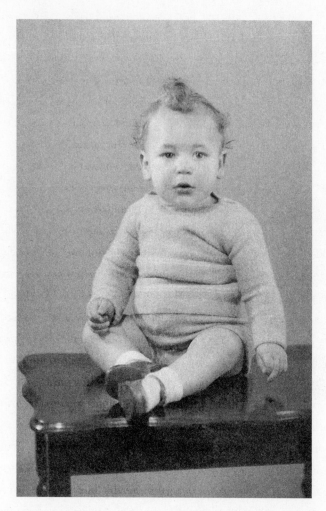

Infant Tom.

The Front Room

My grandmother could neither read nor write, but she knew what to do with dead bodies. When there was a death in Treforest, someone would go to fetch Mrs. Jones. She knew how to lay out the dead—dress the corpse, bind the jaw with a bandage so that it wouldn't hang open, place the pennies on the eyes. These skills she handed on to my mother.

My grandmother knew what to do with newborns, too, which is lucky for me. When I was born, they thought I was dead. I didn't move and I didn't cry. But my gran took me from the midwife, plunged me in a tub of cold water and then shook me. With that, I moved and cried and got started.

This was June 1940, in the front room of my grandmother's row house at 57 Kingsland Terrace. Nobody round our way seemed to go to hospital to have a baby. It happened at home. The women of the family gathered; the men of the family disappeared. My gran at this time was sharing her small, narrow house with my mother and father—Freda and Tom Woodward—and my six-year-old sister Sheila, as well as my Uncle Albert, who was blind. Not long after I arrived, we four Woodwards moved to a rented row house of our own up the hill in Laura Street, a mile or so closer to the adjacent town of Pontypridd. There, in turn, we would briefly, while I was very young, find room to lodge another family, the Wildings, whose mother would, in turn, give birth in our front room. That was the way of things in the community I grew up in. It was understood that you might, every now and again, be required to squeeze up a bit.

They named me Thomas John, after my father, and called me Tommy. Tommy Woodward: as a kid I can remember having a feeling that there was something unusual about that. In Wales, people had names like Jenkins or Griffiths or (like my mother) Jones. Woodward, not so much. What's more, my nana, my father's widowed mother, Annie, had an accent that wasn't like anyone else's, with this strange, soft burr in it. "Come along and have thy vittals," she would tell me, when I visited her. By which she appeared to mean, "Sit down and eat your tea."

I said to my father, "Why does Nana speak like that?"

He said, "Because she's not from here. She's from Box."

"She's from a box?"

"Box. It's a village in Wiltshire."

My father's father, James Woodward, was an ironmonger's hauler from Gloucester who brought his family west to south Wales for work, which there was no shortage of at that time. His business was loading a horse and cart with dynamite and taking it to the coal mines around Pontypridd, where they called him Jimmy the Powder. He died before I could know him, but the stories lived on, most of them connected with prodigious drinking. It was said that Jimmy the Powder could fall backward into his cart at the end of a hard night, and the horse would see him safely home. One night he rode out to the Three Horseshoes pub in Tonteg for a quiet evening with his wife. Some guy wound him up during the course of the evening, so they decided to settle it with a cart race— whipped the horses three miles back to Pontypridd, standing up at the reins, while the wives clung on in terror.

So my father had English parents—but you wouldn't want to argue with him about his Welshness.

"I'm a Welshman."

"But your mam and dad were English."

"I was born here. I'm a Welshman."

End of debate.

What's also not open to dispute is that sometime in his early twenties my father started seeing a girl called Florrie Jenkins. He can't have been that interested, though, because he wasn't showing up for dates. Florrie Jenkins took her friend, Freda Jones, into her confidence about this Tom Woodward and his manners, and Freda Jones volunteered to go in on her behalf and sort him out.

"Hey, you're not showing up for Florrie Jenkins."

Tom Woodward duly informed Freda Jones that she could mind her own business, and Freda Jones, in turn, duly informed Tom Woodward that as far as she was concerned it *was* her own business, and then they had a flaming row about it and ended up stepping out together. And soon after that, in 1934, they got wed and conceived my sister, Sheila—although not strictly in that order. Hard now to reckon with the level of social shame that came down on my father for getting a girl pregnant out of wedlock. A girl five years younger than him, too—eighteen, at the time, to my father's twenty-three. Women turned their backs on him in the street. A couple of people even spat at him. His place in the community was only restored when he married her and made her "honest."

My father was a coal miner, and, as such, he didn't have a lot of time for postmen. My mother used to say, "Poor old postman. Look at the weather," and my father would say, "Postman? If he wants to get out of the rain, tell him to come and work with me."

He was employed from the age of fourteen at the Cwm Colliery in Beddau, a three-mile walk out of Treforest in heavy boots, my mother getting him up and out in the early mornings, giving him an extra nudge on Mondays when the weekend's drink was still in his system. He spent his days burrowing into deep, cramped tunnels where the mice would have your lunch away if you didn't keep it snapped tight in a tin; clawing the coal out and pushing it back in seams so tight that when one side of the pick grew blunt, you would have to clamber back out completely in order to have enough room to turn the tool around so that you could use the sharper side. There was a bar in a pub in Pontypridd, a tiny room down a couple of steps, which was known jokingly as "the two-foot-nine" in reference to the width of the smallest tunnel that a miner could work in.

Yet my father never seemed to want to get away or push himself forward—never applied for promotion to a lighter job at the surface or sought anything more comfortable. He was a bright man, and capable. But there was something nervous in him, too. A large part of him wanted to keep his world small and contained, where he could cope with it. And mining did at least spare him from going off to fight in the Second World War. Miners were exempt from the call-up because the coal supply needed to be maintained. So my father did his National Service at the coal face, and I think he thought he was lucky.

As far as the war was concerned, we were certainly lucky in our location. Cardiff was hit hard by German bombing raids and Swansea was blitzed—the German planes heading west across the mainland, cheered on all the way by the English, as the Welsh liked to imagine. But the mining village of Treforest and the adjacent industrial center of Pontypridd, which had expanded outward until it all but connected with it, escaped almost entirely unscathed. To the extent that the area was struck at all, it was with stray incendiary devices, which could be nasty, but were better than the kind of high explosive bombs that would quite happily put your bedroom in your basement without bothering to ask you first. Consequently the first five years of my life took place during a violent global conflict, but, beyond the occasional droning of planes and the appearance around the town of American soldiers, billeted in the barracks of the Fifth Welsh regiment on the Broadway, I was mostly oblivious to it—which is probably the best state to be in, when it comes to violent global conflicts.

So my earliest childhood memory is a relatively peaceful one: me, in the kitchen with my sister, just before my father is due back from his shift, with my mother hurrying to get the tea ready, and talking to us, but distractedly, while looking out of the back window, watching for my father with his dust-blackened face to come through the gate, because if he comes into the kitchen and the cloth isn't on the table . . . well, that's a failure of duty on an epic scale, as far as my mother is concerned. Later on she tells me what her mother always advised her: "Get the cloth on the table. Even if the food isn't ready, make it look as though it is."

Another piece of domestic wisdom passed down by my gran to my mum—and later handed by my gran to my sister, too, to her surprise, on the eve of her wedding: "You should never refuse your husband. But you can always try to make sure you're out of bed before he wakes up."

My mother was a housewife. She held a part-time job very briefly in a factory at the Treforest Trading Estate. This was when I was in school. She had pleaded with my father, who very reluctantly agreed to it. But one Saturday night we were queuing as a family to get into the pictures, and a man in the line—someone from the factory whom my father didn't know—called out, "Hello, Freda." The tone was no more than casually friendly, but it sent my father into a spin. It was the familiarity that got to him: not "Mrs. Woodward," but "Freda." My mum's adventures in the world of work ended shortly after.

So she went back to doing everything around the house—including papering the walls and painting the woodwork. My father, by contrast, didn't do anything at all at home, nor did he seem to be expected to. He'd simply sit in his dark-green armchair and say, "Oh, well, Freed—nice cup of tea, then?"

"Yes, Tom."

And she'd be there.

My parents were good-looking people—the best-looking couple in any company, or so it seemed to me—and they liked to be well turned-out. My mother would put on dresses that showed off her small waist and would wear lots of carefully applied makeup and teased hair—a Welsh Lana Turner. My father would wear a pin-striped suit—inspired by George Raft in the Hollywood gangster movies of the thirties and forties which were his abiding passion. My parents went most Saturdays to one of Pontypridd's four picture houses and brought my sister and me along with them as soon as we were old enough. My father would see George Raft in these handsome suits and he would try to dress like that, inasmuch as he could afford to. Whether George Raft ever burned a hole in the inside pocket of his jacket with an inefficiently extinguished cigarette, as my father did, I don't know. Whether George Raft was in the habit of quickly putting out and hiding freshly lit cigarettes in order to increase his chances of being given another cigarette by someone who had just walked into the room (the sharp practice which caused my father to end up singeing his pocket), I equally don't know. But Raft was the role model. And I, in turn, longed for a while to dress like my father, because I liked the way he looked—smart and strong—and I liked the way people looked at him, not least the women in doorways as he passed. "All right there, Mr. Woodward?" He was getting a reaction, and I noticed it.

My father also had strong feelings about shoes, exclusively favoring brown brogues for many years and frowning on crepe soles, which grew to be the rage in the fifties, and which he, in common with a high percentage of his generation, seemed to find morally dubious. "I don't want to be creeping around the place," he used to say. "I want people to hear me coming." To this end, he had his soles fitted with nailed-on metal caps, which announced him with a decisive click on the pavement. He was a mostly quiet man, formal and reserved, until beer made him jovial and talkative and brought his stories out. But he liked to hear himself walk.

My father soon added a trilby hat to his look, or sometimes a flat cap, to hide his quickly thinning hair. Self-conscious about that baldness, he would continue to wear a hat while sitting indoors. At the end of one Saturday night at the pictures, when everybody stood for the playing of the National Anthem, someone had a go at my father for not removing his hat, and the pair of them squared up and almost came to blows about it.

Movies were the family's biggest window onto another world. There was no television—just the radio, offering news and *Dick Barton: Special Agent*. There were newspapers in the house—the *News of the World* on Sunday—but there were no books. My mother read but did not write. My father could read, and apparently did well in school, but neither of my parents were what you'd call readers. The only books in the house were my schoolbooks. The general feeling was that reading turned you in on yourself and was anti-social—unlike smoking. Father would send me running out to get cigarettes for him—which was often a complicated errand involving a trip round several different shops, tobacco remaining in short supply well after the war ended. In the absence of cigarettes, my father would smoke tea from a clay pipe. When I was a baby in a high chair, his pipe was given to me to play with, and I whacked it on the table and snapped off the stem. Undeterred, my father simply stuffed the bowl with tea leaves regardless and sucked away at the pipe's stunted remains— creating a comically desperate image of himself which my mother teased him with for years afterward.

My mother was openly affectionate with my sister and me, and my father wasn't, which was absolutely the standard way of things in the families I knew. There were few people less touchy or feely than a Welsh coal miner in the forties. Fellas in south Wales didn't grab one another— unless they were going to hit each other, in which case they felt free to grab what they liked. Even when I got hold of him later in life, to give him a hug, my father would tend to be awkward and stiff about it. It wasn't done. Shaking hands was as far as it went, and you'd do that once, when you first met the person, and then never again. That was one of a number of culture shocks I experienced when I went to London in 1964.

Peter Sullivan, who was the producer on some of my earliest records, would shake my hand every time I walked into the studio.

I said to Gordon Mills, who was my manager at the time: "Why's he keep shaking my hand? I've already met him."

Gordon said, "That's what people do."

Not where I came from.

PONTYPRIDD IN THE FORTIES: industrial, smoky, frequently wet. Row houses ascending hillsides. Coal stacks and slag heaps. Gas lamps at the ends of streets, lit at evening-fall by a red-faced man on foot in a camel-colored overall. Babies carried "Welsh-style" in a shawl. Thoroughfares sprinkled with dropped coal. Discomfort put up with. The water in the River Taff runs black with coal dust. The mud on its banks is dark and greasy. You don't go near it. Legends abound that rats the size of cats, or worse, dwell in those inky depths. The water is too dark for anyone to prove otherwise.

Heavy industry. The Taff Vale Iron Works. Crawshay's Steel and Tin Works. Brown & Lenox, the chain and anchor foundry, whose giant link chains formed the backdrop for that famous photograph of Isambard Kingdom Brunel, the great British engineer, before the launch of the SS *Great Eastern* in 1857. Brown & Lenox also made the anchor chain for the *Titanic*, which didn't get quite as much use as they must have been hoping.

The Maritime Colliery. More than a dozen deep-mine collieries in the area and numerous trial shafts cut without fuss into the surrounding hillsides. A coke oven in the town, smoking away. The slaughterhouse down by the railway track, connected by a tunnel to the station so that the animals can be herded straight in off the trains. Horses and carts. Rationed food. Local characters: Ned Grono, the chimney sweep; Dut Hobbs, who sits just inside the door of the Wheatsheaf pub at the bottom of Rickards Street and who, for a small fee, will dock the tail of your dog with his bare teeth. (For a party trick, and if there are a few coins in it, he'll do the same to a rat.)

We are a little more than ten miles north of Cardiff, the Welsh capital, but fiercely independent of it and willfully self-contained. "You can't get anything in Cardiff that you can't get in Ponty," is the local mantra, which we say until we believe it. The truth is, in these days, you can't get much in either of those places. Everything mined in the Rhondda Valley passes out through here, making it the mouth of the valley, or the other end, depending how you want to see it. A tough, work-hardened place where there always seems to be a metallic tang in the air. This is where I spend the first twenty-four years of my life.

Our house in Laura Street: back and front parlors on the ground floor; two small bedrooms and a box room upstairs; kitchen in the basement, giving on to a small yard with a back gate out to the alley. A bunker in the kitchen filled with free coal—the miner's perk—dropped down directly via a hatch from the street. A tin bathtub on the back door to be taken down and filled on the floor of the tiny scullery beside the kitchen, where my father washes himself nightly in two stages: top half while kneeling beside the tub, and then bottom half by climbing in. Wednesday is wash day—done by hand on the scrubbing board and in that bathtub and hung out in the yard, or draped around the house if it's raining, which it often seems to be. Coming home from school, that washing waving outside the house will work like a warning flag for my sister and me, signaling the likelihood that Mum will be in a dark mood and may need to be tiptoed around.

Everything in the house kept obsessively, oppressively neat by my mother.

One day, when I am still small and wrapped Welsh-style to my mother's chest, a gypsy comes to the door, selling clothes-pegs. My mother says you never refuse a gypsy because it's bad luck. So, as she takes the pegs, the gypsy looks down on the top of my head and notices that I have a pronounced crown. Using her skill and judgment, she tells my mother, "This child will travel all over the world," and my mother believes her.

For now, though, I am going no further than our neighborhood. Across the road from us lies the old quarry from which the stone for our houses had been cut. It's now an in-fill site, and trucks come and go on the far side of it with gray industrial waste from somewhere or other. What is it? We don't ask. All we know, as kids, is that if you get there soon enough after the truck has tipped its load, the ground will be powder-soft—like a fresh dump of snow, except warm and gray. Periodically, as you slide and jump and dust-up your clothes, you might uncover pieces of glass test tube. The unbroken ones are treasures which we take home and hoard.

Mostly, though, we play in the road—the boys of Laura Street: me, Dai Perry, Alan Wilding, Brian Pitman, Brian Blackler, Jimmy Herbert. There's no traffic to keep out of the way of because nobody owns a car. We play "Best Falling" to see who can drop to the ground in the most gruesome and/or realistic manner—who can die the best death. We kick footballs against walls. We pull down washing lines and steal milk. We fight kids from the Graig, the row houses down by the railway—and win. The Christmas that everyone gets roller skates, Dai Perry and I work out that if you skate downhill while straddling a broken broom handle, the stick can do service as a rudder and a prod and, if you're lucky, a brake, all in one. And off you go, the bottom of the stick scraping and thwacking on the ground behind you, out of Laura Street, on to the Wood Road, downhill all the way, gathering to a proper lick, past the Wood Road Non-Political Club, where the adults go, down past Marney's post office and general store, down past the Infants School and the Treforest Hotel, bottoming out now, left at the Cecil Cinema and on to the Broadway, which leads you eventually into Pontypridd and where Dai one day has to take sudden evasive action against an oncoming bus and slams himself dizzy against the window of a greengrocer's shop. Now, that's a ride. You won't see many people roller-skating back up.

Like my mother, my father is the youngest of six, so, between the Woodwards and the Joneses, my family is not short of numbers. Round the corner in Tower Street, Auntie Lena and Uncle Albert alone have seven children. Uncles, aunts, cousins—the place throngs with them, and nearly all of them are within walking or shouting distance at any moment. If I come home from school and my mother is out shopping and my father is at work, I can always go somewhere else. The positive consequence of this is that, as a child, I rarely, if ever, feel alone. I feel secure, not just in my own house, but in the neighborhood. There are allies about the place—always somewhere to go, someone to see, somebody to help you out. So if I mess up my shoes and clothes playing football on the way back from Sunday School, I can go over to my grandmother's house and get sorted out before my mother sees and clips me round the ear for it.

Because her legs are bad, my gran cooks sitting down in her basement kitchen, on a chair between the table and the coal-fired oven, swiveling from the one to the other. She defies the rations, conjures batches of rock cakes out of next to nothing. "How many eggs do you think are in there? One! One egg is in there!"

Her custard tastes like nobody else's. I tell my mother about it. My mother says, "It's because she can't whip the mixture up properly, sitting down like that. It sticks and burns." I don't care. I like the burned taste.

Gran takes snuff from the little tin box that's always with her. The ritual has its own closely observed etiquette: the pinch of snuff on the wrist, the gentle, rather refined sniffing and then (the final flourish) the concluding light swipe at the nose and at the wrist with her handkerchief—although Gran can't say "handkerchief," so we all refer to it as her "hanchercuff."

In the parlor, above the wind-up gramophone belonging to my blind uncle, which must not be touched, my grandfather, Albert, continues to look down from inside a frame—a handsome fella in a company sergeant major's uniform with a long neck, a swizzle stick under his arm and a waxed handlebar mustache. Because my gran can't read, when the telegram came telling her that her husband had died in a trench in France in the First World War, a neighbor had to read it to her. Albert was the son of the landlord of the Treforest Arms, which was known as "the Cot" because it was more like a cottage than a pub. My gran would be sent there by her mother to fetch beer, and Albert, who hadn't yet enlisted with the Royal Engineers in Cardiff, would serve her and try to engage her in conversation. But she was shy and kept her head bowed and never looked up. One day a girlfriend of hers said, "I wish he would ask *me* questions. Have you seen him?" So the next time she went there, my gran found the courage to look up, and that was that. She talks about him so much that I think I will be able to find him. She says she can "feel" him in the house, and I come to think that if I stare at him long enough on the wall I will be able to summon him up.

I say to my mother, in fits of pique or when she has stopped me doing what I want to do: "Why aren't you more like Gran? She's so lovely to us."

To which my mother replies, "You didn't know her when she was younger."

I'm coddled by my gran and doted on by my mother and I'm diligently overseen by my sister, Sheila, who is a mild and placid little girl but fiercely protective of me while I'm a baby. When she comes home from school one day to find that Pauline Rogers, the girl from next door, has wheeled me up the road in the pram to quieten me down, she chases straight out and takes me back because wheeling me up the road in the pram to quieten me down is Sheila's job. Later we will squabble seemingly interminably, as siblings who are going to be close forever often do.

"Mam! Sheila hit me with the broom!"

Mum: "Well, you must have deserved it."

I go to Sunday School because Mrs. Rogers from next door is the teacher, so it's hard not to. We aren't, though, a strongly religious household. My father was born into a Baptist family but he doesn't practice as a Baptist. He says he doesn't believe in it, but when he was dying, he was praying. My mother told me that. So maybe he believed in it more than he realized.

My mother is Presbyterian and, on that account, we attend Presbyterian chapel, in a routine, dutiful way, in our best clothes, which I never seem to mind putting on, as some kids do. However, at heart, my mother feels herself to be a spiritualist first and foremost. She believes she can sense things. When she was a little girl she woke up one night to find a man in a sailor's uniform sitting silently at the bottom of her bed. She discussed this with her mother, and they both became convinced that she had seen the apparition of her uncle, who was a sailor who died at sea.

My mum attends spiritualist meetings for a while, with her sister, Lena. But they both get frightened away. The medium keeps asking my mum to be the messenger and to go and inform someone in the town that a dead relative is coming through from the other side, or that some terrible fate awaits them. I don't know why the medium doesn't pass on these messages herself—or send them through, even. Less work this way, I suppose. Anyway, it puts my mother off, and her spiritualism becomes a mostly private matter again.

The one place members of my family attend devoutly is the Wood Road Non-Political Club, known simply as "the Wood Road," just down the hill from our house. It's a plain, two-story working men's social club, used mostly by miners, with a bar downstairs, a singing room above and a lounge to one side for "the ladies," who are only allowed in on certain nights and are never allowed in the bar. Like anywhere that working men go to fill up on drink, the place can get boisterous and, indeed, when I'm a young man, a friend is goaded into a fight and he accidentally kills a man in the street. The word is, the punch wasn't thrown to kill; it was thrown to teach the fella a lesson. But the fella bangs his head when he hits the ground and is done for. This story does the rounds while I am young, and it haunts me—leaves me worrying about the place where a fight can end up.

Men on both sides of the family, the Joneses and the Woodwards, gather at the Wood Road, drawn by the special cachet the place has as somewhere you can get a drink on a Sunday, when the pubs of Pontypridd are closed, in observance of the Lord's day. So, on a Sunday morning, Uncle Edwin, my father's brother, will call at the house with two of my older cousins, Kenny and Alan, to take my father (who, as likely as not, is still hungover from Saturday) to the Wood Road, and I will look longingly at the sight of them all, suited and booted, setting off together. This dressing up and going off to drink seems like the mark of maturity to me—what it means to be a man, in fact—and I long to be old enough to go with them.

Meanwhile, though, there are the occasional Saturday nights when members of the family spill out of the club and come back to Laura Street for an impromptu party. Alcohol is never kept in the house, but beer will be brought back from the club, and my mother will cut sandwiches, and our rooms will fill with relatives in various shades of pissed. Then someone will sit down at the piano in the parlor (which neither my parents nor me or my sister could play, but which turned into something more than just a prestige ornament on these nights), and the singing will start.

The one time my father gets openly emotional is when he sings. It takes a drink to get him up, but once he's there, the emotion will pour out—to the point where it might actually bring the performance to an early halt. He does "Besame Mucho," the Mexican bolero, and, above all, the sentimental ballad "A Beggar in Love." If he can make it all the way through that, you'll be surprised. He'll reach a certain distance, and it will get to him, and his eyes will fill up, and his throat will go, and he'll have to stop and sit down.

My mother is more flamboyant. She loves to get up. She can carry a tune but she is more about the flair than anything else, and will move around when she sings. Her big song is Eve Young's "Silver Dollar," and she'll be giving it all the actions, the hips and hands.

Then there's my sister, who has a very nice voice but will have to be coaxed. And then there's me, who never requires any coaxing at all.

Getting up and singing seems to come easily to me. It's not something I have to work on or think about. Put up to it by my Uncle George—who's known as Snowy on account of his white hair and has a fine, rich voice himself and a different attitude to the prevailing one about children not being seen or heard—I might stand on a chair in front of the company and do a song from the radio like "That Lucky Old Sun," or "Ol' Man River" from *Show Boat*, or cowboy songs like "Mule Train" and "Riders in the Sky," the galloping-horse rhythm of which my father has shown me how to slap out on a table with my fingers and the flat of my hand. I work out pretty quickly that I like the getting up in front of people—and equally quickly that I like the fuss that gets made of me afterward.

By the age of eight I have seen Larry Parks play Al Jolson in the movie *The Jolson Story* and been struck deep down by the glamour of it, the showbiz, the effect a singer can work on an audience, if he plays it right. It has sown some seeds, as will its sequel, *Jolson Sings Again*, where Jolson gets a ramp built out into the theater to bring him closer to his audience. It has inspired a game where I climb up on the kitchen windowsill, draw the curtains across myself and then jump out as if onto a stage. Sometimes I will persuade my mother to introduce me: "Ladies and gentlemen—Tommy Woodward." Then I'll swish the curtains apart and drop to the floor.

Those films have put some thoughts in my mind. Then again, I've also seen John Wayne and Montgomery Clift in the greatest Western of them all, Howard Hawks's *Red River*. Internationally fêted professional singer or slate-faced cowboy? From the kitchen of 44 Laura Street in Pontypridd in the forties, the odds on becoming one appear to be about as long as the odds on becoming the other.

Tom, school photo.

3

Uneager to Please

I attend the Wood Road Infants School and then the Wood Road Junior School and beyond that the Pontypridd Central Secondary Modern on Stow Hill. It's fair to say that, in terms of academic achievement, I end up setting none of those institutions alight. On the other hand, praise where it's due: I end up setting none of those institutions alight—and not everyone can say that about the school they went to.

At the Wood Road Junior School, Miss Jones has been on the staff long enough to have taught my father. She looks at a piece of my work and says, "Your father would be disgusted." Apparently my father was neat and diligent about his schoolwork, and Miss Jones doesn't mind me knowing about it.

I don't mean to disappoint Miss Jones: I just find the things she is asking me to do very hard. So many of the lessons seem to involve copying things down off the blackboard. And the act of copying, which other pupils around me tear through, is a monumental effort for me. My eyes travel from the blackboard to the page in front of me, where I set down the word, or frequently just the single letter, that I have managed to commit to memory. But then when my eyes go back to the blackboard for the next bit, they are lost. The board has become a soup of letters through which I will have to swim to find my place again. "Just copy this down," the teacher says. But there is no "just" about this, as far as I'm concerned. It is agony.

This is the forties, and nobody is using the word "dyslexia." Instead, people are using the word "slow." And once you have been "slow" for long enough, you are "backward."

I'm so embarrassed by the struggle—embarrassed and baffled. I feel stung by it, sitting at the desk, hot and irritated and, at some level, worried. I know it's a fault in me and I don't like it. Avoidance feels like a better option: don't bother with the copying. Look out the window instead. Tell the teacher, "I don't want to" or "I don't feel like it"— become a bit stroppy, a bit defiant. Or make mischief of some kind: flick some paper around, distract the others.

I learn to read, though. It doesn't come easily, but I get there, and it's thanks to Roy Rogers, really. I'm in the newspaper kiosk one day, looking through a comic book. I'm about six years old and I'm using the pictures to figure out what's going on. But there are speech bubbles with the pictures, and they have started to nag at me. It occurs to me that the world would be a more interesting place if I knew what Roy Rogers was saying. So reading I decide to stick at until it doesn't feel difficult anymore.

School dinner is quite all right, usually a meat and veg followed by treacle pudding. I give it about a week before I plead with my mother to be allowed to go home for lunch, and she agrees to let me. It's not the food so much as the ritual—the queuing, the sitting bunched up at the long tables, eating to command. Plus, it stands to reason that if you go home, you're at school for less time in total, which can only be good.

One day I don't go in at all. I set off in the morning but carry on walking and head instead to the barracks of the Fifth Battalion of the Welsh Regiment, on the Broadway between Treforest and Pontypridd. The war is over, but the barracks are still home to a platoon of American GIs, awaiting demobilization, whom we see around the streets at the week-ends and to whom we are drawn as if by magnets. They have cool accents, like in the movies. Also sweets and gum. Also buttons and badges and chevrons from their uniforms, which they dish out to me and which I insist that my mother sew on my old jacket, to the point eventually where I become the most militarily decorated five-year-old in south Wales. It doesn't seem to bother the GIs that I'm knocking about on a school day, and it doesn't seem to bother me, either, so I do it the next day, too, and the one after that. "Mitching," we used to call it—playing tru-ant. Eventually a teacher calls on my mother to ask why I'm not in school. On my return home, I am dressed down and stripped of my rank—or at least warned not to try anything like that again.

To nobody's particular surprise, I fail my eleven plus. Then again, if you pass, you end up at County School, which is not where I want to go. If there's one thing we know about boys from the County School it's that they can't go out to play in the evenings because they have to stay in and do homework. They are therefore clearly the deprived prisoners of a cruel regime organized by vindictive teachers and parents, and worthy only of our pity.

No homework for me. I am off playing in the evenings, mucking about with the other Secondary Modern kids in the streets round our way, flirting with the girls from the Catholic school, who, unlike the Protestant girls, wear earrings—little gold crucifixes—and are therefore exotic. There's one I've noticed who's blond and very pretty. Her name is Melinda Trenchard, and she seems a little shy and she lives in Cliff Ter-race, the unpaved street down the hill. Sometimes I go out of my way just to walk down there—see if she is outside her house with her friends, playing marbles on the pavement, so I can glide by and maybe catch her eye. Often I'll have a friend with me, for cover—Dai Perry, maybe, or Brian Blackler, whose parents own a radiogramophone and whose older brother, Cliffy, does an Al Jolson impression. Cliff Terrace is also where Phyllis Williams lives, who's pretty, too, and has a following. But she's not the one I'm interested in. The one I'm interested in is Melinda. I seem to know this with great clarity—not least when a game of kiss-chase breaks out, and we're both in it, and I chase her round behind the black shed at the end of Cliff Terrace and snatch a kiss and run away.

Sometimes I might see her in the distance with her friends around the cinemas where all the kids go on Saturday mornings for Gene Autry and Flash Gordon, sneaking in when we can. One afternoon, just for a change, me and Georgie Hobbs from Tower Street go over to the movie house in Hopkinstown, across the river on the other side of Pontypridd, and sneak in through the fire exit. Then the lights go down and the film starts: *The Beast with Five Fingers*, with Peter Lorre as a librarian in a mansion, haunted by the severed hand of a pianist. This is our comeuppance. It is the first horror movie either of us has ever seen and it scares the living nine-year-old wits out of us. Afterward we run, propelled by terror, back over the bridge, all the way through Pontypridd and up the streets to our houses.

The next day at school, still feeling the fear, I am sent to the corner for not working and, as I stand there with my face to the wall, all I can hear is piano notes—repeated piano notes, going up and down the keyboard. I am badly spooked. Is this film to haunt me forevermore? No. Only until the piano tuner, at work in the hall next door, finishes and goes home.

At secondary school, I like Art and discover that I can draw a bit. I enjoy History, so I get on okay there. We do Welsh as a second language, which I never get to grips with—and in later life will wish I had. But, again, things are being written on blackboards, so that's my cue to start looking out of the window.

One day in Religious Instruction the teacher hands out an exam paper. There's a space under the questions for your answers. I don't even bother trying. I devote myself instead to drawing lines through the questions, one after the other. Thick, strong, black lines. Sitting next to me, Brian Blackler sees what I'm doing and does the same.

The following morning we are hauled up, amid disbelief, for this act of wretched contempt. "TWO BOYS have not answered the questions! TWO BOYS have spoiled their exam papers!" We are named, shamed and sent to the headmaster's office, where we each receive six across the arse with a cane. The headmaster has a selection of canes of various widths hanging from a hat rack in his study and seems to take pleasure in asking you to make your choice. I will get to try out most of the range during my time, never ultimately settling on a favorite. Frankly, though, I prefer this to writing out lines, which is the other popular punishment. Caning is, literally, a pain in the arse. But lines are murder. At this stage in my life, I would rather be hit with a cane than have to write.

There are some Grade A hard cases knocking around in the upper years, hunting in packs for amusement, and any of the younger boys are easy pickings. The bullies' big number—their showpiece—is to select a victim at random, carry him to the school wall on the edge of the playground and throw him over it. The street below being considerably lower than the playground, it is a surprisingly long drop—as I discover one day, descending through the air to land in a heap on the pavement.

One day, in the wrong place at the wrong time, I am escorted to a corner, where one of them spits thickly on the wall and instructs me to lick it off. I won't do it, so there is a struggle, with some of them pushing my face toward the splattered bricks, and me kicking back until eventually it devolves into a fight, which was the point of the provocation in the first place. And then I just have to throw my punches blindly and cling on until the teachers come to break it up.

I learn to look after myself, because it feels like you'd be better off doing so, all in all. I do a bit of sparring at the Treforest Boys Club on a Thursday night—learn how to throw a punch, ensure I can handle myself if I have to. And one day I have to, with one of the kids that have started being bussed into the school from Taff's Well, a couple of miles away, and with whom there's some inevitable conflict because they're not from round here. One of these kids has been put up to have a go at me while we're playing football, in order to provoke something, and the provocation works, and we set to it in the street, a suitable distance from the school gate, with an audience comprising a set of my friends and a set of his friends. And I win, by which I suppose I mean that he stops fighting before I do. And then, with my fists badly scuffed up, I go home in triumph—and burst into tears in front of my mother. Which is not conduct you necessarily associate with the world's great hard cases, although I could be wrong. The point is, though, that I hate it. I don't like myself, that I could do something like that: hit someone in the face and carry on hitting them there until they lie still. And it's pretty obvious to me at that point that fighting, though it may be something I'm going to have to do from time to time, is not going to be something I'm cut out for on any major scale. Too upsetting. Too big a deal.

So this is secondary school—and, likely as not, my days are set to run on like this, in an ordinary enough fashion, with me not learning much, reporting to the headmaster's study for the odd beating, landing in the odd scrap and regretting it, getting thrown over the odd wall and surviving. But then, suddenly, it all stops.

At the age of twelve I fall ill and have to go to bed. For two years.

With Mam and Dad and a caravan at the seaside.

4

Pastimes of Youth

I started being tired—tired all the time, completely without energy. More tired than a twelve-year-old ought to be. It was proving hard to shift me from my bed in the morning—but that's true of a lot of people. Still true of me, actually. This was different. I was drained—listless in the evenings, concerned to sit around and do as little as possible. I also seemed to have a cough the whole time.

My mother said, "We'd better get you looked at."

We went on the bus to Cardiff Royal Infirmary, which ought to have been an anxious journey, and must have been for my mother, who clearly sensed where all this was most likely heading. But for me it meant a bus trip and a day out of school, so it wasn't all bad. We got off the bus at Glossop Road and walked to the infirmary, an imposing, towered Victorian building with something of the look of a prison about it, to my child's eyes, an intimidating place with dark, gleaming corridors, down which I was ferried into a room that smelled of disinfectant. I had to take off my shirt, which I didn't much want to do, and press myself against a cold metal plate while everyone else left the room momentarily and the clanking X-ray machine did its business.

I don't remember whether we were told then and there, at the hospital, or whether we had to wait for the results to come through. Either way, the X-ray showed a small dark patch on the left lung.

Tuberculosis.

When I try to remember the impact that this diagnosis had on me, my memories aren't really of fear or worry. Partly this was because it was made very clear to me very quickly that the disease had been identified early, so my chances of recovery were always good. Also I was twelve years old. In the main, if you're lucky, it's not an age where you are much given to dwelling on things or seeing as far as the worst. Certainly I wasn't always tactful when I passed on the news to others.

"Guess what, Gran—I've got TB!"

She practically passed out.

My mother took it very badly, though. Aside from the worry, she couldn't understand how this had come about. Was I not properly taken care of? I was fed; I always had shoes on my feet; I was always wrapped up. It bothered her because she felt it reflected on her in some way—called her care of me into question and revealed her to be a bad mother. Which wasn't true. It was just bad luck—literally something in the air. Wales at that time had the highest rate of TB infection in the UK. It clustered around industrial towns. One of my cousins, Marie, died of it at twenty-one. Her sister, Valerie, spent almost two years in a sanatorium near Penarth and recovered. My future father-in-law was to die from it in his forties. It was around. And now it was around me.

Again, though, my anxieties were offset when I heard what the treatment would involve. There was medicine: injections of an antibiotic called streptomycin. That didn't sound great. But then there was bed rest and quarantine. And bed rest and quarantine meant, over and above anything else, no school. No school! As far as I was concerned, at that point in my life, that was fate doing me a favor.

The doctors wanted to send me away, though: somewhere where the air was fresher than in industrial south Wales, and somewhere that would minimize the chance of me infecting anyone else. This was the standard procedure, and a convalescent hospital in rural Wales or possibly in Scotland seemed to be the options. But my mother wouldn't countenance this—even though it would have reduced the risk to the rest of the family. She thought that I would pine and that I wouldn't get well, and I think she was right. I had never once left home for even a night. The furthest I had ever traveled at that point was twenty miles due south on the steam train to Barry Island, for family days out in the summer— various combinations of Woodwards or Joneses sitting resolutely in their clothes on the beach, or entirely taking over one of the shelters on the promenade and brewing up tea there while the rain lashed down, before getting back on the evening train and going home again. The idea of now leaving Pontypridd and everything I knew and going to live among fellow TB sufferers in the Highlands for an indefinite length of time seemed about as plausible to me as boarding a rocket bound for the moon.

Somehow my mother persuaded the authorities against it. She pleaded with them to come and look at our house. It wasn't as though we lived right by a coal mine and spent our days choking on dust. We were on the street at the top of the hill and you could see out through our back windows to the common and the mountain beyond. Two inspectors pitched up one day and walked round a bit while my mother flapped around them. And they decided that I could serve out my period of confinement in my own room, in my own home.

Some changes had to be made, though. At first when we moved into Laura Street, I shared one of the two bedrooms with my sister. But when we got older, I was moved into the box room next to it, which was just big enough for a single bed. That wouldn't work for a long confinement and nowhere on the top floor would be convenient for my mother because it would give her two flights of stairs to climb from the kitchen in the basement. So my bed was moved down into the back parlor, one of the two rooms on the middle of the three floors, and that's where I saw out my period of convalescence, with the window permanently open so there was fresh air coming in.

For nine months I didn't get dressed. I wore nothing but flannel pajamas and a dressing gown and was at home only to the doctor, who called weekly for my check-up. There was something quite aristocratic about it, I suppose—something quite lordly. I had an empty bottle on the floor beside the bed which was my equivalent of a servant's bell. I only had to lean down and thump the thick base of it on the carpet and my mother would be upstairs running. Even after I was better, she said she was still hearing that bottle banging on the floor.

The doctor told her I was to be spared all distress, and my mother took this instruction extremely seriously, arriving with food and drink on command. It wasn't that long after the war, so things were still scarce, but we got a supplementary allowance on the ration on account of my illness. So, yes, I had an infectious and potentially crippling or even deadly disease of the lungs, but, at the same time, we were eligible for extra eggs. Positives and negatives.

As for school, it turned out that I wasn't completely off the hook. I had to have a tutor, sent in by the local authority. Her name was Mrs. Warren. She was a slight, middle-aged woman in glasses with a pleasant face and a gentle manner and she came in for three hours every afternoon. She was firm and would have me read something and write about it the following day, which would bother me. But she saw that I struggled with writing so she also gave me lots to read and imparted knowledge without always insisting that I write things up afterward.

In the absence of Mrs. Warren, I lay on the bed or sat on the floor and drew. Cowboys, airplanes, battle scenes, explosions—images absorbed from movies and comic books. My cousin Idris was going with a girl who worked in a pencil factory, and he kept me supplied.

I had a large brown electric-powered radio, which I tuned to the BBC and to Radio Luxembourg, which had *The Adventures of Dan Dare*, pilot of the future, and Pete Murray playing the Top 20. This would have been the first time I heard Mahalia Jackson sing, and Louis Armstrong, lying in bed in the evening. Big Bill Broonzy, too—things filtering in and getting stored away for later. This would also have been the first time I really started listening to music properly—not just hearing it, but attending to it, absorbing it. There was plenty of time for that.

What's more, after a few months, I had a television—an amazing acquisition. In 1953, televisions were still new: fewer than one in ten households had one, and fewer than that in poorer areas. In fact, ours was the first one in our street—and it was situated in my bedroom. This was luxury like you couldn't believe. Where did the money come from? I'm guessing Uncle Snowy. Snowy was a bookie's runner, which it didn't do to talk too loudly about, because gambling was illegal. It meant that there were times when Snowy was flush, and there were times when he wasn't. And this must have been one of the times when Snowy was flush—flush and ready to do something for young laid-up Tommy.

They had television sets to buy outright in Stone's electrical shop in Pontypridd, but they were too expensive, so my father rented one from Balls Radio Shop, which later became a branch of Rediffusion. The screen, made of thick, curved glass, can't have been much more than a foot tall, but it was set into its own brown floor-standing cabinet, forming a substantial lump of furniture that would have done you some serious damage if you had ever been under it when it fell over. Engineers came to put an aerial on the roof and fed the cable in through the open bedroom window, and I was away.

To be honest, there wasn't a lot on—just the one BBC channel, operating in bursts: children's hour with Andy Pandy at lunchtime, which was too young for me, though I watched it anyway, because it was there; Patrick Troughton as Robin Hood later on, which was much more like it. Now visiting relatives had to make a judgment call: was it worth the risk of catching TB off Tommy if you got to watch the telly? More of them than you would think weighed this one up and came down on the side of watching the telly. I noticed that Cousin Idris's knocked-off pencil deliveries started coinciding with the times when sports were on.

What stays in my mind from that early television watching is one Saturday night, a variety show, and Frankie Vaughan appeared—this handsome guy, with his big voice. Seeing someone sing rather than simply hearing them sing was a big thing. Frankie Vaughan was an Al Jolson–style performer then—straw hat tilted to one side, a cane, gloves. But he still had a rawness I hadn't seen in movies. This wasn't Fred Astaire. He had some punch. In those pre-rock'n'roll days, Frankie Vaughan made a big impact on me. And the whole idea of a variety show, all sorts of people coming on a stage and doing their bit—that was new to me, and enthralling, too.

No school, a bigger bedroom, my mother at my beck and call, a telly—being confined with TB was just a long string of untold delights. Until it wasn't. Inevitably, within weeks of my solitary existence beginning, the novelty had largely evaporated and given way to feelings of isolation, frustration and raking boredom—a cabin fever set to last for months. When the tiredness left me, which seemed to happen relatively quickly, I was simply restless and desperate for distraction. I'd get glimpses of the life going on without me. Kids from school would come into the back lane and wave up to the window. Terrible to be disconnected from them, to be the boy who couldn't come out. They might be carrying rolled towels under their arms, because they were on their way to the swimming baths, or else they were heading off to fool about on the common or up in the hills, and the desire to go with them was so strong. Sometimes Melinda Trenchard was among them and sometimes she smiled up at me, and I liked that, though it frustrated the hell out of me, too. Forcefully separated from her, my crush on this girl that I barely knew only deepened, became a constant ache. I couldn't put a number on the hours of my confinement that I spent thinking about Melinda. I used to wonder what she might be doing, worry that she would take up with some other boy and that I was up there missing my chance. All the agony of those early yearnings was compounded by the fact that I was locked away from her, unable to do anything about it.

And then, in the second year of being bedridden, puberty arrived, which didn't make things any easier. To all the other varieties of frustration was added sexual frustration. I was starting to notice things developing in that area and wondering what that was all about—because nobody really talked about this stuff back then or warned you what to expect. And I was shut away in any case. The first time I took the situation in hand, I wasn't ready for the consequences. I thought I'd broken something. I resolved, there and then, never to touch it again. Or certainly not until the following day.

The days succeeded each other in an unchanging, monotonous pattern. I was, at least, getting better. After about nine months, the doctor decided I wasn't infectious anymore, but I still had to rest up. Eventually, I was allowed to get out of bed and be around the house for a certain number of hours each day. Then I could go and stand at the front door and look up the street. This was when I discovered the sensation of standing in an open doorway when the rain is coming down outside. I still like that sensation, and it dates all the way from then. I would look across to the lamppost up the street, where the kids my age would gather. This was almost more agonizing than waving to them from the window, though at least I had the sense that I was mending and would soon be able to join them. I have the strongest image from this time, still sharp in my mind, of Melinda Trenchard walking by in a pair of blue three-quarter-length pants, turning briefly and smiling across the street at me. I couldn't wait to get well so that I could pursue her.

Finally the doctor came and said I was free to go out into the world again, as long as I took it easy. I celebrated by running to my grandmother's house. Big mistake. I crossed her threshold in agony. I thought I was dying. Every part of my body ached. She lay me on the couch and massaged me. There was no strength left in the muscles at all. I hadn't grown much in this period, except outward. I was short and slightly plump and my brown hair was now black. I would spend the next year losing weight, growing taller and reacquiring muscles.

IN THE EARLY DAYS of my convalescence, I was sent on errands to Marney's general store on Wood Road—a tiny place, no more than the front room of a house. And if I timed it right, I could bump into Melinda, running errands for her mother. Marney's was halfway between our two houses. And when we met there, we could talk. It was the beginning of getting to know her.

She was half a year younger than me—thirteen to my fourteen at this point—and yet contained and self-possessed in a way that was powerfully attractive to me. She was in the A-stream at the County Modern Secondary school—a cut above me academically, clearly, and maybe she was a cut above me socially, too. Her house was no different to ours: in fact, it wasn't as well positioned, being lower down the hill and on a gravelly strip of unmade road. The difference was, we, like most people, rented our house, whereas the Trenchards owned theirs.

Bill Trenchard's family owned a group of cinemas in Ponty, and if needed he filled in for the projectionist in the County Cinema down on the Broadway. My father could remember the place when it was still a music hall, the Royal Clarence Theatre, the first of its kind in the Welsh coalfields, and members of the Trenchard family would stand out on the pavement, trying to bark up an audience. Now it was one of three cinemas that the Trenchards owned, making them a pretty big family in the area, with some money behind them. Melinda's Uncle Charlie always seemed to have a tan when you saw him around the swimming baths, and a certain swagger. But when Bill first met Violet she was a cinema usherette—moreover, an usherette from a broken home: with the father nowhere around, Vi's mother had gone to America, leaving Vi to be raised by her grandmother, whom she knew as her mother. Bill's choice of partner didn't seem to meet with the family's approval. They thought he was marrying beneath himself. After the wedding, Bill and Vi moved in with Vi's mother and were, if not shunned by the rest of the family, then at least quietly left to one side to get on with it.

Vi now worked in a café in the center of Pontypridd. Bill was a quiet, private man who didn't drink and he wasn't mixing with the same people as my father. I'm sure there were people, similarly, who eventually thought I shouldn't have been mixing with his daughter—that I was a bit rough for her, a bit uncouth. And Bill definitely came to be one of them. I think that was the impression some of Melinda's friends had, too— Anita Thomas, Jean Batten, Jean Jones, fellow A-stream students who wore their blond hair in the same bob-cut Doris Day style as she did and chose the same pencil skirts.

Still, in Marney's, on those first meetings, Melinda and I talked about school and movies and TB and the fact that her father had a radiogram and some records. It wasn't surprising to us that people in our families knew one another: her grandmother, who smoked a clay pipe, used to bump into my grandmother around the Treforest Arms, back in the day. We talked about radio shows and television shows and the fact I had a television in my bedroom while I was ill. We talked about anything we could think of that would keep us talking to each other. Once we talked so long that my mother got tired of waiting for whatever she had sent me out for and came after me, down to the shop, to haul me out. That same time, Melinda ran home to find that the water on the stove that she had been left in charge of had boiled away and the bottom of the pan had burned. We seemed pretty quickly to be occupying each other to the exclusion of all else. And I realized that I hadn't simply dreamed up what I had felt while I was shut away in my room for all that time, and that I hadn't missed my chance, either, and that we were going to be together.

Formally marking the end of my TB period, the television set was removed from my bedroom and installed downstairs in the kitchen. A maneuver beset with anxiety and stress, this involved my father creating a hole in the kitchen window frame through which to thread the cable from the outside aerial. Lacking a drill, he punched it through with a poker. Even then the cable wouldn't fit through on account of the connecting plug at the end of it. My Uncle Edwin was summoned to disconnect the plug.

"Are you sure you can put it back together?" my mother asked.

"We'll deal with that when we get to it," said Uncle Edwin.

In an operation which involved a kitchen knife and seemed to owe as much to guesswork as to electrical know-how, my uncle successfully detached and reattached the plug, and the telly had a new home—albeit that when my father went to switch it on for the first time and test it, my mother took the precaution of going upstairs to stand by the front door.

Did TB change me? Did I come out different? Being separated from your peers and playing with no other child for eighteen months is bound to stay with you in some way. It's going to produce something in you—a strong independence, maybe, a degree of introversion. I've read people who've said this period was where I learned the single-mindedness and the focused determination that I needed to go out and do what I later did. I may even have said that kind of thing about it myself, in interviews, because it certainly sounds okay and it's more polite than saying nothing. One can pour analysis onto these things, make shapes out of them afterward, and the shapes might be right or the shapes might be wrong. For the most part, I'm just trying to tell you what happened.

But one thing I think I can honestly say about the effect of those days of isolation is that I felt singled out by it—and not in that sense of "Why me?," which would have been one way that I could have gone with it. On the contrary, this episode allowed me, in some measure and for at least some of the time, to feel special. I knew that people were asking, "How's Tommy?" I knew that people were thinking about me, and I liked that.

I went back to the Central Secondary Modern at fourteen, for the one remaining year of my formal education, and was placed in the C stream. All credit to Mrs. Warren, my tutor. Below the C stream there was a D stream.

Early days with Dai Perry.

5

Raise a Ruckus

I leave school in the summer of 1955, at fifteen, without fanfare. Also without qualifications. Also without a single backward glance. I'm glad that it's over. I feel released.

But released into what?

Spared the mines (thank you, TB), I go to the Youth Employment Office in Pontypridd, where, in a dusty cubicle, I announce to a tired, gray public servant in a tired, gray suit my passionate and lifelong ambition to work with leather—an ambition no less passionate or lifelong for having been conceived pretty much there and then, in that dusty cubicle, on the spot. (It is true, at least, that I have always liked leather jackets.)

This declaration seems to throw a switch behind the eyes of the tired, gray public servant, and when he sets off to a nearby iron filing cabinet he does so with the energy of a man empowered to make dreams come true. Moments later, I am being issued with a card and dispatched to Polya Glove in Treforest, where I am to find the employment I have so desperately longed for these past fifteen years as an apprentice glove cutter. In the pursuit of this trade, I will work five days a week, from eight in the morning until six in the evening, as well as a shift on Saturday morning, efforts which will reward me financially to the princely tune of £2 per week, before tax.

My place of occupation is a featureless, single-story building divided into two workshops: the glove-cutters' room, with about twenty men working in it, and the sewing room, staffed by thirty women. Here, on the strictly male side of this labor divide, as one of a team of three school-leaving apprentices united by the glove-making dream, I will learn to stretch leather—to dampen down the freshly unrolled cowhide with a wet rag and then pull it by hand across a big desk until it is optimally thin. I will discover how to use the giant guillotine. I will also learn how to wield a wooden ruler and a large set of shears, to calculate the number of pairs of glove linings a length of velvet will yield and, eventually, to cut the required shapes of those linings ready for sewing.

All of this seems okay to my fifteen-year-old mind. I am indoors, where it is warm, rather than outside in the rain. Leather is a pleasant thing to work with, to handle and to smell. So is velvet. I am acquiring a trade. But I chafe at the slowness of it.

I am bored stupid.

Across the road from the factory is a Ford garage. When they have too many cars on site, they use the field behind the glove factory as an overspill parking lot. Lunch breaks on fine days will find me out the back, cupping my hand against the glass and stooping to peer longingly through the windows of Consuls and Zephyrs, climbing into them if the doors are unlocked, getting behind the wheel and dreaming.

But at least I am earning. And there's good news in this respect, early on, one Saturday morning, when, with orders backing up, the foreman takes me aside and offers me the chance of a one-off extra Sunday shift—double time. "Keep it to yourself," the foreman says. "I can't offer this work to everyone."

The next morning, I cycle in through the quiet Sunday streets, hang my coat in the cloakroom, enter the empty workshop. I'm the only apprentice there. In fact, I'm the only worker there, apart from the fore-man. Still, we set to work—him pulling the material tight down the desk-top and holding it there, me dropping the guillotine onto it—and we chat a bit, a little awkwardly, senior-to-junior. After a while, he says, "You're not using the guillotine right."

So far as I'm aware, I've been using it the way I was taught.

"No. Let me show you."

So he comes and stands behind me and places his hands on mine, in position on the handle of the guillotine. And then he leans his body into me and leaves it there.

I freeze. A very long and still moment passes. My first naive thought is that the foreman must have brought me here to kill me. When his grip doesn't tighten, however, that thought quickly passes, to be replaced by a slower, dawning realization of the more likely truth: that I am here to be seduced into the not-much-talked-about in Pontypridd and still tech-nically illegal practice of homosexuality.

He says quietly, "I don't want you to feel odd about this." I don't want me to feel odd about this, either, but he is sweating lightly, and "odd about this" is pretty much exactly what I feel. I extract myself and head for the exit, where he follows me, inserts himself between me and the door and makes a second grab at me. I push him in the chest. "You've got the wrong idea," he says. But we both know that I haven't. There's a brief, silent face-off between us. Then he says, "I'll put a full day in for you if you promise you won't say anything to the manager."

For more than a decade this will stand as the best-paid hour's work that I have done. The exact events of our Sunday morning are not spo-ken about between the two of us again, but its legacy is an immediate and radical change in the balance of power in our relationship. You are meant to call the foreman by the title "Mr." and his surname, but from now on I feel free to address him informally by his first name, knowing that this will irritate him and that I can get away with it. I do not report him to the manager, nor do I share the details of the incident with my co-workers—or, at least, not for a couple of days, after which the urge to tell the story gets the better of my embarrassment about it.

"You aren't going to believe this," I tell a select audience one lunch-time. "He tried to touch me up."

I wait to see the shock explode across their faces.

They couldn't seem less surprised if I had just told them that there were two gloves in a pair.

"Oh, yeah," somebody says. "He does that."

THE BEST THING about the glove-cutting room is the radio. And the best thing on the radio in 1955 is Bill Haley and His Comets doing "Rock Around the Clock." In my opinion. But my older, fellow glove cutters, particularly the two or three of them who are musicians in dance bands in their spare time, don't agree.

I have the wooden ruler in my hand. And the desk we stretch the leather on has a great deep sound to it, if you strike it right. So "Rock Around the Clock," which has been drifting in and out of the charts for almost two years at this point, starts up—kicks off in that great stop/start way, like so many rock'n'roll records, beginning with a slap, and then the voice is out on its own: "One, two, three o'clock . . ." And then it sets off and takes you away with it. So I'm smacking this ruler on the desk in time with the snare—that wonderful, loud snare drum, louder than any snare I've heard on any record to this point—and shouting, "Wow! This is great." But around me people are turning up their noses. Someone says, sniffily, "It's just a twelve-bar blues." "So what if it is?" I say—although I don't have a clue what they're talking about. Twelve bars? Where? And who's counting anyway?

"You're completely wrong," I say. "That record there is putting everything else to shame."

Because of the sound of it, more than anything else—a noise like you simply haven't heard. People are disliking Bill Haley because they're hating the actual sound of what he did. But not me. He's hitting the nail on the head, right here.

One of the men in the workshop plays sax in a band led by a guy called Norman Holt. Funnily enough, somehow all the glove cutters are musicians. So this sax-playing glove cutter tells me, "You want to come and listen to some proper music." So I do, one Saturday night soon after. I go to see his dance band in Caerphilly. And then I very quickly wish I hadn't. Old farts everywhere. Foxtrots and waltzes. Boring. Safe. This thing is horrible to me. "Now, ladies and gentlemen, it's time for an excuse-me." Give over.

On the Monday, at work, I go for the glove cutters: "You're condemning 'Rock Around the Clock' and you're playing that crap? That's not Count Basie you're playing there, you know, that's Victor Sylvester. I know crap when I hear it, and that was crap."

There's a divide coming, clearly. People only slightly older than me, people in their early twenties, think dance band music is wonderful. That's how close I seem to be to the boundary at this point, the musical and cultural gulf that is opening up right in front of our eyes. And I know as clearly as I know anything where I want to be standing when the ground finally opens up, which is on the side with Bill Haley, not on the side with Victor Sylvester, not to mention the Norman Holt Band.

Bill Haley's on the radio and I'm thinking, right: once rock'n'roll properly kicks in, it's going to kill all this other stuff. And for a brief, fantastic time it does.

Out for a dance with Linda and friends.

6

Take My Love

If you want to hear some rock'n'roll in Pontypridd in the mid-fifties, you can go and stand outside Freddie Fey's record shop in the town center on a Saturday afternoon, just across from the ornamental fountain, near the entrance to the indoor market. There's a speaker above the door there that sends the music into the street. They've got records, sheet music and instruments, so it's a proper music shop. Also up the road is Stone's electrical shop, managed by Frank Ride, who is a saxophonist and runs the dance band that plays in the Coronation Ballroom, and he's not too thrilled about rock'n'roll music, and you can tell. Freddie Fey's, on the other hand, is going with the times, and, in among its racks of brand-new shiny-sleeved records, even has a blues section. And Freddie himself, behind the counter in his shirt and tie, or his daughter, who works there too, will thumb through catalogs and tell you about release dates and play you things you want to hear.

Things like Elvis Presley's "Heartbreak Hotel." That's the first Elvis record I set my ears on, at some point early in 1956—not the Sun recordings, which I'll have to catch up with later, but his first session for RCA, with Chet Atkins on guitar. And once again, like with "Rock Around the Clock," there's that slap-you-in-the-face start, and the voice out on its own briefly, so you know who you're meant to be listening to, who's meant to be getting your attention.

Or things like Clyde McPhatter singing "Treasure of Love," the man's round, rich voice floating right at you, with the backing singers lifting skyward behind it, the whole thing somehow finding space to swell from a single strummed guitar to a big choral finish in just two minutes.

No question at this point in my life, I would be one of Freddie Fey's best customers—if I had any money. But records are luxury items on an apprentice glove-cutter's wage, and I don't have anything to play them on, in any case. Uncle Edwin has a radiogram in his front room and in the summer will let it ring out through the open windows. But my father thinks that kind of thing is a waste of money and won't be persuaded otherwise. You can hear music on the radio, after all—lots of different music. So why would you buy a record? You'd only play it a few times and then get fed up with it.

The thing is, though, we *can't* hear rock'n'roll on the radio—or not much, and certainly not enough. Band music dominates: Vera Lynn still rules the waves. Her and Vic Damone. So we go to Freddie Fey's on a Saturday afternoon and stand around outside, or we go to the dance halls on Friday and Saturday nights—the British Legion at Rhydyfelin, or a place at the top end of Pontypridd we call the Ranch, which is actually just a repurposed Nissen hut where troops used to be billeted. In both those places they'll only play rock'n'roll, which I think is wonderful because I don't have to hear any shit. And that way we won't need to own records in order to hear records. That said, a guy called Kenny Rees buys his own copy of Lonnie Donegan's "Rock Island Line," this thumping skiffle number that everybody seems to have by heart in these days, and carefully carries it under his arm to the Ranch to get it played there. I say, "They've probably got it, Kenny," and he says, "Well, just in case they haven't."

It's outside Freddie Fey's that I first hear something which, for me, puts even Elvis and Clyde McPhatter in the shade: a piano rumbling away like a steam train, a voice bawling above it, two minutes of syncopated mayhem. It sets the hair up on my neck straightaway.

I've heard boogie-woogie piano before now, caught scraps of it on the radio: Moon Mullican doing "Cherokee Boogie," or on those Tennessee Ernie Ford records, "Blackberry Boogie," "Catfish Boogie," "The Shot-Gun Boogie." But not like this. This is Jerry Lee Lewis doing "Whole Lotta Shakin' Going On" and it's pretty much going to change the air I walk around in.

The boogie-woogie flow was, to my mind, what Jerry Lee had over Elvis Presley. You get it in the contrast between the way Elvis did "Mean Woman Blues" and the way Jerry Lee did it, which flows and has syncopation. You get it again on their different versions of "Don't Be Cruel." Jerry boogies it up, and it just flows—flows like water from a tap. "Get-on-get-on over here and love me!"

God bless Elvis Presley, and nothing against the man, but he seems calculated in these early rock'n'roll days. It's going to open the door for everybody else, of course. But he knows what he's doing. The choreography, the moves, lifted from chorus girls. He knows how he looks, knows where the camera is. He's working on it. "Contrived" isn't the right word, because there's a freedom to it, too. But he knows what he has to do, and there's a sense of artifice there. Jerry Lee doing "Whole Lotta Shakin'," on the other hand—bang, that's it. There's a flow and a feel that doesn't seem like it's manufactured, or even rehearsed. It sounds like someone just sat down at a piano and let rip. And I'm thinking straightaway: Jesus Christ, who's that?

Much later on, when I get to know Elvis, I'll tell him how I always liked Jerry Lee Lewis. And he'll say, "So do I, Tom. But trust me, he's crazy. I've avoided this man for fifteen years." Jerry Lee didn't give a fuck. He doesn't now and he never did. And it's a shame for him, because not giving a fuck destroyed his career. And the destruction of his career left him bitter. He didn't get what he should have, but he was a fool to himself.

Right now, though, the fact is, "Whole Lotta Shakin'" sets light to something in me that only burns still hotter when "Great Balls of Fire" comes along after it. Those breaks again—whap! "You shake my nerves and you rattle my brain!" Those two singles spark a passion for Jerry Lee Lewis that's never going to desert me, no matter what I hear afterward. In the spring of 1962, me and Roy Nickels will buy tickets to go and see Jerry Lee in Bristol, at Colston Hall, supported by Gene Vincent. And wouldn't you know it, right in the break between opener and headliner, I get a message that a session time in a Cardiff studio has opened up and I had better get over there to take advantage and do some recording. I had to grab these opportunities when they presented themselves, no matter how frustrating. So I had to leave seeing Jerry Lee until the next time, when I managed to get tickets to see him in Cardiff at the Sophia Gardens, supported by Johnny Kidd and the Pirates. Johnny Kidd pretty much tears the place apart, so I'm actually wondering how Jerry Lee is going to follow it. No need to worry. I can still feel the thrill of being down near the front and seeing him walking out onto that stage, his band already on and playing the intro to "Move on Down the Line," and he's looking out into the crowd and holding out his fingers in the shape of the chord he's about to hit, as if to say, "This is what's coming, you motherfuckers." And then, boom, he's into it and the whole room is along with him.

At this stage, however, Jerry Lee Lewis is just one glittering aspect of a world in which everything seems to be changing dizzyingly fast. Early in my childhood I longed to dress like my father but at this point, sixteen going on seventeen, I want—and in fact need—to be a Teddy boy, with the drainpipe trousers and the beetle-crusher shoes. As of now, the desired look is exactly the opposite of what my father, and everybody else's father, is wearing. They're in short jackets? We'll go for long jackets. They're in baggy trousers? We'll have tight trousers, then. They're wearing wide ties? We'll wear our ties bootlace thin. They're in slight, thin-soled shoes? We'll have big, clonking ones, thank you. It's revolution in its crudest form, in a way. See that? Do the exact opposite. But it sure as hell works.

Same with the hair. My father has a short back and sides, and I have long hair, combed back, with grease down the sides—a Tony Curtis with a big quiff of curls.

You can't get suits off the rack in a fashion store at this point, you have to get them made-to-measure by a tailor, and there is no way I can afford that. But my dad has a jacket that he doesn't want anymore, and it's too big for me but perfect in my mind as it's the height of fashion, and that's a start. It drapes low to the thighs in the necessary manner. But it's not quite there. So one day I lift a patch of velvet from the glove factory, take it home and plead with my mother to sew it on the collar for me. The effect is transformative: without the velvet, I was just some bloke in a too-big jacket that used to be his dad's. With the velvet, I am a bona fide, dyed-in-the-wool, jiving, thriving, twenty-four-carat Ted, and you'd better fucking watch it.

One Saturday afternoon, I'm standing in the town center in my new rock'n'roll finery, talking to a girl I know from work, and my mother and sister come by. I give a friendly wave. They walk right by me, eyes firmly on the horizon. Back at home, I say to my mother, "What was that about?" She says, "The worst thing I ever did was put that velvet on your jacket. When I saw you talking to that tart . . ."

Disowned in public by my own mother. This is a result.

Meanwhile I am going out with Melinda Trenchard, or Linda, as I can now call her. She, too, has left school at fifteen and has gone to work as a window dresser in Harvey James, the clothes shop in Pontypridd. I've gone from trying to plan my trips to the shop to coincide with hers, to hanging out on street corners and talking, to going with her to the pictures, where she gets in free on account of her family connections. There's a period when I'm chasing her a bit because she's going to the

Catholic church dances at St. Catherine's Church, and other boys are bringing her home, walking her to the door, and I have to do a bit of running around to ensure that I'm in the right place at the right time to make sure nothing develops there. There's one fella in particular that seems to be making some headway, but I am persistent about planting myself where she can see me. And fortunately she seems to be as keen on me as I am on her, so it happens between us fairly smoothly, without too much anxiety and heartache.

I'm not sure how pleased about it Linda's father is, though—her father, who is, I have learned, now at home, unable to work, battling TB. Apparently when I whistle for her, outside her house, he'll say: "That bloody whistling crow is out there again."

One night, when everyone has gone to bed, I stand outside Linda's house and sing to her. There's a broken plinth left over from what used to be an air-raid shelter in her street, and I climb up on it and, in the direction of her curtained bedroom window, I sing "Irene, Goodnight," except that I change the words to "Linda, Goodnight."

Do you see what I did there?

She doesn't come to the window because if her father sees her she'll catch it. But she tells me later that she heard me as she lay there in bed. Heard me singing out there, not knowing, of course, as I stood in the dark on that crumbled concrete platform, that I would be singing to this person for the rest of my life.

She's started wearing her blond hair short with a DA in the back— very similar to the boys, really. One of my mother's friends reports back to her, in a scandalized tone of voice: "I saw Tom at the cinema with his girlfriend the other night. Her hair's shorter than his!"

She's dressing in tight sweaters, tight skirts and pumps. All the girls of her age are, showing off their developing shapes, because suddenly they can. Then they might wear a studded belt, which is frequently two dog collars, fastened together—quite a tough look, all in all. We don't know it, but we're inventing the teenager. No such thing before now.

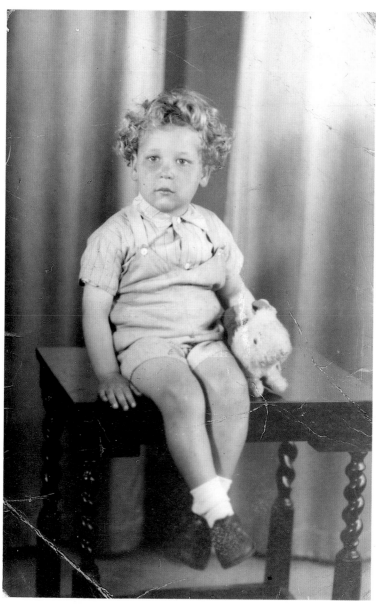

Me, at about two years old.

57 Kingsland Terrace, where I was born.

My grandmother, Ada Jones.

My parents, Freda and Tom.

My parents and sister, Sheila.

At ten years old.

The Wood Road Infants School.

With my family at a cousin's wedding.

Stow Hill, Pontypridd.

With my cousins
at the seaside.

On a lunch break with my workmates at Polya Glove.

Some serious drinking in Ponty.

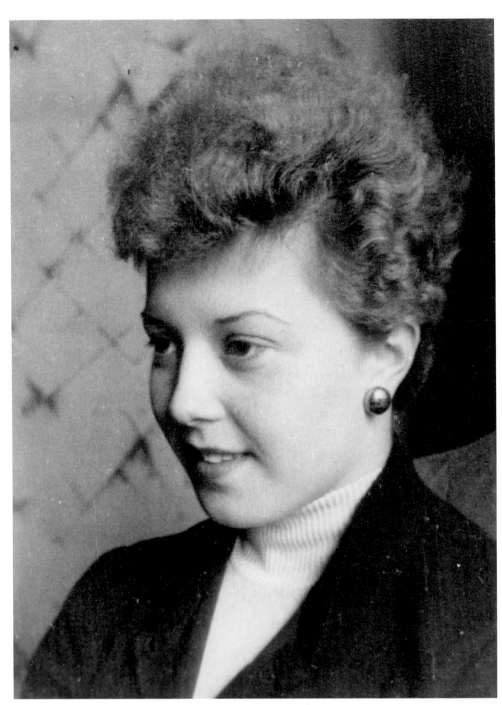

Melinda Rose Trenchard in about 1954.

That's for the social historians to work out later, though. Meantime, the boys are all villains and the girls are all tarts, as far as the grown-ups are concerned.

Linda loves dancing. She's been working on it while I've been laid up in bed. She teaches me how to jive. It's always either the jive or the creep, which is the one where you hold on to each other. We do it at the Ranch and we do it at the Legion—we hit the floor and dance like crazy to the rock'n'roll records.

Being totally wrapped up in each other, it seems like we may look a bit older than we are because at the Legion one night the woman who runs the place comes up to Linda and me when we're doing the creep and says, "If you don't mind, please don't dance so suggestively." We look at her, baffled, and that's when we absolutely know we're doing it properly.

Dancing is for weekends, but we're seeing each other pretty much every night. We do a lot of kissing in the phone box at the end of Laura Street. Periodically someone will want to use the box to make a phone call, of all things, and start rapping irritatedly on the steamed-up glass with a coin. At which point we dutifully step out, wait until they've finished and then go back in.

There's an engagement party at Laura Street: my sister Sheila, at twenty-two, is getting married to Ken Davies, who's the groundskeeper at the golf club. Linda comes, all dressed up, and sees my family together for the first time, and I am proud as hell—of her and of them. And there's drinking and noise and singing, and Linda is taken with the exuberance of it, and also with the contrast of it, because her father is ill and doesn't seem to be getting any better, and the mood in her house is somber and nothing like this.

It's high summer, and when the weather's good we walk out to the hills, where we can be alone. She is the first girl I go with, and it doesn't feel anything other than right because it's not just sex, it's love. Even here, at this young age, I feel sure I know the difference. I know the sensation of looking at a photograph in a magazine, or setting my eyes on the appropriately named Rosalie Butt from round the corner, and feeling lust, pure and simple, without any emotional attraction. I know the difference between sex and love. And this is love—a warm feeling, more than anything else, that I simply have to hold her as often as possible for as long as possible. And it's a wonderful thing, and what I can say with absolute certainty is that wherever else my life has taken me in the years since this, I have never had that feeling with anyone else. I don't think you do ever find it more than once, in all honesty. If you're lucky enough to fall in love, and to fall in love properly, that's it. Forever.

My father takes a week of holiday from the mine, and he and my mother lock up the house and set off with my Uncle Edwin and Aunty Violet to Wiltshire to visit some of the Woodward relatives who didn't join the Welsh exodus. I am instructed to spend this week at my grandmother's and, my parents being no fools, I am very specifically not given a key to Laura Street. But I have planned for this and got ahead of the game, and I leave my bedroom window unlocked. On the Friday night, I tell my gran that I will be spending the night at Dai Perry's house. Linda tells her parents that she will be sleeping over at Veronica Taff's house. Veronica's her friend, who's going out with Dai. Then, on the appointed evening, I shin up the drainpipe, climb in through the window, go downstairs and let Linda in through the kitchen. We spend the night in the single bed in the box room and then leave as carefully as we can. The following week, Mrs. Rogers, the Sunday School teacher from next door, tells my mother that she swears she heard noises in the house while they were away. My mother says that's impossible and tells her she must have imagined it.

We're stuck to one another, Linda and me, in that fantastic, wide-open teenage way—not seeing much else. And this is me as the summer of 1956 wears on: work is a pain in the arse, but I'm young and passionately in love and completely sold on a girl who is young and passionately in love with me, and life couldn't really be very much less complicated.

She is fifteen and I am sixteen when one day she tells me she is pregnant.

Pontypridd, South Wales.

7

I Wish You Would

I remember Linda, worried, saying one evening, "I haven't seen my period." This was at the end of the summer in 1956. And me trying to be casual about it and saying, "Maybe you will. Maybe it's late." Brushing it off.

But it wasn't late.

No Sex Education lessons in school in those days. You figured it out for yourself, or you didn't. My understanding was that if you took it out, there was a good chance the girl wouldn't become pregnant. What I didn't realize was that you shouldn't put it back in again. So that's where we came unstuck. As it were.

What I did know, and very clearly, was that the shit was now going to hit the fan. I feared the reactions of my mother and father. I feared, even more, the reaction of Linda's father. I knew that he didn't approve of me—the "bloody whistling crow" who lingered hopefully in the street outside his house. And now the bloody whistling crow had got his prized eldest daughter pregnant.

But one thing Linda and I agreed before we told our parents was that, whatever their response, and whatever the outcome was, we would see it through. We would find a way somehow. Because for all the worry and the fright and the sense of responsibility suddenly dawning large on my sixteen-year-old horizon, where there was no doubt in my mind was about my feelings for Linda, nor Linda's for me. We were completely in love. No question. I wanted to be with that girl and take care of her more than anything in the world. Her being pregnant only made me feel that even more strongly.

I told my mother. She was shocked and upset and then, typically, almost immediately concerned to relieve me of the worry by taking it on herself, assuring me that whatever we needed to do we would do. My father wasn't angry, he was quiet and thoughtful—anxious, clearly, but sympathetic. You would think this might have been a good moment for him to point out that he knew very well what Linda and I were going through because he, too, had got a woman pregnant out of wedlock— namely, my mother. But their own experience wasn't brought up. My father never said, "I know what you're going through because it hap- pened to me." I didn't even know that it had happened to him at that stage. I only worked it out much later. It wasn't spoken about. My assump- tion, growing up, was that everybody in the family talked about every- thing. That was the way it felt to me. Absolute openness. But clearly, as so often in families, there were certain things that simply didn't get discussed.

However, my and Linda's situation did get discussed. There was a meeting at our house—a kind of family convention, organized to deal with the situation and settle on a course of action. My Uncle George, my grandmother, Linda's mother, Vi—they all came up to Laura Street to join with my parents and sort this out. Not Linda's father, though. He stayed away, because he was either too ill or too angry, and maybe both.

The meeting took place in the kitchen. It was a strange and confusing and crowded occasion. The grown-ups sat in chairs in a kind of circle. Me and Linda sat on our own, holding hands, the subjects of the discus- sion but seemingly not a part of it. There was a lot of concern in the room—concern that we shouldn't be about to make a mistake at such a young age. Everybody seemed to have an opinion. We listened powerlessly as various options were raised and dismissed. There was marriage, of course, but nobody seemed to be giving too much weight to that because we were obviously too young. Abortion? Not a chance of it. The temporary disappearance of Linda to stay with a relative somewhere, where she could have the baby, surrender it for adoption and then return as if nothing had happened? Not impossible, but complicated. Let Linda have the baby here and then arrange for its adoption? . . .

My mother, God bless her, eventually looked up from the conversation and said, "We're all trying to say what's going to happen to these children, and we're talking about them as if they're not here."

My father then asked me what I thought should happen. I said that I wanted to get married to Linda, and that Linda wanted to get married to me. Surely we were going to get married anyway, at some point. Wasn't that understood? It was certainly understood by us. So we might as well do it now as later.

It was again pointed out that we were too young to be married—and not just emotionally or temperamentally. Linda was legally too young. We would have to wait until she was sixteen, in January, at the earliest. And just supposing we did marry, how would it work? Where would we live? There was no way that we could afford to rent a place of our own. Sheila, my sister, was marrying Ken, and they were going to live on the middle floor until they could find a place of their own, so Laura Street was out . . .

On the discussion went. But ultimately, our wishes and feelings were heard. After Linda's sixteenth birthday, we would marry: not in a church, obviously, with a white dress and morning suits and people flinging confetti. But we would be married. And then we would live apart. I would stay where I was, in Laura Street, Linda would carry on living at home with her parents and her younger sister Rosalind, where Vi, her mother, would be able to help her with the baby.

Soon after this, in advance of the wedding, I went to see Bill Trenchard. It was the most awkward conversation I had ever had. He seemed frail, withdrawn—the TB destroying him, though I wasn't to know it. I told him I loved his daughter. I told him I would love his daughter's child, too, and that I would always do my best to look after them and make sure they were okay. He said he hoped that was true. If he seemed unconvinced at the time, you could have understood it.

ON SATURDAY, MARCH 2, 1957, Linda and I walk down the hill into town and get married in a plain room smelling of polish and floor cleaner at Pontypridd Register Office in Courthouse Street. We are accompanied by my mother and father, my sister Sheila and her new husband Ken, and Linda's Aunt Josie, who lives next door to them in Cliff Terrace. Linda's mother, Vi, is working in the café, and she joins us in her lunch break for the signing ceremony. Bill, Linda's father, is not well enough to be there. I wear my best suit, and Linda is in a navy-blue dress. She is eight months pregnant, and no photographs are taken.

When I sign the marriage certificate, I go to put Thomas J. Woodward along the line and I cannot remember how to write a capital "J" in "real writing," as we called it at school, rather than simple printing. I turn to my brother-in-law, Ken, to ask him to remind me and he makes the shape with his finger to show me how.

Afterward, Vi returns to the café, and the rest of us go back to Laura Street and have some drinks. That night Linda and I take a short train ride to Cardiff and go to the movies. Linda's feet are swelling, and on the walk back to the station at the end of the evening she has to take off her shoes and go barefoot for a while, and she stays that way while we're on the train. Then I walk my bride home to her house in Cliff Terrace, say good night to her and go on up the hill, home to my parents, alone, for my first night as a married man.

BECAUSE I WOULD SHORTLY HAVE a child to support, I needed a better-paying job. Given how little the Polya Glove factory was paying me, it wasn't going to be too hard to find one. One of my cousins told me that they were taking on laborers at Wiggins Teape, otherwise known as the British Coated Board and Paper Company Limited, who had a big factory on the Treforest Trading Estate. Without faking any reluctance, I cut short my apprenticeship in glove-making and signed up.

My job, at first, was to offload the reels of uncoated paper that would arrive on trucks and then push them around and set them down, ready to be wound on to the coating machines and put through the color processes. I was to work there for a little over four years, until I was twenty-one.

The factory ran for twenty-four hours a day, except at weekends, so I was on a shift rotation: the day shift, from 6:30 a.m. to 2:30 p.m.; the afternoon shift from 2:30 p.m. to 10:30 p.m.; and the one that I really dreaded, the night shift from 10:30 p.m. to 6:30 a.m. I was working a night shift, pushing reels, on the evening that Linda went into labor. An ambulance went to the house and took her to the Royal Infirmary in Cardiff, accompanied by her mum. During the course of the night, I went into the front office and asked if I could use the phone to call the hospital and see if there was any news. The bloke in the office was beaming all over his face.

"They just called through," he said. "Great news! It's twins!"

Fucking joker.

I called, and the baby hadn't come. So I finished work and went home and washed up and at midday I went to the telephone box at the top of Laura Street and called again. And that time the woman on the maternity ward said, "Congratulations. Your wife has given birth to a baby boy."

That afternoon I caught the bus to Cardiff and went to see my wife and our brand-new son. I took a shopping bag with some fruit in it, because that's what you did when you went to see people in hospital: you took fruit, in a shopping bag.

He was in Linda's arms when I first saw him. I thought, "My God, what's wrong with him?" He had a dent in his head. I didn't know that babies quite commonly get a bit squished on the way out. They said, "Don't worry, it will soon round out." They were right.

And then I held him for the first time, and that's not something you forget—that feeling, that overwhelming rush, right through you.

My son.

Linda said she wanted to call him Mark Stephen, because they were names that she liked. That was fine by me. I was merely relieved that the names she liked weren't unusual names, because the way I saw it, it was your first duty to your son to spare him from having an unusual name.

I stayed at the hospital until the evening. On the bus back, I came past the British Legion club. And I'm not sure why I did what I next did, but something was clearly driving me to. I got off the bus and walked back into this dance hall because it was Saturday night and I knew that a lot of people who knew me, and who knew Linda, would be in there, and I wanted to put myself in front of them and find out if anybody had any objection to my having a child. Because, if they did, we could sort it out, there and then.

With me was the shopping bag in which I had taken the fruit to Linda in the hospital. If you fancied yourself as a bit of a Ted in Pontypridd, the shopping bag was not a part of your everyday wardrobe—not if you could fucking help it. You were inviting derision or worse by carrying a shopping bag. But right now I seemed to be filled with feelings of defiance, like nothing or nobody could touch me, and good luck to them if they tried. I walked up to the cloakroom and put the shopping bag down on the counter, almost as if willing someone to make a comment about it. Then I went in to where people were dancing. Dai Perry was there. He tapped me on the shoulder, said well done above the noise. But Dai was my closest friend—he was always going to be fine with it. It was other people I was testing out—people who didn't know me well, yet might have an opinion about my situation, and might want to voice it. It's like I was looking around the room and asking the question, "Who's got something to say?"

Bryan Pittman joined us, and at one point we went into the toilet. There were about half a dozen other guys in there who, as we came in, seemed to be sniggering about me, making fun. I asked Bryan to close the toilet door and stand by it. And then I asked each of these fellas, one at a time, whether they wanted to say something to my face. One of them was Reggie Owen, in his army uniform. He'd always had a crush on Linda, and I knew it. When I confronted him, he just mumbled, "I don't want any trouble." But then there was Colin Evans, and he did seem to have a bit to say—came on a bit bolshy and taunting. So I backed him up, got hold of the scruff of his neck and pushed him up against the wall. And then I asked him again: "What do you have to say, Col?" And now he said, "Nothing." And with that point established, Dai, Bryan and I turned and left the toilet.

Strange. My son was a few hours old and my sixteen-year-old hormones were in a dance hall in Rhydyfelin, looking for a fight. There was pride in there, but something deeply defensive as well—like I was trying to demonstrate that my life had changed now, but only for the better, and I was still me, whatever anyone else might want to say about it. And luckily nobody said anything I didn't want to hear, because I dread to think what might have gone down if they had. I felt huge, indestructible at that point.

I look back on this now and I feel how young I really was. I didn't look like a kid, and I didn't think I was a kid and I sure as hell tried not to behave like a kid. But I was a kid.

After a couple of days, Linda was ready to come home from the hospital with Mark. I was going to go to Cardiff and bring them back with me on the bus. But Mr. Hughes, who lived in Linda's street, had a car. We barely knew him because he kept himself to himself and didn't really speak to anyone, but he surprised me by stopping me in the street and offering to drive us. So that's how Mark came home: in style, in the back of a car belonging to one of Linda's neighbors, whose voice I can still hear now, saying, as he dropped us off, "Good luck to you and God bless you."

THOSE EARLY WEEKS of a baby's life are pretty exhausting. Anybody who has been through it will tell you that. But I guess that phase is a little easier if you happen to be living around the corner from it all, in another house. I would finish work, go home to my parents' house, have something to eat and then walk down to Cliff Terrace and, depending on which shift I was on, be there with Linda and Mark for a few hours in the day or in the evening. Linda and I would walk out together with the pram, wheel it down to the shops or out to the Common, which I expected to feel sheepish about but which I actually got a real kick out of. It made me proud. But I'm not going to lie: the real baby business—the feeding, the getting up in the night, the changing of nappies—was done by Linda and her mum. In fairness to myself, though, I was a man, and it was 1957: nothing much different seemed to be expected.

Mark was only a month old when TB finally got the better of Bill, Linda's father. He was just forty-two years old. Bless the man, he had used some of the last of his fading energy to try and knock the house around a bit, decorate some of the rooms for Linda and the baby. I wanted to help him, but he wouldn't let me. Nurses were coming to give him injections, but I couldn't understand why he wasn't in the hospital, giving himself a chance to get better. Before he went, I would have liked to have been able to stand in front of that man and assure him that everything was going to be okay, that it would all work out and that I would end up being able to take care of his daughter. But I couldn't.

The day he died, I went around the town to pass on the news to members of Linda's family. It was a terrible thing for Linda's mum, Vi. She had seen this man disintegrating and now she was widowed, and I don't think she ever really got over it. Impossible to find words for how hard it hit Linda, too. Life threw so much at her in that short space of time: pregnancy, marriage, childbirth and the death of her father, all in her sixteenth year. So much to carry on such young shoulders. The strength with which she bore it outwardly was a lesson for the rest of us, but you can't take all that on and not stagger a little under the weight.

Bill's death meant that there was now room for me to live with Linda at 3 Cliff Terrace. I packed up my clothes, which were pretty much the only things I owned, and moved down the hill and finally began to live with my wife and child.

I'm not sure how impressed my father was by this change in my circumstances. He said, "You remember that gypsy who came to the door and said you would go round the world? Fat lot she knew. You've ended up going round the corner."

Mark taking his first steps.

8

Coat Full of Singles

Cliff Terrace in the late fifties. An unpaved cul-de-sac of joined housing down a slope off Wood Road, just above the railway line. The Baptist church at one end of it, the synagogue at the other. No tarmac: stones and pebbles. Goods trains rumbling past below. Narrow houses with basement kitchens and concrete backyards, all the same, laid out like the houses in Laura Street. Two bedrooms. A tiny gas immersion heater above the kitchen sink for hot water. A marble slab in the kitchen to keep the food cool, in the absence of a fridge. This is the house I move to in 1957, and where I live for seven years until 1964.

Linda and I have the bedroom at the front of the house, with Mark sleeping in a cot. Linda's mother shares the back bedroom with Linda's younger sister, Roslyn. When Mark is old enough, he will have the box room, as I did in Laura Street—though at first he'll keep coming back to our bed in the middle of the night and climbing in. Linda always lets him stay, I always put him back—so he soon learns that it pays him to go quietly to Linda's side of the bed—until the night he slowly peels the covers back and is horrified to find we've fooled him by changing places.

Linda's mum says, "Don't call me Mam, call me Vi." So I do. Vi, who continues to go out to work at the café, is friendly, outgoing. We get along fine. I feel accepted by her, which is just as well, given the intimate circumstances in which we are now living. One morning she says, "What was all that noise last night? Don't you two go to bed to sleep?"

Still, there is a part of me that longs for us to have our own space—the three of us, me, Linda and Mark—and which is desperate to be able to provide that. So I compensate. The middle floor, as it stands when I move in, is unfurnished and a bit of a building site. Linda's father, Bill, had started to knock the two rooms into one but didn't live to finish the job. I restore it to two rooms—fit a plasterboard partition wall one weekend, with the help of my father. Bill has taken down the ceiling and I don't fancy putting it up again, so we'll have to make do under the bare rafters for a while until we can afford to get the job done properly. But nevertheless I convert the front room into a workable living room. My mother gives me a small table and four upright wooden chairs from Laura Street, which I put in the bay window. There's also room for two armchairs and a settee around the fireplace. I think of this as our home within a home.

I also decide that this is the room where I want to eat. This is the cause of some friction. "Why here?" Linda says. Eating in this house has always taken place in the basement kitchen, which is where the television is. But I decide I want to come home from work and have my dinner at the table in the sitting room. I prevail, and the plates of meat and boiled vegetables, prepared by Linda in her new role of sixteen-year-old mother and wife, are carried upstairs.

It's not obscure what my motives are here. I'm marking out my territory: "This is our place." Even though it's not our place. It's my mother-in-law's place.

My other contribution to the décor at 3 Cliff Terrace: at some stage I box in the staircase—fit board panels to the banisters, entirely enclosing the actually, on reflection, rather nice polished newel posts. For that oh-so-modern boxed staircase look, obviously. For some reason this seemed important to me at the time.

Five days a week, I leave the house and cycle the four miles to work. It's that or the bus. I have an old drop handlebar bike that I have picked up from somewhere, and I wear a trilby hat crammed down on my head to keep my ears warm. Coming back is tough, but going is easy— downhill all the way at first so that, by the time you reach the Cardiff Road, heading out of town, you can really have your head right down and be barreling along at a lick because at 5:45 in the morning you can always rely on an open stretch of road at that point.

Which is how come I don't see the parked baker's van that morning— don't know it's there until I ride smack into the back of it and come to an immediate, shuddering halt. Fortunately I hit the van's back door, which has at least got some give in it. Even so, the next thing I am lying face-up in the road, a mess of lumps and grazes, with a concerned baker peering down into my blinking eyes.

"Look what you've done to my fucking back door!"

"Look what your fucking back door has done to my bike!"

Over in the gutter, what used to be my bike cuts a pitiful spectacle. The frame is almost L-shaped. I think the sight of it awakens some pity in the man. The baker shoves the shattered bike in the back of his van and runs me up to the paper mill, where I limp in and report sick for the day, because I might as well get something out of this. And then, very decently, he drives me home to Cliff Terrace.

Where Linda opens the front door to a bruised and forlorn-looking bloke in a battered hat, holding a bent-in-half bike and saying, "Look what happened to me." She probably would be more sympathetic if she didn't find it so funny.

(The bike was a write-off.)

Daytime might find me sleeping off a night shift, doing my best not to be disturbed by the sound of the world carrying on regardless. Because apparently the world doesn't care that you've been up all night working. One day I am woken by the sound of singing and clickety-clacking from the street. It's a group of girls, out on the old concrete foundation from the air-raid shelter—the one on which, a couple of years before, in the dark, I stood to sing "Linda, Goodnight" to the tune of "Goodnight, Irene" to Linda when she'd gone to bed. These girls are rehearsing a song and tap-dance routine to "Winter Wonderland." And rehearsing it, and rehearsing it . . . Eventually I have to throw open the window and ask them as politely as I can if they would mind shutting the fuck up. It sets me against that song for, without exaggeration, the rest of my life. About forty years later, doing a private Christmas show for employees of Apple at Cupertino in California, I will be asked if I would mind throwing in a version of "Winter Wonderland," in keeping with the season. The chill will go right through my spine, and suddenly I am back in Cliff Terrace—clickety-click, clickety-clack.

"I'll do anything else."

EARLY ON AT THE PAPER MILL, I get a big break. Cliff Llewellyn, the manager, asks me if I think I could run one of the paper-winding machines. One of his machinists has dropped out for some reason and left him in the lurch. Llewellyn says, "If you can double-back tonight, you can have that machine from now on. And you'll get the pay."

I agree without a beat, because this is a gift. Ordinarily, you'd be twenty-one before you got paid at a machinist's rate—and I could more than use this money right now. I come back that night at 10:30 p.m. and clock on. The foreman, who is a miserable bastard at the best of times, has a problem with me being there. "You can't run that machine, you're too young." He wants to send me home. But I am on to a good thing and I know it, so I sit firm. "The manager told me to come in tonight, and I'm staying here." It would have taken horses to drag me out of there.

The next day the union guy kicks off about it with Cliff Llewellyn. And the union guy is a second cousin of mine, so thanks for that. Cliff Llewellyn, though, who maybe has taken a bit of a shine to me or who perhaps knows something about my circumstances, can't be persuaded to change his mind. And suddenly I am going home with a slightly fuller pay packet.

Some of the other fellas hate the fact that I'm getting this special treatment. If it isn't already enough that I have a Ted's haircut . . . One hard case in particular starts to give me grief over it. This is a big, broad-shouldered guy, a machinist who comes into work in a camel-hair coat and a brimmed hat—he'd look like a toff, really, if it wasn't for the scarred face. As it is, he looks like a hit man, without the gun. And he's really unhappy about my new position. If he's on the machine before me, he'll deliberately fuck up the settings before my shift starts. He's trying to get me fired and trying to goad me into fighting him, which will have the same effect. I'm on edge whenever I'm around him, feeling threatened. One night I leave work on my bike and see his big, hulking shape up ahead, walking toward me. It's dark, and my mind fills with doomy thoughts. Now is going to be the time. There's no one to see. This is where it's finally going to go off. If he just steps off the pavement, makes a move toward me, I'll know it's coming. I cycle on, closing in on him now, trying not to speed up or slow down or in any way betray my fear, the two of us about to pass, and me waiting for him to walk into my path or for his arm to reach out . . . And he does nothing, just watches me out of the corner of his eye with a satisfied look on his face as I glide by. He's playing me and getting to me badly, and he knows it.

I start having nightmares about this guy—hate it when we're on shifts together, am almost permanently paranoid. I take to avoiding him like the plague because I am too frightened that something will start up, and he'll somehow work it that I'll end up losing my job, which I cannot afford to do.

The hit man without a gun adds an extra strain to what is a strenuous time altogether. I always feel better on the afternoon shift. The morning shift I get heartburn and feel tired all the time. And the night shift is just a pain in the arse. But I am earning money to keep my wife and my son, and something about that makes me feel powerful and keeps me at it.

Flush with our newfound wealth, Linda and I get a record player to play in the evenings—a Bobby Soxer. It's more like a hat box than a gramophone: you have to take the lid off in order to put the record on and, if it's an LP, the record overlaps the box on all sides. The first record I buy to play on it is "Treasure of Love" by Clyde McPhatter. I buy records by Elvis and Jerry Lee, by Brook Benton, Ray Charles and Chuck Jackson. I am ashamed to admit that I also have a few records which don't come from Freddie Fey's in this period. Which is terrible, because I like Freddie Fey and he deserves better. At the same time, even though money is less tight than it was, it's still tight, and I have a big winter overcoat and I realize that I can stand at the bins and surreptitiously slide items into the lining, then casually walk out. No question, the advent of the seven-inch 45 is revolutionizing popular music. It is also revolutionizing petty theft. Those thick old 78s you would never have got away with.

Linda notices how absorbed I am when music is playing—stolen or otherwise. I never want to put it on and just have it in the background. If it's on, I'm listening to it because, for me, it's the loudest thing in the room.

Music also seems to work some kind of magic on our baby, too. Sometimes we prop Mark between cushions on the sofa with his bottle, and I'll stick a Jerry Lee Lewis album on, and he seems content as anything. He cries when it stops—calms down again when it goes back on. He's taking after me, then.

I also spend five pounds on a steel-strung Spanish guitar that I have seen hanging in the window of an instrument shop at the top end of Pontypridd. It's a piece of shit, and I have to file down some of the frets to stop them buzzing louder than the strings. But I sit with this thing in my lap in the evenings and I fiddle around and teach my fingers to straddle the neck in the shapes of what seem to be the necessary four chords: C, Am, G, F7. They sit with my voice, and some of the records I'm listening to seem to be in that key. I know I'll never be able to play the piano like Jerry Lee but I figure that I might be able to play the guitar close enough for rock'n'roll.

Looking tidy for the photo at about eighteen.

9

Bring It on Home

On Friday nights I would go to the Wheatsheaf on Rickards Street with Dai Perry or Brian Blackler to play darts and toast the weekend. And Saturdays were for serious drinking and, every now and again, for what can famously be the upshot of serious drinking, which is fighting.

I'm not trying to paint Pontypridd in the fifties as some kind of Welsh Beirut, but it could definitely get a bit sparky on a Friday night, and a bit more sparky on a Saturday night, and it was certainly somewhere you would never step off the pavement to get out of somebody's way. To step aside was to lose face. So, inevitably, there were comings-together, shoulder-to-shoulder, and then there was conflict. However, let me be clear that the fighting that ensued was all fists and heads: no knives, darts, bicycle chains, car parts . . . We kept it honorable.

The cause of the fighting was generally the usual one: booze, leading a person, as it so often has, to ponder the question that man has been asking himself since the dawn of time: "What are *you* looking at?" People got sozzled, and then things got bent out of shape, and before you knew where you were, you were in it.

The drink which caused the sozzling in my case was beer: in

particular, Fern Vale, a Welsh beer, and the appropriately named Brains, which is brewed in Cardiff. When I started drinking, the landlord would be tapping your pint direct from the barrel, racked up or on the floor behind the bar, but not long after that came the arrival of pressurized beer pumps in Pontypridd, which was celebrated like a breakthrough equivalent to the advent of electricity. Occasionally, I might order a chaser or two of rum and black, which I once got horribly, hopelessly sick on. (And there are few worse sicknesses than a rum and black sickness.) But the staple drink was beer. Lots of beer.

Because it was a coal-mining town, the pubs in Pontypridd stayed open until 4:00 in the afternoon, unlike in poor, benighted Cardiff, where they were only open until 2:30. So you would drink from Saturday lunchtime through until 4:00, when the pub would shut until 6:00. You would fill those two hours in a café—sometimes the one that Vi served in. She didn't seem to mind us boys coming in and she would slip us a cup of tea if she could. Or you might go to the Italian coffee shop, where the pies were heated with hot steam off the espresso machine, making them moist. Then, at 6:00, it was back into the pub, where the drinking would continue. By the end of a typical Saturday session, I would probably have got through about ten pints, which might seem like a lot of liquid, but such was the way of life.

Occasionally those ten pints, or the pursuit of them, would land me up in fights. I could handle myself and I never got beaten to a pulp. I was never a hospital case. The tale, often recounted, that I was once thrown through the window of a fish and chip shop, and stood up brushing shards of glass off myself, is one of those stories that has grown shaggy in the retelling. It didn't happen and nor, for the record, did I ever throw anyone else through a fish and chip shop window. Nor through any other window, come to think of it. But I did get my face bent out of shape one night in the street outside a pub, thereby creating the boxer's nose behind which I would eventually launch a career in show business and which I finally had surgically corrected at considerable expense in Los

Angeles. I think the guy who bent it was a friend of mine, but, alas, the episode is sunk in a pool of alcohol and the details are elusive.

One night I'm paying the bill in Pontypridd's premier Indian restaurant, and some guy that I don't know decides to lean all over me as he's putting on his coat. I don't know what, precisely, has caused him to single me out. Maybe it's my hair, maybe it's the shape of my nose. Maybe it's the desire to save me a fortune further down the line and fix my nose for me here and now. Maybe it's nothing more than a keenness to end the evening with a punch-up in the gutter—a desire that this fella would not be the first or only man to experience, and certainly not in Pontypridd. Whatever it is, he won't leave me alone, and I realize, with the familiar surge of adrenaline, that something is going to have to happen. As soon as we get outside the restaurant, some kind of movie-inspired "you messed with the wrong guy" vengefulness gets hold of me and, without any preamble, I pile into this fella as properly as I can. And when I have finished piling, he is lying motionless on the pavement.

For the rest of the weekend, I have the same cloudy feelings of guilt and unease that I had after that schoolboy fight. These feelings by no means lift on the Monday, when I get into work at the paper mill, and see the headline on the front page of the newspaper: "LOCAL MAN FOUND DEAD."

The whole of my chest ices over in horror. I have killed someone. I have brutally, stupidly got carried away on a pavement at the end of a drunken evening and now I am a murderer.

It's not him, of course, as I find out when I read the story and my heart rate eventually drops back down to normal. This coincidence gives me an almighty jolt, though, and slows me right up. Street fighting isn't always about how much muscle you're carrying. It's about what you're prepared to do, how quickly you're prepared to do it and how long you're prepared to carry on doing it for. What if the person who's laying into you has trouble locating the cut-off valve? What if you have trouble locating the cut-off valve yourself? Where does a stupid scrap over nothing outside an Indian restaurant land you then? Weighing this up, I begin trying to step around the vicious temper in other people— and to step around the vicious temper in myself.

Meanwhile, on Sundays, I'm going to the Wood Road Club with my father and my uncles and cousins—because I have graduated into that company now. I have come of age and am a married man with a child and can drink with the men of the family, as I always longed to. We wear our suits, with white shirts—always white shirts. But I only have one of those and one week Linda burns the collar, ironing it. That Sunday I have to wear a colored shirt to the Wood Road, which is simply not done, and I moan about it loudly.

Sunday nights are men-only in the Wood Road, and when fellas get up to sing during those evenings, it's a different thing from Saturday nights. Nobody's trying to impress the girls, nobody's forcing it. There's a different feel to it, something a bit more bare-bones. A fella called Teddy Protheroe gets up and sings "Looks Like I'm Never Going to Cease My Wandering," a thirties-era Depression song, and I'm completely en-thralled by it—by the song, and by the heart in his delivery of it. And then there's Glynog Evans, who we'll often see in there, a big, imposing former rugby player, about my father's age, in his late forties. And people will urge Glynog to get up and sing, half taking the piss—because he is so serious about it, and a bit puffed up in his blazer, and that makes people want to mock him even more. The Wood Road Club has recently acquired a microphone on a stand. Glynog will put the mic as far away from himself as possible, making a point—like, his voice is powerful enough to fill this room on its own.

You'll hear a few people pipe up: "Yeah, go on, Glynog. You don't need the microphone."

And then he draws breath and sings "My Mother's Eyes" (written by L. Wolfe Gilbert, with music by Abel Baer), the ballad from *Lucky Boy*, the 1929 George Jessel movie, which Frankie Valli later recorded:

One bright and guiding light
That taught me wrong from right,
I found in my mother's eyes.

And by the end of it, some of these guys who have mocked him are crying. There's an experience there, and a power, and by the end, you cannot dispute the fact that this man can get through to people. This affects me. Other people my age might not want to give Glynog the time of day. In fact, of my friends, Dai Perry shares my interest and will come to the Wood Road on a Sunday with me, but the others, not so much. They're after somewhere younger and they leave the Wood Road and its singing workers to me and Dai. That singing speaks directly to me, though. "My Mother's Eyes" feels as real to me as "Whole Lotta Shakin'" or "Rip It Up."

I STARTED SINGING IN PUBLIC at this time. At first, I might just get up in pubs where there was a pianist and do a number for the hell of it. In the Wheatsheaf on a Friday night, there was a blind piano player, Blind Johnny, who would sometimes play the battered upright in the upstairs bar. I loved to sing with that guy. Most pianists you came across would just play the song's melody—play along with you. Blind Johnny was a proper accompanist, who would listen to you and play around you, leave gaps for you to sing in. That felt great. I might ask him to play Frankie Laine's "I Believe," or Conway Twitty's "It's Only Make Believe." And I noticed when I started to sing that I didn't seem to have too much trouble getting people to listen. Generally, upstairs in the Wheatsheaf, even though there were a few rows of wooden chairs lined up to form an auditorium, there would be a lot of background chatter—people not really giving the singer the time of day, tuning in casually if they wanted, carrying on their conversations for the most part. Or they could get merciless if they didn't like you, slap you down. But I noticed, when I sang, that I could get the room to sit quietly. I didn't get heckled. People wouldn't even get up and go to the bar. That felt great, too.

The first time I got on an actual stage, though, was at the Wood Road Club, when I was seventeen, going on eighteen. Sunday night at the Wood Road was guest night. There would be some kind of musical act booked in by Charlie Ashman, the vice president and entertainment secretary. That particular Sunday night, for some reason, the entertainment didn't show up. Charlie, who was clearly in a bit of a fluster, collared me at the bar and said he had heard I played guitar and pleaded with me to go home and get it and help fill in.

I didn't really need to be pleaded with. I ran back up to Cliff Terrace, grabbed my guitar out of the sitting room and ran back down again. There were about sixty people in the room expecting to hear a banjo trio from Gwynedd. Instead, they got me and a cheap Spanish guitar, doing "Blue Suede Shoes" and Tennessee Ernie Ford's "Sixteen Tons." I don't suppose the guitar playing impressed anyone. But the voice seemed to do so. I'd listened to these songs a lot, knew them inside out, and I could phrase them. At the end of the night, Charlie came up and said, "You were bloody great." Then he gave me £1, which I thought was generous until I heard the banjo trio from Gwynedd would have been getting four.

The next day, the local papers were full of glowing reviews of this unknown singer who had stepped into the breach, and by the afternoon you could barely move in Pontypridd for talent spotters down from London, trying to find this new singing sensation who had come from nowhere to send shock waves across south Wales.

Okay, not really. In fact, the next thing that happened was that I got approached by a fishmonger. This was Bryn Phillips—Bryn the Fish. Bryn doubled in his spare time as a mime artist—as so many fishmongers do. His act was to put on records and do funny, slapstick mimes to them—impersonating singers, tripping over, falling around. He might come on in a Hawaiian skirt and a long black wig, with a brightly colored bra attached above his large, bare belly, and do some very straight-faced but entirely inept Hawaiian dancing. Maybe you had to be there—but trust me, he was funny. Bryn ran an outfit called the Misfits, which was from the old "concert party" tradition. There were quite a lot of "concert party" acts around. They would provide a mixture of entertainers in one revue package: a comedian, a tenor, sometimes a juggler, making up a self-contained variety show, and there was plenty of call for those in the working men's clubs at the time.

Bryn wanted me to come along as the rock and pop singer—someone for the younger people in the room. I was going to need a better guitar, though, so I bought a more solid one that buzzed less off a bloke at the paper mill and joined the Misfits.

Now I would have to get my drinking with the boys done on a Friday night because Saturday night and Sunday night were often gig nights. Bryn got bookings for us all round the valley towns. Glenda Ford's father had a car so he would drive us, or, if he wasn't available, we would clamber into Bryn's green Morris delivery van, with its sliding front doors, and turn up for shows smelling lightly of haddock. Our destinations were working men's clubs, where you might, if you were lucky, get a dressing room and a stage but where very often you were just directed to a small patch of floor in the corner. I would be singing Elvis, Jerry Lee, Buddy Holly—new stuff. The younger guys liked me because I was the thing they could connect to. The older guys were more of a problem. Rock'n'roll wasn't always what a working man's club wanted to hear. In fact there was enormous resistance to it and suspicion of it. It wasn't "proper singing"; it was "just a racket," "a bloody noise." I pretty quickly learned that just the sight of a bloke with a quiff and a guitar moving toward the microphone would be enough to trigger shouts of "Pay him off!" So I made sure I had some ballads up my sleeve for when they weren't into the rockier stuff and might need some calming down.

Besides Bryn and his comedy miming, the Misfits offered Les Morton, who was a self-taught tenor, and a classical soprano called Glenda Ford, who had been a few years ahead of me at my school, some Roy Orbison things, some Conway Twitty, some Frankie Laine. With a ballad, I would show these miserable old bastards that I could actually sing. What never seemed to fail me was "My Yiddishe Momme," in A minor, a vaudeville number from the twenties which my father used to sing when I was a kid and which was a song I loved. If the situation got heavy, and the room grew restless, I could pull that one out, and it would normally bring them round. It was what these guys wanted to hear, and I could give it to them and I didn't mind doing so.

Sometimes, though, it didn't matter what was happening on the stage. In the valleys you came across tough, edgy places where it could all kick off at the drop of a hat—or, more likely, at the drop of someone's pint. Gilfach Goch, in particular, was renowned for being nasty. We went to a club there. Glenda was on stage singing something lovely, and I went to the bar—because when you weren't on stage, you would tend to get a beer in with everybody else and be part of the audience. There was a bunch of lads in the corner of the room, about my age, starting to play up, making themselves heard above Glenda. In the working men's clubs they always had committee members looking out for the drunks and the row-dies, keeping some order. One of the committee members, a big fella in a Prince of Wales check suit, with a carnation in his lapel, went across to this group of lads and said, "Now, now, boys: one singer, one song."

They began to tease him about his nice suit. "Where did you get it? Suits you." They were playing him along, and he was falling for it. "Did you grow that flower yourself?" one of them said. "Could I smell it?" The committee man leaned in and, right out of nowhere, the kid punched him hard in the face.

I had no idea what this man would do—this formal committee man in his smart suit, now with blood streaming from his nose. I certainly didn't expect him to react the way he did. With a roar of fury, he picked up the table the lads were sitting at and pinned them against the corner with it. Then he stepped back a bit and began to crack the edge of the table against them, again and again, beating the hell out of these upstarts with the furniture. Other club members were trying to pull him back, shouting at him to restrain himself.

"Mr. Roberts, think of the committee," one of them said.

"Fuck the committee," roared Mr. Roberts, continuing to bang away with his table.

That was my first taste of the rougher side.

After a gig, we would go out to the van and divvy up. My split of the fee after a typical appearance with the Misfits would be between £2 and £5. After expenses and your drinks, it would just about cover the night. But you couldn't make a living at it. I used to stare out the window of the van on the way home and wonder how anybody ever did.

Christmas gig with Vernon in the early days.

10

Escape from Wiggins Teape

In 1961, I turn twenty-one: a husband of four years, the father of a four-year-old boy. Mark is about to start school in Wood Road, the same place where I went, and my father before me. Money is tight. God forbid that Linda should ever need to get a job, because that would be proof to me that I had failed. But it's okay because I have a steady income as a machinist with Wiggins Teape so I am able to provide.

Until I get fired.

It would be true to say that I have grown disenchanted with the job—if I was ever particularly enchanted by it in the first place. I have worked on this winding machine in this paper mill for four years now. I have a lot of friends who are laboring on the building sites—working outdoors, getting strong. I sometimes feel pale and pasty by comparison with them—a factory worker with a factory worker's pallor. I used to think that having a job which kept you out of the weather was a good thing but recently I'm not so sure. Maybe I want out. Escape from Wiggins Teape. Which sounds like a war movie. But maybe I've decided I'd be better off elsewhere.

Maybe I'm slightly spoiling for it when it happens.

There's a Scots foreman. Used to be a perfectly nice, friendly bloke when he was a machinist—one of us. Then he made the grade to foreman and overnight he turned into a prick—by no means the first man to walk down that particular path. He comes by one night and tells me I'm not paying enough attention to my work.

Bloody insult. Okay, I might have been reading the paper. Even so, everything's under control, isn't it? Nothing's going wrong. I don't take well to his criticism. I especially don't take well to it coming from him. I tell him to fuck off.

I'm at home the following morning, sleeping off the shift, when Linda wakes me up with a telegram. It's the first telegram we have ever received—a bit of a landmark moment, the guy in the uniform, on his bike, coming to the door; something that happens in the pictures. Except that I know the balloon has gone up because the telegram tells me to report that afternoon to the manager's office at the paper mill. And I know this meeting isn't going to go well when the manager is already shaking his head as I walk in.

"We've had a complaint."

I try to make a case for myself. I point out that nobody at the paper mill has ever had a problem with the quality of my work. But I'm no lawyer and I make a big mistake when I say, "When I come in later tonight, I'm going to have it out with that prick."

The manager says, "I'm afraid you won't be coming in tonight."

Sacked for foul language and insubordination. I'm paid off with a week's notice.

Linda is distraught and worried. I reassure her as hard as I can. I'll sign on for the dole. I've got my singing work with the Misfits—which doesn't really pay much, but it's something. I'll find shifts on the building sites—cash in hand. It'll be okay. I'll make it work.

I say all this firmly in the hope of believing it.

ONE FRIDAY NIGHT in the spring of 1962, I am drinking in the Grey-hound near the railway station with my mate Alan Barrett when a guy called Vernon Hopkins walks in. I know Vernon a bit—see him knocking around the place. He's from Rhydyfelin, plays bass guitar. Father's a piano tuner. Vernon has sometimes been upstairs in the Wheatsheaf when I've been singing. He works as a typesetter at the *Pontypridd Observer* but he's also got a group going called the Senators, who do Cliff Richard and Buddy Holly songs and a few Elvis numbers, as well as some instrumental Duane Eddy stuff—"Dance with the Guitar Man," "Shazam." The Senators are a bit of an item in Pontypridd—perhaps, in these early years for the concept, the town's first and only proper pop group, complete with blond maroon Burns electric guitars and tiny, floor-standing amplifier units and hair grown determinedly over their ears. They've done a midweek gig at the Regent Ballroom in Hopkins-town, formerly a cinema and the scene of my childhood spooking by *The Beast with Five Fingers*. The Regent was solidly a traditional dance band venue until the Senators marched in, flying the flag for this newly emergent brand of pretty-boy pop.

They have even been on telly—on the TWW (Television Wales and the West) show *Discs-A-GoGo*, recorded in Cardiff on a set designed to look like a coffee shop and labeled "GoGos, the gayest coffee bar in town," which you could say in those days without creating any confusion. The show was fronted by Kent Walton, the Canadian DJ who would later make a bigger name for himself by commentating on the wrestling for *World of Sport*, and the Senators appeared the same week as Screaming Lord Sutch, the barking-mad English rock'n'roll singer, whose act at the time involved him emerging from a coffin and who, in a few short years, will start being a serially unsuccessful parliamentary candidate. But this one piece of heady television exposure doesn't seem to have radically altered the Senators' fortunes or opened the door to stardom, and they are still doing a regular Friday gig in the relatively humble surroundings of the Pontypridd YMCA, a red-brick building over where Taff Street meets Crossbrook Street. Not that I've ever been to see them over there because I'm not that interested. Not my kind of music, really, that light-end pop stuff. And in any case, the crowd in the YMCA is too young, and they don't serve alcohol.

The first thing Vernon does in the Greyhound is offer to buy me a pint. So I know straightaway that something is up and that's he probably going to ask me to do him a favor.

"Could you do me a favor?" says Vernon, and he asks me if I would come up the road with him and sing a couple of songs.

I say, "Vernon, it's Friday night boys' night out."

I don't need to say any more. Friday is drinking night. An important night. Self-explanatory.

Vernon says he realizes that it's a long shot, but if there's any way that I could help out . . . the Senators have a singer called Tommy Pitman, a guy I remember from school, who's not long back from National Service in the navy. Tommy does a more than decent Elvis impression, with the leg-moves thrown in, but this particular Friday—and not for the first time, apparently—he hasn't shown up. The story that emerges later is that he was deep in a game of cards and just couldn't be arsed. Three card brag, allegedly. Doesn't really matter what's keeping him at this point, though. The fact is, he's not there, and the Senators are short of a singer.

Still, the other fact is that you can't get a drink at the Christian Union–run YMCA, whereas you can get as much drink as you can afford at the Greyhound, so I voice some reluctance. Vernon says, "What if we could sneak a few bottles behind the curtain?"

This clinches it—although, to be honest, deep down the idea was already appealing to me anyway. Up to now, I've sung with pianists or with my own guitar, or I've simply sung unaccompanied. But I've never stood in front of any kind of band and sung, let alone in front of a newfangled pop group with proper guitars and amplifiers, and I'm bound to be curious to find out what that would feel like.

So we walk to the YMCA, about half a mile away. It's a big room, holding about 200, and it has a proper stage with dark red velvet curtains, behind which I find my new bandmates.

I can't work out exactly how pleased the Senators are to see me, even though they're in the lurch and I am ostensibly the cavalry. I don't exactly detect relief. On rhythm guitar is Keith Davies, a big Hank Marvin fan, which is also true for the lead guitar player—Mike Roberts from Taff's Well. Mike can play a solo with the guitar up behind his head, a skill which seems important in these early days of pop. He went to the County School and seems quite middle class. That's all right with me, but I'm wondering whether he's looking down on me here, at the YMCA. Bear in mind that I'm still wearing my hair in a greased-up quiff at this point. I'm still fundamentally a Ted, and I don't know whether Mike is that thrilled to see me come on the scene—bringing my Jerry Lee Lewis attitudes into his Hank Marvin world.

And then there's Alva Turner, the drummer. Alva's a tiny chap with sticky-out ears and therefore inevitably known as "Dumbo." He's obviously a very nice fella, but perhaps not a rock'n'roll drummer. My first impression is that he's the drummer because he has some drums—one of those situations. But Alva looks a little bit afraid of me, too.

They are all a little younger than me—just two or three years—but a little seems to make a big difference in these times, when the mood and the fashion seems to be changing every hour, on the hour. They're all keen on Cliff Richard and the Shadows, the Ventures, Duane Eddy— the pop stuff, at the lighter, safer end of the spectrum, as it seems to me. I think Cliff is all right; I quite like "Move It." But there's no danger there—no rock'n'roll menace. He's a nice fella, clearly, and he sings like one, whereas if I'm looking for anything from this experience at the YMCA, it's for an opportunity to fucking rip it. Actually, this would pretty much define my attitude to singing, both at this point and in the coming years: "Wait till you fucking get hold of this." Doesn't matter what the song is. Won't matter if the song is "I've Got a Lovely Bunch of Coconuts." My approach will essentially be: "I'll fucking have it."

Okay, it's a philosophy which will eventually lead to a succession of record producers telling me: "Try not to be as . . . large?" Trying to get me to calm down a bit. But there it is. At this point, in 1962, Cliff Richard and the Shadows seem to me to be part of that gentle, undercooked, British pop-copyist thing that isn't as good as the American original, and certainly isn't ripping it. Nobody's getting hold of anything when Cliff sings, to my mind. "Endless Sleep" by Marty Wilde got close. It had some edge there. But I prefer Little Richard, every time.

However, for the members of the Senators, Buddy Holly is all right. The Everly Brothers are all right. And anything British that's trying to sound like Buddy Holly or the Everly Brothers is all right. But Little Richard, Chuck Berry, Jerry Lee—they're a touch too strong. And a little old, they would no doubt argue. A little bit behind the wave, here at the start of the sixties, with the pop thing really beginning to happen and everybody getting ready to scream at the Beatles. So that's the situation at the YMCA on Taff Street that night: I'm in a band that's suffering from a bad case of musical differences the moment I walk through the door.

Still, it's just a one-off, isn't it? I'm just here to help out. A temporary fix. A one-night stand. Vernon sensibly suggests that, in the absence of any rehearsal, we keep it as simple as possible: do some twelve-bar blues—"Linda Lou," "Lawdy Miss Clawdy," "Johnny B. Goode," stuff that can be easily jammed. I'm up for that. It sounds good. Then there'll be a passage of the show where they play some instrumentals—their Shadows stuff, their twiddly Duane Eddy bit. Vernon says I can go off during that. And that sounds good, too. He asks me what I'd like to start with, and, making a point, I suggest "Great Balls of Fire." The band, with various degrees of reluctance, demurs.

The Senators are organized: they have stage outfits—matching black trousers and pale blue shirts. No uniform for me, of course, and I probably would have told them where to shove it if they'd asked me. I'm in a suit, with a white shirt and tie, because you get dressed up to drink on Fridays. I sense it's a little formal and restricting for what's coming, so I decide to take off the jacket and the tie and go on in the white shirt, unbuttoned.

When the curtain goes back, I get my first proper view of the room. It's a really young scene: school kids, drinking lemonade. Boys in open-necked shirts standing around the walls, trying to look cool; girls in party dresses clustered in the middle of the floor, pretending not to notice the boys. It's a school prom, frankly.

Still, what are you going to do? I don't hold back. I go in bawling. "Great Balls of Fire," in C. "You shake my nerves and you rattle my brain . . ." I realize how liberating it is not to have a guitar strung around my neck, just to have a microphone to hold. I realize how much this frees up my body. I get the hips going. I swing my arms around. There's nothing particularly calculated or worked out about it. It's just how singing this stuff makes me feel. I do some head-shaking and a bit of stamping and I open my throat and rip it, leaving the audience . . .

. . . well, quite frightened, actually. A bit cowed. "Goodness gracious," indeed. It's pretty clear, early on, that what this crowd is getting from me with their lemonade on a Friday night is a bit less reserved than what they are used to getting from Tommy Pitman—possibly to the extent of being a bit upsetting. Indeed, I think the general feeling is: "How did this animal get in here?" There's definitely some wide-eyed fear in the room. Isn't it the first-time performer who's meant to be afraid? In this case, it seems to be the audience. And perhaps one or two members of the band.

But what do I care? I carry on. Over the following twenty minutes or so, I sing the tits off our improvised, twelve-bar repertoire. And gradually the fear in the room seems to melt a bit, and people start to dance—girls first, then, eventually, the boys. Then I take a break, while the Senators play their instrumentals and have their Hank Marvin moment. I go behind the stage during all of that and put a couple of smuggled bottles of light ale away. And then I go back out for "Lawdy Miss Clawdy" and "Long Tall Sally." And the dancing continues, and we get cheered off.

I mean, big deal: they're just kids. But it's uplifting. It's the best fun I've had with my clothes on in quite a while—in fact, maybe ever. That night I end up thinking: actually, this could be okay. If I had a band, I could sing the things I really want to sing—things beyond my very narrow abilities as a guitarist, things with a proper thumping beat under them. I can't do Chuck Berry on my own. But a band makes Chuck Berry an option. And I seem to have found one. Even more convenient than that: a band has come and found me.

Backstage, Vernon gives me a pair of £1 notes—my share of the fee. I check my watch and notice that it isn't yet closing time and that therefore it is still, technically, Friday night. I leave the Senators and go back to the pub to drink.

TOMMY PITMAN WANTED HIS PLACE in the band back. But what had happened at the YMCA had clearly got into Vernon's head. There was the wider issue of Tommy's unreliability, of course. But I think Vernon had also liked the way the band looked and sounded with me in it, that he could see some possibilities there. There was a band meeting in the front room of Vernon's parents' house—everybody there, including Tommy and me. Vernon's two sisters made tea and cut sandwiches—all very civilized. I don't think I said much—just concentrated on drinking the tea and eating the sandwiches. Tommy suggested we could both sing: me the rockers, him the ballads, a dual front man thing. I wasn't too keen on that. The idea of sharing singing duties had never appealed to me, in any context. I guess that's why I had never seen the point of singing in choirs. A wonderful Welsh tradition, of course, and I never minded listening to a choir—but how would you get heard in the middle of all that? Too many voices. Lord knows, even back in the days when a bunch of us used to go out carol singing, I would end up breaking away and going off to sing on my own. Not really a team-player, in that sense. Not really a willing sharer of the limelight.

Fortunately, Vernon did the talking. He basically called Tommy Pitman on his overall commitment to the project, and Tommy Pitman, who didn't really have a leg to stand on in this area, backed down. And that was that. I was in. They had a choice of Tommys. And they went for this one—something for which I would always owe Vernon. And something for which, I guess, I would always owe Tommy Pitman, too, who developed an interest in three card brag at just the right time from my point of view. I told Bryn Phillips that I wouldn't be turning out for the Misfits anymore, and I threw in my lot with Ponty's finest, and only, pretty-boy pop act.

Rock'n'roll with Tommy Scott and the Senators.

11

Revenge Is Not Necessary

Vernon Hopkins was organized—ambitious for the band. It was never the limit of his plan for the Senators to be big in Pontypridd. He was thinking about record deals and stardom way beyond the valleys. In that respect, London was where it mattered at this point, of course. Liverpool and Manchester, too, with the Beatles coming out of one, and looking like they might be something quite big, and Herman's Hermits coming out of the other. But it was mostly about London, in terms of where the deals were made and the fortunes earned. And London seemed light-years away at the time. No Severn Bridge in those days, bringing it closer. It was a city in another country that had no obvious connection with our lives at all. How you made a noise that could be heard that far away—that was the problem that faced us, in the seemingly walled-in world of south Wales. And there didn't seem to be any obvious answers.

Still, one step at a time. Vernon decided that I needed a stage name. Tommy was fine, in his opinion, but Woodward wasn't going to do any of us any favors. Vernon had been typesetting something in his job at the *Pontypridd Observer*, and the name "Scott" jumped out at him. Tommy Scott. We both agreed that it sounded good, that the name "Scott" explicitly wasn't Welsh (which might have undermined our global ambitions) and that it was altogether more starry than Woodward.

Vernon's job at the *Observer* was handy in terms of getting articles into the local paper, and also in terms of getting the odd printing job done. He duly had some business cards made up: "The Senators, with Twisting Tommy Scott." Beneath that was Vernon's phone number for bookings.

When I joined, the band was only playing dance halls and youth clubs. I suggested to them branching out a bit and going into working men's clubs. They were very hesitant: it was a different, older crowd— most definitely not a pop crowd. But it was a crowd that I felt comfortable with, and I knew it was wide open, an untapped market where there was money to be made if you got it right. And I had played all these places with the Misfits, so I had an in.

We'd need to play it slightly differently, though—adapt the act. My idea was to bring Bryn "The Fish" Phillips in, to help bridge the gap between the dance halls and the working men's clubs. He could do a comedy routine before we went on. People knew him and accepted him, and he was good at it. Nobody better in the area for getting his belly out and doing a Hawaiian dance. If trouble started, he could maybe lighten it up a bit, if he got in there quick enough. In the clubs, we didn't have to think of ourselves as auditioning for a record deal, so we could afford to be broader. We could turn "Long Tall Sally" into a comedy skit—bring on Bryn the Fish to fall about a bit. It was just a way to get across to those audiences and it didn't mean we couldn't still do the Empress Ballroom in Abercynon.

I'm not sure how excited the Senators were made by this commercial vision of mine. I think it might just have confused them about me even more: here was this guy who came on strong as a Jerry Lee Lewis fan and all-round rock'n'roller—yet who seemed just as keen on getting a dewy-eyed reaction from oldsters by delivering some ancient ballad or other in the dusty bar of a men's club. Vernon certainly got the idea: he bought into it straightaway. But I think, for a couple of the others, the first question in those days was always: "What would Cliff Richard do?" And if you had asked Cliff at that point whether he was ready to risk a bottling at the Fochriw Social Club near Merthyr Tydfil, I reckon he would probably have said no.

Still, under pressure and however reluctantly, all of the Senators eventually came round and agreed to it. We had our first working men's club booking on a Saturday night in one of the local places where I was known. But even so we attracted immediate suspicion, on sight, just walking in with the gear. "Oh, Christ—electric guitars, is it? Rock'n'roll now, eh, Tommy?" As we were setting up, some of the fellas were already shouting, "Pay 'em off." But I asked the old fellas to just give us a chance and a listen. The audience was, as usual, seated at tables around the room and more than ready to be appalled. But we kept the volume down. I said, "Let's do 'I Believe'"—a ballad that I knew would go over. We eased into it, played the sparkier stuff later, when everyone was onside. At the end of the night, the secretary of the club said he was going to move the chairs and tables aside and asked if we would play a few extra songs so they could have a dance. At which point we knew we had won.

That was it. We were in business. Alva Turner, our not-so-hot drummer, had a dad who didn't mind doing the booking and a van he didn't mind us using for gigs, so we were happy with that. We could go into the working men's clubs and get it across there. And then we had the dance halls, where we could hit the younger crowd. Word of mouth goes ahead of you, and before long we were getting booked all over the place: from the Cwm Welfare Hall in Beddau to the Memorial Hall in Tredegar, and from the ballroom at the end of Penarth Pier to the Empress Ballroom in Abercynon, where we played in the summer of 1962 and where the poster, printed up by the venue and slapped on the wall outside, read: "The Fabulous Senators featuring Tommy Scott, the Twisting Vocalist. Admission: two shillings."

People got off on it. And, on a good night, about 200 people would happily part with two shillings to be there.

The dates kept coming. Club Union Beer was injecting some money into nightclubs at this time, financing some places to sell their beer. So some of these smart clubs were coming up, with glass fronts, purpose-built stages—a cut above the old run-down places. We had our share of those. We were getting three or four bookings a week, at anything up to £15 a throw. I might get to walk away with three or four quid in my pocket at the end of the night, so I was making some useful money.

And the reaction you got was great because there simply wasn't much of this kind of thing in the area. Over in Cardiff, there was a trio fronted by someone called Dave Edmunds—the Raiders—and they seemed to be doing okay, playing the dance halls. There were a couple of other bands over there, too, doing the same. But otherwise, at that point in time, south Wales was a pretty open field. We were a rare thing: young people, playing young music to young people: the pop and rock stuff they'd seen on the telly and heard on the radio. People jumped on it and jumped around to it.

With the exception of Vernon, the makeup of the band would change entirely over the next couple of years. Mickey Gee from Cardiff replaced Mike Roberts. Mickey was more of a rock'n'roll guitarist, and could play like Chet Atkins, finger-style. Keith Davies didn't fancy playing in the working men's clubs so much, so we got another rhythm guitarist, Dave "Dai" Cooper, whose father, conveniently, had a pub, the Thorn Hotel in Abercynon, where we could rehearse. Dai was so small that he could fit himself into a bass drum case—and often did so. It became a little feature of the club show. In the interval, Dai would put on a gorilla outfit and then squeeze himself into the drum case, which we would casually place on the edge of the stage. Then, when we were playing Neil Seda-ka's "I Go Ape," Dai would burst out of the case, just for effect. It's hot in a gorilla suit, and even hotter in a gorilla suit inside a drum case, so Dai would end up drenched in sweat and, if possible, even smaller.

As for Alva, the drummer, for a while his father, Horace, was driving out to some of these clubs that we played and seemed to be interested in managing us. He got us a gig or two—one in a posh hotel in Cardiff—and appeared to have some plans for us and some capital behind him, which was all very intriguing while it was in the air. What scuppered all that, though, was the plain fact that Alva wasn't quite the forceful drummer that we needed and he was eventually replaced by Chris Slade-Rees. Chris's father, Danny Rees, was a tap dancer in a concert party that I used to see. Chris was only sixteen, just out of school and working in Clarks shoe shop in Taff Street. He had a kit in the front room of his house, and Vernon and I went to listen to him and took him on board because he was so clearly hot. Chris went on to have a really successful career, playing all round the world with me after things took off, and then with Manfred Mann's Earth Band, Asia and AC/DC, among others.

In due course, in a declaration of real seriousness about things, the Senators even had their own roadie—Chris Ellis, a TV repair man who lived in Nantgarw and started showing up at the Bedwas Working Men's Club, known as the Green Fly, where we had a residency for a while, playing Tuesday and Thursday nights for a fee of £11 per show. Chris just seemed to like being around us. If any of the equipment started playing up, he would hop on stage with a screwdriver and sort it out. Eventually he offered to start driving the gear around in his works van, a cream-colored Morris J, the back of which he tarted up with some old carpets and, for extra seating, a beaten-up sofa that somebody who lived near him had junked.

On the evening of a gig, Chris would drive round picking up the band. He would pull over at the Blue Star Garage, down on the Broadway, where there was a set of steps up to Cliff Terrace, and someone would run up and call for me. If I was down in the kitchen, getting ready at the sink, they would stamp on the grille above the basement window. Vernon has claimed since that I was never ready—always kept the rest of them waiting while I finished shaving. There may be some truth in that. What's beyond dispute is that, once in the van, I seemed to have an uncanny ability to fall asleep, ignoring all discomfort. Because, despite the carpets and the sofa, Chris's van remained a formidably uncomfortable place, not least when stuffed full of blokes and their guitar cases and amplifiers, and driven round winding south Wales roads. Didn't seem to bother me, though. I would be asleep as soon as my head hit the side window.

I was very happy. If we were playing a working men's club I would be putting in some songs like "My Mother's Eyes," which I loved to do; and if we were in a dance hall, I could do "Good Golly Miss Molly" and fling myself about a bit and let it rip. Okay, we were still doing Cliff's "The Young Ones," which I hated with a passion. But I was out, getting up in front of people and singing and, really for the first time, properly seeing the effect that my voice could have on a room full of people—noting how it excited people and how that, in turn, excited me. I realized, with a new, even clearer urgency, how badly I wanted to do this and nothing else, as remote as the possibility of that still seemed. Let's face it, the music business wasn't exactly rushing to the valleys to sign up any Welsh pop group that could do a kick-arse version of "Good Golly Miss Molly" or, for that matter, a heartbreaking rendition of "My Mother's Eyes." The music business seemed to have plenty on its plate already. But you could dream, couldn't you?

Vernon and I grew to be good friends in this period. He would come up to Cliff Terrace every now and again, and we would sit in the front room and listen to records, picking out material for the band. Generally, the whole group rubbed along pretty well.

Sometimes Linda left Mark at home with her mother and came out to hear us play. She was friendly with Jean Evans, Vernon's girlfriend, so they would come together. I was always happy when she did. I liked that feeling of performing when she was in the room. But the truth was, it made her anxious to watch me. She was caught up in it and would be nervous that I was going to make a mistake or get a bad reaction—a thousand ways she could see in which it might all go horribly wrong. It's a feeling that has stayed with her across the years. The sight of me on a stage just made her tense, which was no fun for her, and she pretty quickly realized that she was more comfortable leaving me to it and staying at home, which I perfectly understood.

One night in particular, though, I was grateful that Linda wasn't there. Some mates came out to see me at the Green Fly—Roy Nichols, in his Austin A70, bringing Johnny Cleaves and Dai Shephard with him. After the gig, I abandoned Chris's van and piled into the car with the lads for the ride back to Pontypridd. We'd been drinking, and there was a fair amount of shouting and singing going on. We were on Nantgarw Hill when we hit a car coming the other way.

I can still hear the bang, after which there was a terrifying spell of spinning and then stillness, followed by the sound of groaning. The other car was fine: we weren't. No seat belts. Blood seemed to be everywhere. Roy broke his jaw. Johnny was badly cut on one side of his head. Dai had a terrible slash across his face that needed thirty-six stitches. I got off relatively lightly with a massive bruise in the center of my forehead where it slammed against the seat in front of me. An ambulance came, and we were all taken to the Miners Hospital by Nantgarw Colliery and patched up. Roy's Austin was written off. We got lucky that night.

Of course, it wasn't just the roads that were dangerous. Some of the clubs could get hairy, too. There were a few bust-ups. Sometimes the band became a target because the girls would get excited, and the fellas would get upset about it. Or sometimes there might be a bust-up because the fellas were excited. On one such night, in the middle of an up-tempo number at the Fochriw Social Club, I saw this beer bottle coming through the air—flung at me from the back of the room. Alas, the guy hadn't put quite enough arm in it, and the bottle fell slightly short, hitting a fella at the front of the audience in the back of the head. The fella automatically assumed the bloke behind him had hit him, so, in line with the traditional south Wales view on punching first and asking questions later, he turned round and smacked him.

Instant chaos. The whole place went up. It would have been entirely comical if it hadn't also been quite frightening. The club was suddenly a heaving sea of violence. Everybody was hitting everybody—and not always with fists: sometimes with furniture. We stopped playing and closed the curtains against the raining bottles, glasses and chairs, standing there looking sheepishly at each other as missiles continued to thud unchecked against the other side of the velvet. Every so often I took a peek out to see if it was getting any quieter, but it wasn't. It continued to look like the Wild West out there, only with more hair lacquer. The police had been called, but they seemed to be staying outside in their cars, having looked through the door, much as I had looked through the curtains, and thought better of it.

"Looks like the end of this, then," Vernon said, and the rest of us could only agree with him. While the battle continued to rage, we loaded our gear out through the back door and drove away to neutral territory.

There's a story that has long since passed into legend that I stole a chicken from a table of raffle prizes on the way out the back door that night. I absolutely insist that this story is not true. I wouldn't do a thing like that. It was a turkey that I stole.

THE BIG THING BACK THEN, working the clubs, was being paid off. That was the signal of defeat, failure and humiliation. And it never happened to me, I swear. Not once. Yes, there was the odd riot and the occasional pause for fighting, occasioned by our music. And there was certainly some early-evening indifference to be battled with. But on no occasion did anyone from the committee have to come up to me, midperformance, and say, "Look, I'm sorry son, but I'm going to have to stop you there."

In the nineties, and at this point resident in America, I will buy a house near Welsh St. Donats because Linda and I want to have a base in Wales again. And one night the two of us are out together at a restaurant, where a wedding party happens to be going on. On my way out, I happily agree to pose for a picture with the bride and groom and I'm crossing the

parking lot when one of the party asks me if I remember playing a particular club in south Wales, back in the day. And I do. I remember this club
clearly.

"Only, my uncle was the secretary there," this person says.

"Oh, that's great," I say.

"Yeah," says the guy, "and he paid you off."

Strange to say, but these words work on me like a red rag works on a
bull. Something hot flashes right through me, like this guy has just laid
on me the worst insult anybody could conceive of. Like he's called into
question my entire reputation and, beyond that, my whole being.

I spin round and reply through gritted teeth: "Nobody. Ever. Paid
me off."

The guy looks a little shocked and doesn't press the point.

This is thirty years later we're talking about. And it still seemed to
matter.

How to use your

Electrolux®

CLEANER

MODEL G

Not a bad job.

12

Door to Door

"Good morning, madam. We're in the area this morning demonstrating Electrolux vacuum cleaners. You're under no obligation to buy, but I'm here to give you a free demonstration. Would you allow me to come in and show you this exciting new product?"

That's me in 1963 in my new role as a door-to-door vacuum salesman. And that's what I hit them with when the door opens: a smile, look them in the eye and give them the patter. If you get through the door, you can do the demo. And if the demo goes right, you can leave with a commitment to purchase and a £5 deposit which is yours to keep.

Along the way you might even have got to wheel out the brand slogan: "Nothing sucks like an Electrolux."

Might not have worked in America, that slogan: seems to be working in Britain in 1963, though.

I owe this new occupation to a man called Geoffrey Bloomer, who's been coming to see me sing in the clubs with the Senators. He's an educated guy and a bit of an entrepreneur, it seems to me, whose father owns property in Pontypridd. The pair of us have fallen to talking after a show one night, and he's asked me what I do when I'm not singing. I tell him I've been working as a laborer on the building sites. There's plenty of new houses going up around the town and I know enough people to get myself taken on. I've been slogging up and down ladders with a hod full of bricks. I don't mind the fact that I'm putting on a bit of muscle, but the work's an absolute pain in the arse, if I'm being honest.

He says, "Have you ever thought about selling vacuum cleaners?"

I haven't, oddly enough. But Geoffrey is very persuasive. He's got this franchise arrangement worked out with Electrolux—takes his Mini van down to the depot, loads it up with boxed vacuum cleaners and then drives out to try and flog them around Pontypridd and the surrounding towns. Then he goes back to Electrolux with the signed-up paperwork. He says there's enough going on that he could use a hand with it.

What have I got to lose? Even if you only manage to sell one or two of these things a week, £5 is a pretty decent sum—not least for maybe only a few minutes' chat. You might even get a cup of tea and a biscuit thrown in, according to Geoffrey, if the person is nice enough or bored enough. Also—and this really is the clincher—a vacuum cleaner isn't ever going to be as heavy as a hod full of bricks.

So one morning I meet Geoffrey, and we set off together in his Mini. As we drive, he runs me through the tactics and the techniques. We don't work as a pair, because, like as not, in the middle of the day, the door is going to be answered by a housewife, and two men on the doorstep could be intimidating. We go up the path on our own. Trust is the key to it, so you smile—make like an honest and sincere person. If she's interested and you're invited in, you take in the demonstration model and a little box of ashes, throw the ashes down on the carpet and reveal how well the Electrolux picks it all up. Because nothing sucks . . . What you really want is for them to have just finished doing the cleaning— and preferably with one of the old deadbeat manual floor cleaners, like a Ewbank or a Bissell, yesterday's technology. If they've just done the cleaning, they're a bit anxious about seeing the ash go down—and that bit more relieved and delighted when you make it vanish again with this new piece of chore-saving electrical magic. Well, that's the theory.

The key thing is, you've got to get them to sign for it—and it has to be the man's signature. As far as the company is concerned, it's not enough to get the signature of the housewife. You need to get the signed permission of the man of the house. That's just the way it is, at this point in time.

So that usually means, if you convince the woman and get the promise of a sale, you've still got to drive back out to the house that evening when the man's home from work. And then you've got to hope that the woman has done a decent job of persuading her husband that their house can't survive without one of these new vacuum cleaners and that he hasn't simply nixed the deal straightaway, before he's finished hanging up his coat and putting his slippers on, which sometimes happens.

One time a woman tells me she'll definitely, no question about it, have the vacuum cleaner and instructs me to come back at 7:00 to get the paperwork sorted out with her husband, who won't have any problem about it, she knows. I'm pretty sure I've never had a firmer sale. You can just tell with people, by the way they are. So I leave the machine with her, head back out there in the evening and knock on the door. The door opens, and I am drawing my breath to say good evening when one slightly used Electrolux vacuum cleaner comes flying out. I have just enough time to react and catch it in my arms before it crashes to the ground. Then the door slams.

Probably not a sale after all, then.

The company warns us off certain areas—one or two blacklisted housing estates in Pontypridd where they've had their fingers burned before and where people have shown themselves happy to take the product, but less happy to pay for it. But Geoffrey and I will make out we don't know anything about all that and head into those places anyway. We'll head into those places first, in fact. Because once we've got the signature and the fiver, we're through. Getting the rest of the money is the company's headache.

We do this for a couple of months, Geoffrey and me, doing okay, picking up a few sales, until we come to feel that we've kind of exhausted the area, and maybe our enthusiasm for vacuum cleaners, too. Not before one particular day, though, when Geoffrey says, "Why don't you have a go at driving?"

"Are you serious?"

"Yeah."

So we swap places, and over the next few days, at the age of twenty-three, I learn to drive, taught by Geoffrey in his Mini van, going around the valleys with a load of Electrolux vacuum cleaners sitting in the back. I take to it pretty quickly and like the feeling. I'm way off being able to afford a car, but I dream of the day when I might.

Meanwhile, there's always my brother-in-law's car. Linda's sister, Rosalind, has married a fella called Tony Thorn, and Tony has landed himself a big win on the football pools—not life-changing money, not Viv Nicholson money, the Yorkshire housewife who pulled in £152,000 around the same time and famously promised to "spend, spend, spend"—but enough to buy himself a red Ford Corsair, which is the business. One day, not having anything better to do, I borrow it and spin over to Vernon's house in Glyndwr Avenue, honking for him outside, just to get a reaction.

"How the fuck . . . ?"

I tell him to jump in, and we head off down to Barry Island for the afternoon, where we knock about on the seafront and eat chips before driving back to Pontypridd as evening falls, feeling pretty happy with ourselves. At least, I'm pretty happy with myself until, as we're coming into the town, a policeman steps off the pavement and flags us down.

Just a routine check. Would I like to produce my license?

Well, of course I would, if I had one. But I haven't even taken the driving test, let alone passed it. I've just been knocking about in the hills with Geoffrey Bloomer.

Done for driving, uninsured and without a license. Made to appear in court on a wet Tuesday morning and fined £5—the price of the commission on an Electrolux vacuum cleaner.

Nice car, though, that Ford Corsair.

THE SENATORS WERE OUT GIGGING three or four times a week in 1963, going over well, putting some decent money in my hand—to the point when I started to wonder whether I was attracting suspicion at the dole office, where I continued to sign on every Thursday morning for my weekly ten shillings and sixpence.

The band was thriving—and yet, at the same time, kind of stuck. Vernon and I used to talk about it all the time, getting more and more frustrated. We were playing the same places, to the same crowds. Were we just a local thing? Was this the limit of it? How could we move it on? It was no clearer to any of us how we could break beyond those boundaries into the wider world where records were made. "Go to London," people said. But how could we do that? I had a wife and a son to think of. The band had jobs. And anyway, just supposing you did go to London: what would you do then? Stand outside the train station and sing until somebody signed you up? The whole thing seemed impossible.

It was at this point that Myron and Byron entered our lives.

Myron and Byron's real names were Ray Godfrey and John Glastonbury, but to us they were always Myron and Byron. Ray Godfrey was the shorter and the noisier of the pair: he was Myron. John Glastonbury was the tall, quiet one: he was Byron. I'm not sure why we called them that, except that it rhymed and it took the piss and it stuck.

They were a pair of County Schoolboys in their late twenties, who seemed to fancy themselves as songwriters. They came to see us one Thursday night at the Green Fly in Bedwas. I'm not sure that any of us particularly warmed to this pair on sight. I'm pretty sure they were in tweed jackets. They certainly behaved as though they were. They came across as a bit square, studious and somewhat nerdy. They were both big fans of the Goons' radio show and liked to imitate the silly voices of Milligan, Secombe, etc.—not always successfully. These weren't rock'n'roll people, that was for sure.

On the other hand, they told us they had some contacts in music publishing in London, which sounded promising, and they said they thought they could help us. And really, at the stage we were at, that seemed to be enough. One evening Myron and Byron brought a management contract to the Abercynon Hotel, where we were rehearsing, and all of us solemnly signed it. I'm not sure any of us actually read it, but we certainly signed it—and would perhaps regret doing so a couple of years later, when this deal had to be unpicked, at some expense, in a court of law. At the time, though . . . well, it wasn't like there were any better deals on the table. People weren't exactly hammering on the door in their hundreds, pleading for the opportunity to manage us.

At first it worked out pretty well. Myron and Byron really did seem to have the wherewithal to change things up a bit. Their first gift to us was a slot supporting Billy J. Kramer and the Dakotas at the Grand Pavilion in Porthcawl. That was a good gig to have. Kramer was from Liverpool, shared a manager with the Beatles—Brian Epstein—and was part of that whole pretty-boy Merseybeat thing which was sweeping the country. He'd had a hit with a cover of the Beatles' "Do You Want to Know a Secret." I didn't mind it. A bit lightweight, maybe, but I'd heard worse.

He had some fans, though. The Grand Pavilion, a white, dome-roofed thirties building on the Esplanade, was rammed with about 600 of them, mostly girls, ready to go up at any moment. It was my first experience of that kind of crowd, up close—and Christ, it was intense. They were there for Kramer, but they screamed for us, too. I have no idea how we played that night, because I couldn't hear a thing above the audience. We just threw ourselves at it for our twenty minutes and got off. Thrilling, though—our own little slice of beat-group action. I knew the acclaim wasn't really for us—that these kids were excited about what was coming their way later, and that we were merely benefitting from the fallout. But it still felt great.

Myron and Byron's second gift to us was a recording session—in a manner of speaking. According to Myron and Byron, we needed to attract the interest of a record producer. And in order to attract the interest of a record producer we needed to record a demo. Which, in an ideal world, would be something you did in a recording studio. But recording studios cost money, so, instead, we got permission from the manager of the YMCA on Taff Street to go into the building one afternoon and set up our equipment in the room there that offered the best acoustics—the gents'. We set up the gear in there and recorded a batch of about eight songs from our stage show, using a single microphone and a reel-to-reel tape recorder, provided by Myron and Byron. Then we listened back to it. I thought it sounded like shit. To my ears, it was the sound of a bunch of blokes making a lot of noise in a YMCA toilet. I couldn't see it impressing anyone at all.

AT SOME POINT IN 1960, I took it upon myself to audition for a singing slot on a television show at the studios of BBC Wales in Cardiff. The show was called *Donald Peers Presents*—a showcase for local talent, broadcast only to the region. Peers, who was by this time in his mid-fifties, was bona fide show business royalty in Wales. He had had a massive post-war, pre-rock'n'roll hit with a song called "In a Shady Nook by a Babbling Brook," had done numerous radio shows and been crowned with an appearance on the Royal Variety Show at the London Palladium. You can gauge how much currency he had in the culture from the fact that he was also the source of a piece of widely used rhyming slang. Your ears, in Cockney slang, were your Donalds: Donald Peers—ears.

For my audition piece, I chose "That Lucky Old Sun"—which is a kind of spiritual, hardship song, which I have always loved. Sam Cooke had recently done it, and so had Ray Charles and Aretha Franklin. I thought I did a decent job on it—decent enough, clearly. Soon after this an envelope arrived at home with the BBC logo printed on it. I took it to work with me and nervously opened it up in a quiet moment on the building site, away from everyone else. The letter thrillingly confirmed that I had passed the audition and that my name had been filed on the BBC books for possible future appearances. Soon after, I was called back for the final *Donald Peers Presents* of that particular season, where I would have happily sung "That Lucky Old Sun" again, except that the producers had other ideas. They wanted me to do "I'm Lookin' Out the Window"—a fucking Cliff Richard song. A Cliff Richard B-side, indeed. I guess this was karma coming round for all the times I'd slagged Cliff off. I didn't have any choice—just had to suck it up, sitting there on a stool in the producer's choice of clothing for me, which included a black shirt with a floppy, built-in bow under the collar. Next to me was a window frame down which the rain played as I sang—except, of course, it wasn't the rain, it was some bloke up a ladder, off-camera, with a watering can. Talk about a baptism of fire—or a baptism of crap, anyway. Still, I was on the telly, which made my parents proud, and Linda, too. It made it seem like I might finally be getting somewhere—TV's mighty stamp of authority. Also, I got to sit in a chair and have makeup put on me, for the first time in my life, which felt kind of film-starry.

But then I got the bus back to Pontypridd, and a mate of mine got on and started looking at me oddly. "Fucking hell," he eventually said. "Are you wearing makeup?"

Even though I'd hated the song and the setup, and even though I knew it was local telly, some small part of me entertained the possibility that my appearance on *Donald Peers Presents* might turn out to be transformative—might be the breakthrough moment. Wasn't that how telly worked?

It wasn't, though. The show came and went, the days went by, and I still seemed to be exactly where I was before it happened.

I'M SITTING IN THE WHITE HART early one evening in 1963 when the Rolling Stones come on the television behind the bar. They're doing "I Wanna Be Your Man." Standing there with a pint in his hand is Glynog Evans, the big former rugby player I mentioned earlier, who gets up in the Wood Road Non-Political and sings the piss-takers into submission. Glynog, in his blue blazer, looks up at the image on the screen of Mick Jagger's skinny figure, clapping and bopping, and for a while is lost in speechless, open-mouthed amazement. Eventually he announces to the room in general, in his booming voice, "Well I've fucking seen everything now. What the fuck is that?"

Then he calls across the bar to me. "Hey, Tommy: when are you going to get up off your fucking arse and move to London and show these English bastards how to sing?"

I laugh and say, "Yeah, yeah. I'll leave in the morning, Glynog."

If only.

Joe Meek.

13

Friend or Foe?

Late 1963. Myron and Byron have some news for us. They've played our demo recording—the legendary lavatory tapes—to an independent producer in London. He's liked it and he wants us to go in and record a session with him. The producer's name is Joe Meek.

We've heard of Joe Meek. He produced "Telstar" for the Tornados, Billy Fury's backing band. Weird-sounding instrumental track: sounded liked the theme for a sci-fi TV show. Massive hit not long ago, though. Hard to avoid it: five weeks at number 1. Big hit in America too, apparently. So immediately we're thinking: this guy can make a difference.

Thank you, Myron. Thank you, Byron.

Chris Rees books a couple of days off from the shoe shop. Vernon has already been laid off by the *Pontypridd Observer* because he kept oversleeping after gigs and going in late, exhausted. My employment situation at this point is, let's say, highly flexible—and nonexistent, if anyone at the dole office is asking. Chris Ellis takes some time out from the TV repair shop and drives round in the van to collect us all, and the gear, and we set off on the seven-hour drive to London.

I'm twenty-three, and this is only the second time I've been there. The first time was a school trip to the Tower of London in my last year at school, traveling on a chocolate-and-cream-colored Great Western Railway steam train. The only one of us who has any experience of the place—of how it looks and works—is Dai Cooper, who was born there. But even he moved away to Wales when he was quite small. Otherwise, we are a bunch of Welsh hicks in our jeans and white T-shirts, trying not to gawp and reveal ourselves. To me, a Cockney accent sounds like an impediment; like a foreigner trying to speak English. They can't say an "l" at the end of a word—"wew" for "well." "Wew oi nivvah!" What's that about?

We stay at a bed and breakfast which Myron and Byron have sorted out for us in Sussex Gardens in Paddington, and in the morning, after the landlady has served us greasy fried eggs and toast, we get back in the van and drive over to Islington.

Meek's studio doesn't look much like the kind of place where multi-million-selling singles are made. It's on a main drag, the Holloway Road, in a flat above a leather goods shop selling handbags and wallets. You ignore the door into the shop, go up a narrow staircase to one side and find the studio on the middle floor—sound room to the front, control room to the rear. It's cramped and messy—littered with wires and tape boxes and mad-looking electrical contraptions—and not particularly soundproofed. Apparently, the people from the shop downstairs will poke up at the ceiling with a broomstick when they've had enough of the racket. Maybe this is what is meant by "independent." But I've only been in the studios of BBC Wales before this, so what do I know?

And then there's Joe Meek himself. My experience of record producers at this point is pretty much limited to photographs of Quincy Jones or George Martin—a smart man in a suit or a cardigan. Very much an adult presence. Meek's not like that. He's in a suit, but it's a mohair one—silver gray—with no tie, and his hair is slicked up and back. He looks like a player: shades of Teddy boy, except that he's in his mid-thirties, a bit old for the look. He has a slight west country accent, a bit of a burr, not unlike my paternal grandmother. He's distant, preoccupied, not exactly excited to see us, as far as we can work out.

His eccentricity and his paranoia—his interest in putting tape recorders in graveyards in order to try and capture the sound of the dead, his belief that major record labels have bugged his studio with microphones behind the wallpaper in order to steal his ideas—these things will become legend in due course, not least after the point in February 1967 when, racked by depression, Meek kills his landlady with a shotgun and then turns the weapon on himself. But to us, at this point, he's just this guy in a silver suit who knows what he's doing and is going to get us where we need to be.

We set up in the sound room, where the drums go in the fireplace to benefit from the acoustics offered by the bare brickwork, and Meek puts his microphones around the place—very efficient, still not really engaging with us. Then he goes through to the control room, and we run through a song so that he can get the sound-levels sorted out. When we've finished, he comes back in.

"You won't need to be so close to the microphone," he tells me. "You have a very loud voice."

After the first take he returns from the control room looking like thunder. In his hand is a gun.

"Didn't I tell you to back off from the microphone?"

He points the gun right at me, at arm's length from himself.

"Jesus Christ!" I shout.

Bang!

My ears ring and the room reels with shock.

It's a starting pistol.

Fucking prankster.

I suppose this breaks the ice—inasmuch as a nutter with a gun is ever going to break the ice. But I'm furious for a while. Fooled and furious.

We carry on and record five songs in quick succession—among them

"Little Lonely One," a popped-up doo-wop song recorded by the Jarmels. The idea is that this might make a single. Meek plays us back to ourselves. It's unmixed, but I'm thinking: wow, actually this is okay. Better than we've ever sounded. Better than the tape from the YMCA gents', definitely. Meek doesn't give us a copy of the recording to take away with us. He says he's going to send us something later, when he's finished with it. And then he'll take it round a few record companies and see what people say.

After the session, when the gear has been packed back into the van and we're about to leave, Meek calls me back into the control room. He says, "I want to have a word with you." I'm thinking he might be about to say something complimentary about my voice. Instead, he looks at me meaningfully and says, "Those jeans fit you well."

I say, "What is this?"

I notice that one of his hands is in his pocket, moving around in there.

He says, "Do you normally move when you sing? Do you want to show me how you move?"

I'm flashing back to that Sunday shift at the glove factory, all those years ago. It's happening again.

I get out of there, gallop down the stairs and jump into the van, where everyone's waiting. "You'll never fucking guess what? He's only gone and started coming on to me . . ."

The band takes the piss, all the way back to Wales.

BACK IN PONTYPRIDD, WE WAIT. And we wait. And then all of a sudden . . . nothing happens. And we go on waiting.

No news. It's agony. Why aren't we hearing anything? What's going on? Where's our record deal? What's Meek doing? It's driving me nuts. It's not like I can just pick up a phone. I don't have a phone to pick up. I haven't even got anything from the session that I can play to Linda, or anyone else. It's like the whole thing with Meek never happened.

So much for the big timers. We've opened our mouths to a few people.

"Off to London, then, is it, Tommy?"

"Yeah. Recording a single. With Joe Meek."

Get me.

And now I'm back.

Where is it then? Where is this record?

Myron and Byron go up and down to London a number of times during this period, but we never quite work out what they get up to when they're there. Certainly nothing concrete seems to come of these trips. Meek appears to be playing the pair of them along quite merrily. I'm not sure how much respect he has for them, ultimately. Meanwhile they say they're still touting the YMCA tape around, trying to drum up some interest on their own. One time they disappear off and are gone for a few days, and my impatience gets the better of me, and I finally lose it. I'm full of righteous indignation and madness and possibly some beer. It's a Friday night, and I ask Chris Ellis to drive me to London.

"I'm going to go up there and sort those fuckers out. And if they're not doing anything about getting us a record deal, I'll do it myself."

We know they're supposed to be staying in Bloomsbury, in the Aaland Hotel. We get there in the early hours of the morning. Chris sits outside in the van while I get the room number from reception and head upstairs, where I immediately take to banging the shit out of the door.

No answer. But maybe that's not surprising because I'm roaring and thumping and I don't sound like someone you'd necessarily open the door to in a hurry in the middle of the night.

However, as I continue to bang and shout, the door to the next room along opens and a tired man, approaching forty, with a neatly trimmed bob of peroxide hair emerges. And suddenly I am staring at the well-known figure of Radio Luxembourg disk jockey, nightclub entrepreneur and national television presenter Jimmy Savile.

In his pajamas.

I don't now recall what Savile's opening remark is, but it's something to the effect that if I would mind not kicking the door down and making such a godawful racket, he, as someone who is trying to get to sleep, would appreciate it.

Calmed down very suddenly by embarrassment, I try to explain myself. "I'm from Wales," I say (which is a good start). "I'm a singer and there's a fella in there who's supposed to be my manager and I can't get hold of him." Savile seems to recognize the face of a desperate man; either that or he just wants to go back to his bed in peace. He says, "Listen, if you're around tomorrow morning, I'll be downstairs. Come and find me and we'll have a chat."

I go back out to Chris, and the pair of us spend the rest of the night sleeping in the van in our clothes. I stew over the irony of my managers being in a hotel in London, on a quest to break their act into the music industry and oblivious to the fact that Jimmy Savile is in the room next door. It seems to say a lot about Myron and Byron.

The following day, unwashed and wearing slept-in clothes, I go back into the hotel to await my meeting, which I'm strongly suspecting will turn out to have been a tactical ruse on Savile's part. But no. He's already there, true to his word.

We sit in a corner of the lobby, and I pour the whole sorry tale out to him: the session with Joe Meek that seems to be coming to nothing, the managers trying to attract a record company, which also seems to be coming to nothing. "What do I need to do?"

Savile looks like he might have heard this kind of story before. He says, "Let me give you some advice. If you send a tape to a record company, they won't even thread the machine. They'll throw it straight in the bin. You need to spend some money, go into a recording studio and make an acetate—a proper, solid disk. Then you give the acetate to me, and, if it's any good, I'll take it to Decca Records."

Savile has one other piece of advice for me, which I struggle to see the relevance of, but which I just swallow as part of the man's eccentricity and his general air of randomness. "Don't get involved with stars," he says, with a wag of the finger, like a bossy teacher. "Go into Woolworths and chat up a nice girl behind the counter because they don't tell stories."

I report this meeting to Myron and Byron when our paths finally cross again, back in Wales. Relations between us are more strained than ever after my failed attempt to dig them out in London, but we battle on, having no better alternative, and we agree to exploit this contact I've made with Savile. In late 1963, or possibly early 1964, using money cobbled together from the fees for some gigs in Wales, we go into Regent Sound Studio in Denmark Street in London and make an acetate. "Breathless," a Jerry Lee Lewis song, and "I Love How You Love Me," a piece of Brill Building pop which Phil Spector had produced for the Paris Sisters in 1961 and which had been going over well in our live act in the working men's clubs. Myron and Byron take this acetate to Savile, who, in turn, takes it to Decca and gives it to Peter Sullivan, the company's in-house producer. And Sullivan likes it enough to invite us up to London for an audition.

Another seven-hour slog by road up to London—I'm getting used to these. But we're optimistic. Decca's a proper label. Okay, they passed on the Beatles, which, in retrospect, looking at it from early 1964, with the band having entirely conquered Britain and on its way over to invade America, was probably a bit of a mistake. On the other hand, the group Decca passed them up for was the Tremeloes, and they're not doing too badly—had a number 1 with "Do You Love Me." And Decca didn't pass up the Rolling Stones, who aren't doing too badly either. So maybe they won't pass up Tommy Scott and the Senators if we play it right. We go to Decca Studios, a well-polished and rather sedate-feeling facility at 165 Broadhurst Gardens in West Hampstead, a number of miles, in every sense, from Joe Meek's flat—and the very place in which the Beatles failed their audition, although we try not to think about that. We do some songs for Sullivan, and it seems to go okay—although, as I'm rapidly learning, it's not always easy to tell.

Afterward, Sullivan takes me aside and says: "Tell the boys to pack the gear up, I want to talk to you."

I'm remembering Meek. I'm thinking to myself, "Oh, no, not again. Is this the music industry? Is this how you get on?"

In fact, Sullivan says he's really impressed with the way I sing. Powerful. Soulful. A lot of rhythm and blues in there. He thinks I've got something that could really work, given the right song. He's very complimentary, and that's great. But he's not saying there's a deal on the table. And he's certainly not thrusting a piece of paper into my hand and begging me to sign it.

During this conversation, I mention to Sullivan about Savile taking the trouble to offer me advice and then passing on the acetate. "Which was nice of him," I say. But Sullivan points out that Savile is effectively working for Decca: he presents *The Decca Chart Show* on Radio Luxembourg. Decca has put him on the lookout for new talent, so it wasn't exactly a favor.

Still, it meant something to me that he would go to the trouble. I appreciate, of course, that subsequent history, and the appalling evidence that came to light posthumously of the man's lifelong evil practices, mean that the name "Jimmy Savile" isn't one that you can go dropping into polite conversation anymore. But I wasn't to know, mad with fury in that hotel corridor in 1963, what a piece of work he was. And it would be churlish of me to deny him his part in this story.

I guess it's a little bit like what Eva Braun used to say about Hitler: "Well, he was always very nice to *me*."

Mickey Gee, Chris Slade, Vernon Hopkins,
Dave Cooper: The Squires.

14

What You Don't Know

After all these trips up and down to London, things seemed to be coming together. We had some stirrings at Decca Records—an ally there, clearly, in Peter Sullivan, the in-house producer. That said, there was still nothing concrete anywhere at this point, and time was ticking on. At this stage it could all have unraveled again, very easily, and drifted away. It needed someone to come in and force the issue. And that was when I met Gordon Mills.

I'd first set eyes on Gordon Mills in 1961, when he was on the telly. I was shaving in the scullery off the kitchen at Cliff Terrace, and Linda called me through.

"Come and see. It's that fella from Tonypandy."

She was watching *Thank Your Lucky Stars*, the ITV pop music show. A three-piece singing group called the Viscounts were wearing tight suits and doing "Who Put the Bomp (in the Bomp, Bomp, Bomp)." Pop stars from Tonypandy, which is about six miles up the road from Pontypridd—there weren't so many of those to the pound, so that was a bit of a thing, all in itself. Pop stars from Tonypandy who used to be bus conductors with Rhondda Transport—there were even fewer of them.

Pop stars from Tonypandy who used to be bus conductors who packed themselves off to London at nineteen to work the vaudeville scene in a harmonica act before forming a vocal group, despite never having sung before . . . well, you can see that Gordon was a man who took his own path.

Linda thought what she was seeing with the Viscounts was great. I wasn't so sure. Good-looking fella, but the number wasn't so hot. I went back and finished shaving and when I returned, they were still singing.

"Jesus Christ—how long is this song?"

After the Viscounts, Gordon set himself up as a songwriter. He had written "I'll Never Get Over You," which Johnny Kidd and the Pirates recorded, and a quick-paced pop/rock thing, "I'm the Lonely One," for Cliff Richard and the Shadows. Both of those were Top 10 hits. Now he wanted to break into management. He felt that, what with the singing and the songwriting and the edging himself into the London scene, he'd had this crash course in the way the music business worked and that, if he could get the right artist under his wing, he could now make it work for himself.

He was down in south Wales for a week to visit his mother. Two old friends of his, Johnny Bennett and Gog Jones, who knew that Gordon was in the market for talent, told him I might be worth checking out while he was around. This was May 1964. The Senators had a Sunday-night gig booked in at the Top Hat Club in Cwmtillery, a small, stone-walled mining village about thirty miles northeast of Pontypridd. The Top Hat was a remote social hall, standing beside a road called Wood-land Terrace, with a bar and a concert room that had a small stage at one end of it. It wasn't exactly the London Palladium, but it could get rammed to the rafters with people coming out from the local towns and was usually pretty lively when we played there.

I think it was Johnny Bennett, acting as a go-between, who thought it might be a good idea for me and Gordon to hook up before the show, just to shake hands. So an arrangement was made to meet on the Sunday lunchtime at the Lewis Merthyr Club, a working man's place in Porth.

Gordon turned up at the wheel of a maroon Ford Zephyr convertible. You didn't see a lot of convertible cars around our way. Soft-tops were swanky—definitely the mark of a person who had made it. He was wearing a dark-blue mohair suit, looking pretty smooth. Pricey wristwatch, I noticed. With him was his wife, Jo Waring, who was quite far pregnant. She was a model. I'd seen her in Linda's catalogs. She'd been a Bluebell girl in Paris—done the feathers-and-legs thing in cabaret at the Lido, worked the clubs in Vegas for a bit. You couldn't deny that there was an aura of mid-sixties London glamour about the pair of them, not least against the backdrop of a relatively quiet working men's club in south Wales on a Sunday lunchtime—like these people had some kind of extra sheen to them that other people in the room didn't.

You couldn't deny, either, that Gordon was incredibly sure of himself—confrontational straightaway, grinning and accusing me of looking a bit rough and ready in my leather jacket and jeans.

"You look like a fucking Rhondda-ite!"

And me straight back at him.

"You're the fucking Rhondda-ite!"

Just like that, connecting pretty fast. He was only four years older than me—twenty-eight at this point, to my twenty-four—but the confidence he had about him added another ten years to that at least, it seemed to me. And he wasn't just confident, he was also stubborn with it—nicknamed by his London mates "The Mule." We were the same height, the same size. He could have been my older brother. My very dominant older brother. In some respects that was the kind of relationship we would go on to have.

After that meeting—just a handshake and a hello, really—I was desperate to impress him with the show that evening. It put me on edge at home during the afternoon, in a way that I never normally was before a gig. Linda sensed it. She didn't often come to see me sing, on account of the anxiety it caused her, but on this occasion she decided that she would. After I had gone on ahead with the group in the van, she left Mark at home with Vi and came in a Mini driven by her friend Jean Evans, Vernon's girlfriend.

The evening didn't get off to the most promising start when Gordon and Jo arrived at the Top Hat and the bloke on the door tried to turn them away. "Sorry, mate. Full." Brilliant. I've got a VIP down from London and some bouncer is making him and his pregnant wife stand in the parking lot. I had to do some pleading to get them inside and then, once they were in, tried to get them installed somewhere where they wouldn't be too badly jostled about. I didn't want them getting pissed off after two songs and walking out.

The show we did that night was the standard Tommy Scott and the Senators social club appearance. A bit of rock'n'roll, a bit of pop, some ballads. We had done a lot of this. We were pretty slick at it by this point. We opened with "Spanish Harlem," as I remember, and then took it from there, me getting into it as much as the space on that stage allowed, coming across big in the ballads. We went over okay. We usually did in the Top Hat.

I stood at the bar with Gordon after the show. It was unnerving. He wasn't giving much away. There was no gush. He said something like, "I like what you do. If you ever come to London, look me up." Cool as that. Very even tone of voice. No particular excitement.

It was only later that I heard from Jo, his wife, about the way Gordon spoke about me in the car going back to London that weekend—really fired up, full of it, talking about how he couldn't believe I was still only working the clubs and how he was convinced he'd found a potential star, saying, "I've got to do something with that guy, Jo, I've got to do something."

Only later, too, that I heard what Jo had said to Gordon: "I've never seen anything so *male* in all my life."

I, meanwhile, had a more pressing concern: finding my wife. After Gordon had left, I couldn't see Linda anywhere in the club. Jean Evans knew where she was. Apparently Linda had decided, early in the evening, to take the edge off her nerves with Babycham. It's one way to deal with it. But then the Babycham ended up taking the edge off Linda, which can happen if you give it the chance to, and midway through the show she was forced to head unsteadily for the ladies'. Which was where I eventually found her, flat out in a cubicle. I had to laugh about it—my moral support. She had sat down and then slid forward so that her feet were halfway up the door, blocking it shut. Fortunately the cubicle was one of those ones that was open at the top. So I jumped up in the stall next door, climbed over, unbolted it and carried my wife out of there and home to bed.

NOT LONG AFTER THAT WEEKEND, word came back that Gordon wanted another conversation with me. The arrangement was that he would call me at the phone box at the top of Laura Street at a set time, late one afternoon. I had to hang around outside the phone box and wait for it to ring. Thus do futures in show business get decided. When it rang, his voice at the other end said, "I'd like you to come to London and have a meeting."

I went up by train. Gordon showed me around the place a bit, took me into the offices of his music publisher, Leeds Music in Denmark Street, off the Charing Cross Road. Short and narrow, Denmark Street in those days was London's Tin Pan Alley, the nerve center of the songwriting trade. At Leeds Music, we went into a little writer's room with an upright piano in it, and Gordon played some songs that he was working on. Afterward we went out to the Gioconda café—the usual kind of little Italian place, with the espresso machine and the Formica tables, but a big Denmark Street hangout, the place where the publishers and musicians from the recording studios spent their breaks. Gordon bought me a coffee, and we sat down at a table in the corner. And it was there that he said, "If I'm going to become your manager, you must trust me"— choosing this moment to place his hand on my knee. Which was no more than a gesture of reassurance, though, again, not for the first time in my formative relations with the music industry, I found myself experiencing a moment of uncertainty.

The point is, though, I was already convinced. I related to Gordon. We came from the same place, seemed to share the same attitudes. I liked the way he talked and I felt understood by him. Mostly I felt he understood my voice, recognized that there was some versatility in there. At this stage I think he thought of me principally as a blues and soul guy. But he made clear to me that he also saw me as someone who, once established, could almost certainly sing anything and make it work. All I was waiting for was the right song. He said, "If I can't write you that song myself, then I'll do everything in my powers to find it for you."

He said he knew promoters, too, that he could get me out performing with the band all over the country, not just in south Wales, get my face properly out there. With everything he said, I was always aware that he had been there and done it, so he was coming from a position of authority. For the first time since I had set out on this journey, I felt I was in the presence of someone who genuinely knew the ropes. I was entirely persuaded by him.

"But you'll need to be here, in London," Gordon said. "You and the band."

I guess I had seen it coming, although the thought still caused my heart to sink, thinking of Linda and Mark, wondering how the hell this could be made to work. Gordon told me that if I stayed in Pontypridd, it would almost certainly never happen for me. In his opinion, I had pushed it about as far as it would go there. Now I had to move it on— come to London and make an impact on people who could make a difference. It was the way Gordon had done it himself. Now it was my turn.

So there I was, facing the decision that I'd been dodging for years.

True, the prospect of moving away to London felt more plausible now that Gordon was behind me. It felt like there was a bit of structure to it. But it was still daunting. A leap of faith. And weighed down with practicalities. How would it work with Linda and Mark? There was no question of all three of us taking off for London—moving Linda away from home, dragging Mark out of school, no money, no job, no house . . .

So what I would be effectively saying to Linda, by going along with this plan, was, "I'm off, then. Going to London to try and become a star. Look after our son, now, won't you? And I'll see you when I get back." She was troubled by the idea, and who could blame her? Okay, it helped that Linda believed in Gordon. He was so self-assured, so convincing, how could you feel anything other than sure about him? But how certain of him would she have to have been to be happy to see her husband disappearing off up the road, promising to be back when he could?

And then there was my mother, urging caution and putting thoughts in my head that I'd rather not have had. "You, leaving a pretty young girl like that," she said, when I was getting ready to go. "You'd better be careful."

I guess at some point along the road you find out how much you really want something, and what you're prepared to do to get it. And this was that point.

The last gig Tommy Scott and the Senators played in Pontypridd was in the room on the top of the White Hart Hotel in June 1964, and the following day I put my clothes in a brown holdall, kissed my wife and child good-bye, climbed into the van with the rest of the band and left for London, taking with me the rabbit's foot on a keychain which my sister-in-law Roslyn had given me for luck, presumably on the basis that I was going to need it.

One thing I noticed about Gordon at that meeting in London that maybe I might have made more of at the time: his nails were chewed down to the quick. If I had thought about that, perhaps I might have wondered whether he was less at ease with everything than he gave the impression of being. And I would have been right. What I didn't realize was that, at this point in his life, Gordon needed me as much as I needed Gordon.

LADBROKE GROVE, LONDON, in the summer of 1964. Acres of cheap housing, much of it in disrepair. Students in bedsits, bohemian types and artists. Corner shops and fruit stalls. Music playing from windows. A cosmopolitan edge to the place. A big Afro-Caribbean community, a large Irish contingent. Graffiti on the walls. "No Color Bar Here." Construction and destruction going on in equal measure—the raised Westway road overpass going up to the north, ground being cleared . . . An emerging underground scene, the sixties counterculture taking root—though not so much with five blokes from south Wales in their two-bedroom flat at 6 Clydesdale Road. We're spared any worries about fitting in, though. In this setting we don't stand out as Welsh rubes, or new kids in town. We're just a few more immigrants lobbed into the mix.

The flat Gordon has rented for us is in the basement of a Georgian row house. It is dark and basic with worn and stained carpets and it smells of unwashed bedding; we quickly christen it "The Black Hole of Calcutta." But it's not that awful, in all honesty. In retellings of this story down the years, the flat will quickly acquire rats and damp and will soon be well on the way to earning a demolition order, but actually, in my recollection, it's not so bad. Short of daylight, but hardly a slum, which can't be said of every house in Ladbroke Grove in this period. It does, though, have only two bedrooms to split between the five of us. A cozy fit, then. Two bedrooms, five blokes. Someone always ends up on the floor, and someone else on the couch. Not me, of course. I'm the singer. I always have a bed. Singer's privilege. Or something like that.

Opposite the house is a church with a function room attached to it in which we can rehearse and occasionally, at Gordon's instigation, audition for people—such as Colin Berlin, for whom we play a few songs one day. Colin runs a booking agency within the European division of the American music company Acuff-Rose Ltd., and Gordon thinks he might be able to help us get more and better gigs, which is the point of our being here.

Chris Slade, the drummer, has quit his job in Clarks shoe shop. Mike Roberts wanted to remain in Wales, so Mickey Gee has come in as guitarist in place of him. Everybody calls him Gypsy. Gypsy is steeped in rock'n'roll records and can perfectly duplicate pretty much any solo you mention. In due course, he will travel to Nashville on a pilgrimage to visit the home of Chet Atkins, his hero—only to discover that Atkins is away on tour. But Gypsy will say that it was an honor enough to sit on Atkins's doorstep. Gypsy was working as a delivery man for Brains brewery, but he has willingly thrown that in and headed for London with us, along with Dai Cooper. Vernon Hopkins and I were already unemployed so we had nothing to quit—except, in my case, a wife and child.

Gordon puts us each on a retainer of £1 per day, which is enough to keep us in food and beer, provided we don't eat or drink very much. Most days we get up late, pull on jeans and yesterday's T-shirts and head to Pete's Café on Ladbroke Grove for lunch—ordering braised beef and potatoes because it's the cheapest and most filling dish on the menu. Or I might buy a portion of chips from the fish and chip shop and a bottle of milk, because I know it will fill me up and the emphasis, at this stage, is very much on basic replenishment and leaving some money aside for the pub at the weekend. To this end, I will also, over the coming weeks and months, perfect the art of the runner by practicing it at some of the numerous Indian and Chinese restaurants in the area, exiting one particular establishment, after a hearty and sustaining meal of chicken curry and rice washed down with lager, by the lavatory window.

Gordon has extracted us from our deal with Myron and Byron—a fairly impressive demonstration of his can-do, it seems to me, and my first experience of what it feels like to have a mess invisibly cleared up on your behalf, so that you can just walk away from it. That said, it later emerges that Gordon has shaken off Myron and Byron by offering the pair of them a percentage of my future earnings, thereby creating a court case in waiting.

Still, Gordon's next move is to make some name changes. Apparently there is already a band out there called the Senators. So the Senators became the Playboys. Unfortunately, there is already a band called the Playboys, too. Such is the mid-sixties beat explosion: if you want to name a band in these days, you have to get in fast. So the Playboys almost immediately become the Squires. There doesn't seem to be another band called the Squires.

As for me, Gordon says we can't use the name Tommy Scott. For one thing, there's already a Tommy Scott out there somewhere, and for another, it makes me sound like a jazz saxophonist. He may have a point. I tell him I'm not going to change my first name, because the thought of that makes me uncomfortable. But it's open season on my surname, as far as I'm concerned. So Gordon thinks about it for a while. And then one day, he says, "I've got a name for you: Tom Jones."

He's thinking of the movie with Albert Finney. Big picture in 1963. Won four Oscars. Based on an eighteenth-century novel by Henry Fielding, if that's your thing, though I've never read it. What I hear in Tom Jones is my mother's maiden name, so I'm perfectly happy with that. It's a name in which I immediately feel I belong.

So now we're Tom Jones and the Squires, and Gordon, with the help of Colin Berlin, is going to get us gigs wherever he can. And wherever he can turns out, in the first instance, to be a dance hall in Swansea in Wales, a mere forty miles from Pontypridd. It's like that gypsy thing all over again: tipped to go round the world and ending up round the corner.

However, in July 1964, either Gordon or Colin steps it right up, in our eyes, by getting us booked into a residency at Beat City. This is more like it. Beat City is a seriously happening venue in a basement on Oxford Street, slap in the beating heart of London. Top of the bill: the Rolling Stones, who are hitting it big at this time. We couldn't be happier at the prospect of getting in there and hoping that something rubs off. Come the night, there are hundreds of fans outside on the pavement, and the police are there in numbers in case it all goes wrong, as it sometimes does in these early and not yet entirely understood days of teen hysteria. When the doors open, the place is immediately rammed with Stones fans—600 of them, sixty of whom will faint and have to be carried out before the end of the Stones' set. That's partly as a result of overexcitement and partly as a result of the heat, because the place becomes a sauna. The paint seems to be dripping off the ceiling along with the condensation in giant globs. There are bouncers at the front of the stage throwing water over the kids to keep them cool. I go on in a white shirt and a state of high anticipation and once again turn in a performance which seems to put fear, more than anything else, in the eyes of those observing it—fear at the sight of this big, broken-nosed Welshman whose top, thanks to a combination of sweat and the water that is being flung about, is growing ever more transparent by the moment.

I leave the stage a sodden and interestingly see-through wreck, passing Mick Jagger in the corridor, who says, in a tone of astonishment, "Look how hot this guy has got—and he's just the emcee."

Thanks for that.

We hang around and watch the Stones whip the place to a frenzy, thinking to ourselves, "Maybe one day . . ."

When we're not gigging, Gordon has me jumping in and out of taxicabs with him, taking me to recording sessions he's involved in at studios around the city. The broad notion is that we're on the lookout for a song—for the number that's going to crack it—and also that I'm learning some ropes. This is how come I find myself standing one afternoon at the back of a session with a group from Scotland called the Sensational Alex Harvey Band. They sound rough as old boots to me, but they have some flair—and will later, of course, record a version of "Delilah," crunching it up and turning it into a rock song. This is also the first time I see Kenny Clare, the respected, seasoned session drummer who I think is great and who will end up playing on a lot of my records.

Sometimes these sessions that Gordon takes me to are for record companies, and sometimes they're private, paid for by the indulgent fathers of rich kids. A real mix, then. And sometimes I will do demo singing, make a little money as a sideline. Nothing comes of any of those demos that I know of, and certainly none of those demos seems to be yielding the right song for me.

This is the problem, though, with which Gordon and I are in a constant wrestling match in this period. What is that right song? And, moreover, what am I? Am I a solo singer? The solo singer thing—at least in pop music—is over, isn't it? It's all groups now. But I have the Squires, so I'm sort of covered in that respect. Except the singer-with-band thing—Cliff and the Shadows, Billy J. Kramer and the Dakotas—is mostly over, too. Groups that write their own material—that's the thing. Groups who have started out playing other people's songs and then moved on. The Beatles, the Stones, the Kinks. And that isn't us. We are slightly out of step. And at this point, everything seems to be happening so fast that to be slightly out of step is to be a hundred miles behind.

I'm a hard sell, is what I am. Gordon is talking to the record companies and hearing all sorts of stuff back: that I'm a bawler; that I'm too much like Elvis, and not necessarily in a good way; above all, that I don't look right. The standard look for a pop star at this point in the mid-sixties is soft-faced, silky-haired, skinny at the waist and wrists, androgynous— less so, a working-class bricklayer who looks like he can handle himself. What did Jo Mills say about me: that she'd never seen anything so male? Well, it's not clear what the pop industry in the mid-sixties thinks about "male."

At one point, Bert Berns is over from Atlantic Records in the States. He's the staff producer—has produced for Ben E. King, the Drifters, LaVern Baker, Wilson Pickett. Longish black hair, greased back—not well groomed, like your typical idea of an American record company person. Gordon arranges for Berns to come and see me sing at an audition at the church hall. Berns passes. He tells Gordon to listen to this new signing of Atlantic's, Solomon Burke. "This guy's the future," Berns says. "He's going to be the new Ray Charles." I listen to Burke and like him, but I'm irritated, too, because I don't think Solomon Burke could sound much more like me. That's a black version of me, right there, surely. But he's on Atlantic, and I'm not.

Peter Sullivan's the one, though—Peter Sullivan at Decca. He clearly feels there's something going on with me, even if he doesn't know exactly what it is yet. Gordon keeps on at him, urging him to take the plunge until, finally—finally!—something like four months after I first auditioned for him, hallelujah, Sullivan makes his move. A record deal! With Decca Records! Okay, a pretty tentative one: Decca agrees in the first instance to release a single by Tom Jones, with an option on a second single and a third one, depending on levels of interest (theirs, not mine). There's a lot of suck-it-and-see built into this offer, no question. And a lot of drop-it-very-quickly-if-it-goes-shitwards, too. But it's the sweetest thing I've heard so far. And it's a record deal.

I've got to be concerned about the feelings of the band at this moment, however, because there's a sensitive issue at the heart of this. The deal is for Tom Jones, not for Tom Jones and the Squires. If the five of us come as a package—singer and band—then it's not how Peter Sullivan and Decca Records see it, and it's not how Gordon seems to see it either. The band's sense of itself as an equal partner on this journey, and the emerging sense, for the people steering us, that the Squires are Tom Jones's backing band—no less, but no more—is going to be a source of tension that will ripple through the coming months and will ultimately create some nasty and still unhealed wounds and divisions between some of the band and me. For my part, inasmuch as I have the power to, now that Decca's corporate machinery is cranking into action behind us, I make it clear that I want them involved—want them on the recording sessions, want them on the shows. And I continue to make that clear until it becomes impossible for me to do so.

For that first single, Peter Sullivan picks out a song called "Chills and Fever," an R&B number recorded with some success by Ronnie Love in 1961. I like the song—think it's quite ballsy, feel that it gives me something to have a crack at. It's one of the songs I already recorded with Joe Meek, not that he has done anything with it. (Meek will wait until I have my first hit, whereupon he will sell those recordings to EMI.) So we end up recording it at Decca Studios in an afternoon and a relatively small number of takes. The Squires provide the rhythm track, but Peter thinks it needs a harmonica solo, so he calls on a session player. Guy named Jimmy Page. Seems quite good. Can play guitar a bit, too, apparently. Wonder what will become of him.

Before long, Gordon is showing me my first single, freshly pressed with that dark blue Decca label with my name on. And this is a big moment because a record with my name on was always the dream and also because here, now, is tangible proof, for any doubters, that I am getting somewhere.

Thanks to the exertions of Decca's promotions department, I am booked to promote my single on *Thank Your Lucky Stars*, thereby making my first national television appearance. I mime, there being no technical facilities to do live music in the studios at this time. I enjoy it, find it easy. And most importantly, even more than the solid fact of the record in its plain black paper sleeve, this is something to put in front of Linda and my mother and father, and the other people looking out for me back in Pontypridd, who can say, "It's working out, look. Tom's on the telly."

I take the train up to Birmingham alone, where the show is filmed on a Sunday afternoon and then screened that evening. Then, in the afternoon, me and the Squires take the train over to Bristol to do *Discs-A-GoGo*, carrying the uniforms that Gordon has got us for the occasion: denim shirts with button-down collars, black leather ties, black leather waistcoats, black pants. (These become our regular stage clothes for a while, with me further accessorizing the outfit by attaching the rabbit's foot keychain to a belt loop at the front of my trousers, where it flaps around when I dance in a manner that could be taken for suggestive, and why not?)

Brian Matthews is presenting and the Drifters, whom I like, are on the bill this particular week, and so, too, are Bill Haley and the Comets, so that's a thrill. In truth, Haley, with the shiny cowlick and the suit, seems to be well and truly from another century at this point. But "Rock Around the Clock" is turning into the song that will not die, and now, in 1964, he is toting a sequel number, "Dance Around the Clock"—which moves it on a bit, I guess. Whatever, it still feels immense and unreal to find myself just across a room from the guy who had come steaming out of the radio and shaken it all up for me, ten years before.

When it's our turn, I have to mime to the single. Not having to think about singing frees me up to think about dancing—which is perhaps unfortunate. I overplay it, jumping all over the place, frantically moving, seizing my two minutes under the nation's gaze. There are two cameras—one catching me against a white backdrop and the other, on the opposite side, catching me against a black backdrop. So, in the broadcast version, as they cut from one to the other, the image goes black/white/black/white . . . All very mid-sixties. All very op-art. Also, a fucking catastrophe, when you watched it back. Almost impossible to look at it without getting a migraine.

Still, something good happens afterward. Bill Haley comes over and says to me, "Wow, you just out-Presleyed Presley." If I take nothing else away from this experience, I'll take that.

I am back on telly almost straightaway. I do *The Beat Room*, which is the first pop show on the new BBC2, only four months old, having opened in April, thereby, at a stroke, increasing viewer choice by 50 percent to the grand total of three channels. As a token of its commitment to the untamed youthfulness of the times, *The Beat Room* has a dancing audience—girls in A-line dresses and blokes in cardigans frugging and chugging around the floor doing the white man's overbite, everybody trying not to look at the camera as it follows them around and only narrowly failing. We go on there with the Kinks and John Lee Hooker, and with Julie Rogers, who is singing "The Wedding," a bona fide, massive-selling hit. I stand off-set in a state of advanced bewilderment and think, wow, look at this show: you've got John Lee Hooker, a black American Delta-blues guitarist, doing "Boom Boom," live, with a British band—really good. And then you've got Julie Rogers, who looks like a beauty queen, with perfect upswept hair and a lot of poise at the mic, singing a huge ballad about getting married. And in between, the Kinks, who are pop urchins, and a bunch of Welsh rockers in leather ties (us). The program really couldn't have ranged much more widely without falling over completely.

So there I am with a single out on a major label and two national television slots on which to promote it, and surely I would be justified in thinking of myself as well on my way to what John Lennon has called "the toppermost of the poppermost," if it wasn't for one fact.

That almost nobody buys the record. Almost nobody at all.

1964.

15

Factory Girl

"Chills and Fever" did not turn out to be a game changer. Indeed, I went from releasing and promoting my first single to playing American air force bases with the Squires around Suffolk and Lincolnshire. Still, at least the American servicemen loved us. We were doing American music, so I guess we fit right in. And we were in uniform—sort of. (The denim button-downs, the leather waistcoats, etc.) Back to being a human jukebox, though. "Play 'Walking the Dog,'" they kept saying one night, in some mess hall or other with the chairs cleared to one side. "Walking the Dog" was the recent Rufus Thomas hit. It wasn't in our repertoire, but what the hell, we did it anyway, with me chucking any old words together to make up the verses, on the way to the safety of the chorus, which was the only bit I knew. The servicemen didn't seem to mind. They dug it anyway.

We went back to gigging and hoping. Colin Berlin got us on to a package tour with Them—Van Morrison's band—at the top of the bill. We had enough live work to summon Chris Ellis, our old driver from Pontypridd, who jacked in his TV repair job and, on a retainer paid by Gordon, committed himself full-time to ferrying us around in a bright red Morris J4 van, rented from somewhere by Gordon. Or maybe it was a Thames Commer. It was one or the other. A little routine of Chris's which he developed during this period: we'd be driving home from a gig in the middle of the night, humming along a motorway, all the band asleep or drifting off, the van quiet apart from the noise of the engine. And then Chris, on a portion of suitably clear road, would suddenly scream at the top of his lungs and jump on the brakes. And everyone would jerk awake in terror, hearts pounding. Most amusing the first time. Less amusing the fourth, fifth and sixth times. Eventually I asked him if he would mind desisting. Or words to that effect.

We now moved out of the Black Hole of Calcutta at 6 Clydesdale Road and into a slightly bigger flat in Lime Grove, Shepherd's Bush, where I at least had my own bedroom. Again, singer's privilege. The rest of the band continued to double up. Big improvement all round, though.

And somewhere around this time we did an audition to play at the Astor Club—a nightclub in Mayfair. That was quite a high-end sixties hangout—a salubrious place, with a less salubrious clientele. Indeed, in 1965, the Astor Club would famously become the venue where George Cornell of the Richardson Gang called Ronnie Kray "a fat poof" during a Christmas party, thereby sparking a fight and a long-lasting turf war that remains legendary in the annals of East End gang culture.

Gordon told us we had to smarten up a bit for the audition, so I wore a suit jacket over a white shirt. But I got hot while we were playing, so I took off the jacket and undid the buttons on the shirt. Gordon, from the other side of the room, said, "That's a good look for you. You should go with that." So that's how that particular look was born. It would serve me well for a number of years.

For now, though, everything seemed to have slowed right down again. Decca wasn't exactly banging the door down for another single. For me, all that energy and anticipation around the release of "Chills and Fever" very quickly dissipated, and in its place there was wounded pride and, once again, a frustrating sense of drift. August, September, October . . . days just leaked away with nothing developing. For all concerned, something had to happen—Gordon included. Because Gordon was getting strapped for cash.

We didn't realize how broke he was, although really there were signs from the beginning. When Linda came up for weekends, Gordon would invite us to stay with him in the spare room of his flat in Notting Hill. That way I wouldn't have to subject her to the lion's den in Ladbroke Grove. Linda got on with Jo, Gordon's wife, so it worked out well with the four of us. But the first time she came, Linda said to me, "Why doesn't he have a carpet on the stairs?" I had wondered about that myself. Even in our house at Cliff Terrace we had a carpet on the stairs. At Gordon's it was bare boards.

Then, one morning, Gordon told me he wanted me to go with him to a meeting at the National Westminster Bank in Notting Hill. On the way, I was saying to him, "What's this about? What do I need to be here for?" And Gordon wasn't answering. The fact was, though, he was tapped out and needed a loan. In the bank manager's office I sat on a chair next to Gordon, feeling like a spare part, while the two of them talked, and Gordon did his best to charm up some money.

Eventually the bank manager said, "What are you going to put up as collateral?" And Gordon said, "Him," and pointed at me. "He's going to be the biggest singer in the world."

I felt the bank manager's coolly appraising gaze—could almost hear him thinking, "Who—him?"

I believe Gordon secured a loan that day, though. Whether it was as big as the one he was asking for, I have no idea. What I do know is that the convertible Ford Zephyr soon went. So did the wristwatch—sold to a music publisher for £50.

Meanwhile I was going home to Wales any chance I could get—but, again, that took money. I would get back there on the train when I could.

Sometimes the other boys would hitch, but I never fancied that. One weekend, I was so desperate to see Linda and Mark that I sold Mickey Gee my prized leather jacket so I could buy a train ticket.

The separation from Linda and Mark was beginning to do my head in. I was worried about other fellas coming after my wife and stealing her while I wasn't around—my mother's words ringing in my ears: "You, leaving a pretty girl like that . . ." I had Dai Perry back in Pontypridd to keep an eye out. Dai wasn't the kind to see people muscling in on his friends' wives and not react. His attitude was, essentially: "If there's anything you want done, let me know." I didn't think it was going to come to that. That said, some bloke from Cilfynydd seemed to be sniffing about at one point. I said to Linda, "A little bird told me somebody saw you home." "Oh, hush," she said. "Nothing happened." I believed her completely. But that didn't stop me worrying about it.

There's a story that has done the rounds a bit from this time that I got so low that I nearly threw myself under a Tube train. It's not quite straight. There was a day when I went round to Gordon's flat and asked him if I could have some money to send back to Linda—not much, just something to help her keep going. And Gordon said he was sorry but he had no money to give me, because there was no money. And I got angry about it and told him that if something didn't happen soon, I was off, because living like this was bollocks. And I stormed out of his flat and went down into the Tube station at Notting Hill to get the train back to Shepherd's Bush. And as I stood on the platform, in a despairing fury, and watched the train come rattling in, it flashed into my mind that I only had to take a step forward to bring this whole dumb thing to an end.

But it was only a flash. And then, much later, in an interview, somebody asked me if I had ever, at any point in my life, contemplated suicide (nice question), and I brought up that moment. I shouldn't have mentioned it, because it got built up: Tom Jones: The Day I Nearly Ended It All. Like I was at the end of my tether. I wasn't at the end of my tether.

I was a good way along my tether, and extremely pissed off. But I hadn't reached the end of it. Just to take the edge off that little myth.

Still, I definitely got down during those months—down low. There were nights I lay in the flat, listening to the other guys snoring, thinking about my wife and son and wondering, "Is this right?" You have to provide. That's what I was raised to believe: the man of the house provides. That was the most painful aspect of this phase. I didn't mind getting along on cheap dishes from Pete's café, hoarding a few pennies for beer at the weekend. I could do all that. It didn't bother me. But my wife and son . . . the thought that they were somewhere else, unprovided for . . . I hated contemplating that, and I didn't like what might be being said about it in Pontypridd, either: that Tommy Woodward's up in London, indulging himself, flapping about with his stupid singer fantasies, and his wife and kid are back here in his mother-in-law's house, struggling to get by. I didn't like that at all. That was the thing, more than anything else, that I was bothered about.

And then, the ultimate humiliation, to my mind. With no money coming in, Linda took a part-time job. A part-time job in a factory that made thermometers on the Treforest Trading Estate. No choice, she said. She needed the money. I hated the thought of her being exposed to that—to the work and the flirting and all the stuff that goes on in factories. And being exposed to that because her husband was failing her. That's the way it felt to me.

The one thing that would cure all this from every angle was a hit record—a hit record that would set me up for life and would bring in money and reunite us—me, Linda and Mark—in a house better than any we had ever known and somehow set us free, as I imagined it. Because that was the dream. But how often does that kind of dream come true, in actual fact? And time was getting thin.

It's Not Unusual *single cover: note lucky rabbit's foot.*

16
———

In My Bones

It's just two chords, really. That's all that Gordon has. I hear him vamp-
ing away at them on the piano in his flat in Notting Hill. The chords, and
then some opening words. "It's not unusual . . ." Nothing else, though.
Two chords and three words. I'm not taking a lot of notice of it, really.
It's just one of a lot of ideas for songs that Gordon has that he'll be fid-
dling around with on empty afternoons while I'm sitting around in there
and drinking his tea.

But then Les Reed gets involved. Les is one of Gordon's numerous
musician friends. He was a member of the John Barry Seven—the instrumental pop group led by John Barry who did all those great film scores.
Les's instrument is the piano, and he is now turning a living as a writer
and an arranger. Gordon knows a lot of these people: guys who have done
some years of performing and have moved on. Les likes to wear suits and
is a jazzy guy—not a rock'n'roll merchant, it seems to me. But he's smart
and opinionated, and his musicianship commands respect. Gordon brings
him to see me sing at a gig in Slough one night, valuing his opinion. Les's
recollection is that I came on with my shirt wide open, which made him
think he wasn't going to like me. But when I sang, he did.

The way it works is that Les has had a call from Eve Taylor. Eve manages Sandie Shaw, who has just had a massive hit with "(There's) Always Something There to Remind Me" and has shaken a few people up with her deeply countercultural habit of going about the place barefoot. Apparently Sandie Shaw desperately needs a song, and Eve Taylor asks Les Reed if he's got anything. Les, in turn, rings Gordon. And for cash-strapped, watch-less, car-less, now-with-a-baby-to-feed Gordon, the lights go on. Get a hit with Sandie Shaw, and suddenly everyone's back in clover again.

So Gordon shows Les his two chords and his scrap of lyric and his melody line, and Les starts to collaborate with Gordon on this song. At first, the way Gordon had it, the two chords under the melody repeated themselves through the verse. They didn't go anywhere. But Les now shapes it so that those chords move on as the verse develops and then come back round. And suddenly the structure comes alive. And now my interest is aroused, because this song that the pair of them are mucking about with sounds suspiciously like a hit to me.

I'm nudging at Gordon about it from the beginning.

"I could do that song, you know."

"No, it's for Sandie Shaw. You can sing the demo, though . . ."

Thanks a bunch.

One afternoon in the autumn of 1964 Gordon and I take a taxi over to Regent Sound in Denmark Street—the studio where I recorded the acetate for Jimmy Savile. We're late, which is often the way with Gordon, so the booked studio time is already eaten into, and the demo gets rushed together with a haste unusual even by the standards of demo recording. Chris Slade plays the drums, Les plays the piano, I sing. There's no bass, because there isn't time for that, and there's certainly no brass. At this point, what will become the song's big brass hook—the "b'dabba-dabba daa" part—is Gordon and Les singing it, like a muted male duo version of the Mike Sammes Singers: camp as Christmas, frankly. I don't give the vocal all that much power because I figure that this is for Sandie Shaw. It wouldn't seem right to be tearing it apart because I don't suppose that's particularly the way that she is going to go with it. The demo is altogether a fairly mild and underwhelming experience. Even so, when I hear it played back, I'm surer than I've ever been that I need to have this song.

After the session, we adjourn to the pub at the top end of Denmark Street—Les Reed, Chris Slade, Gordon and me—pints are ordered, and I start to go at Gordon.

"Gordon, that's it."

"No, it's a pop song. It's Sandie Shaw."

"You're wrong."

I'm adamant. The intro, that opening line, the melody and the lyric—it's instant. Irresistible. If that doesn't lift something up inside you, then you're either dead or well on the way out.

"Fucking hell, Gordon, this is it."

Chris Slade is with me on this. "Tom could have a hit with that."

I get petulant. "If I don't get this song, I'm fucking off back to Wales and I'm not coming back."

And at that point, Gordon and Les both throw their hands up and say, "Oh, in that case, if that's how strongly you feel, scratch that Sandie Shaw plan. The song is all yours. Let's head up to Decca right now and record it."

Do they? Fuck no.

Les Reed books in a meeting soon after this with Eve Taylor, and he and Gordon head off up to her office with the acetate. I'm really pissed off about it. Furious. The only glimmer of a hope left to me is that Eve Taylor doesn't want it and sends the pair of them away with their tails between their legs. But that isn't going to happen. Anyone with functioning ears can tell that this song is a hit record waiting to happen.

They come back from the meeting. "She doesn't want it." Apparently Eve Taylor couldn't hear it at all—not for Sandie. Les and Gordon are really downcast about it. The cash cow just keeled over in the field.

They're wondering how they misplayed it, coming up with reasons. Maybe my version put her off. If they'd had a girl to sing the demo, maybe she would have gone for it . . .

I couldn't be happier. The song reverts to me by default.

"I guess we could always try it with Tom . . ."

"You think?"

Jesus Christ.

We take it to Peter Sullivan at Decca, and, to my further frustration, he, too, is unsure at first—not unsure about the song, but unsure about whether the song is right for me. Weren't they thinking of pushing me in a bluesy, rock'n'roll kind of direction? Something harder-edged than this, surely . . .

Still. The song really is good. He'll give it a go.

We record it at Decca Studios in West Hampstead. Les makes the arrangement fatter. Now the descending "b'dabba-dabba daa" part is played by a trombone. There's a bass guitar on there, obviously, and the sound is rich and full and . . . really disappointing. It's just not firing somehow. The melody still stands out, but there's something missing. There's something soft about it, something a bit gutless. It doesn't come punching out at you. It sounds like an album track, rather than a single. It doesn't sound like the kind of song that launches a career.

We all go away to think about it, and Peter agrees to give it another shot. His notion is that it's too smooth. It needs roughing up a bit. "We need to try and make a rock'n'roll record out of it, even though it's not a rock'n'roll song." He wants to get the guitar more involved. We lift the key so that I don't sound quite so comfortable—put it up higher where I can rip it. Les comes into the studio with a brass part, punching along with the bass drum—ba ba-dap, ba ba-dap. An R&B thing. Now there's a proper snap to it from the kickoff. I loosen the phrasing. I take the line across the rhythm in a couple of places, where the Ivy League, the vocal group who are singing the backing vocals, are right on it, so the arrangement unscrews a little, loosens its tie, as it were. I get excited with it. Even now, to me, I sound fleetingly a bit sharp at the top of the open-ing line—too excited. But the energy is there, and the recording catches fire, and the song goes up.

Myths abound about this session: that I recorded my vocal in the tape cupboard for the acoustics. Not true: I was in the regular vocal booth. That Jimmy Page played guitar on it: the guitarist was Joe Moretti, who played on "Shakin' All Over." But what's definitely the case is that, after a couple of hours, as all these elements came together and took on a life of their own, what we were finally listening back to was a big, thumping, surefire, smash-hit pop song.

The recording took place in November 1964. The release was held over until after Christmas, at the beginning of 1965. And then we'd see what would happen.

With John Lennon in New York City, 1975.

17

I Wanna Hold Your Hand

The press release that went out from Decca Records with the first copies of "It's Not Unusual" urged the media to sit up and take notice of Tom Jones from Wales.

"He's twenty-two, he's single and he's a coal miner."

I was twenty-four going on twenty-five, I had a wife and a son and I had never been down a coal mine in my life. All that aside, though, that press statement was entirely accurate.

Perish the thought that a young male singer with a single to sell in 1965 should be married. What happened then to the dreams that caused young girls to part with their money for pop records? Availability sold. I didn't reflect too hard on how this might have felt for Linda—and for Mark, too: written out of this revised backstory. I ought to have thought about it and told Decca's publicity department to shove it. But I was too busy getting to where I thought I needed to be. If this was the game, then, as far as I was concerned, I had to play it, in all its bullshit. It's a funny thing about how you are, setting out. In some respects, you're a ball of determination, entirely resolute; and in other ways, you're just a leaf for the wind.

Anyhow, when the single came out and before it was clear what its fate would be, this young, single, former coal miner was still busy doing pre-booked gigs. In January of 1965, I joined up with a Cilla Black package tour that was booked into the UK's ABC theater chain. Cilla had made it big with "Anyone Who Had a Heart" and "You're My World," so this was a good gig to get. I took over from PJ Proby, the rock'n'roll-influenced Texan singer who had landed up in London and had a couple of hits, but who was increasingly famous for bopping and crouching in his tight pants until the seams went. Well, everybody needs a shtick.

Also on the bill with Cilla were the Fourmost, a Brian Epstein Mersey-beat band who had a hit with "A Little Loving," and Tommy Quickly, another Epstein act, a nice Liverpudlian bloke for whom it didn't quite take off. Proby's duty, in among this throng, was to close the first half. Unfortunately, he didn't seem to be able to close the first half without simultaneously opening his trousers. And this was the mid-sixties, at the uncertain dawn of the sexual revolution, when the morals of the time didn't look too well on people busting their pants in front of a mixed crowd. The ABC theater chain, which had its reputation to protect, warned Proby that they would drop the fire curtain on him if he so much as strained the cotton in his groin area one more time, but, being a bit of a prat (in my considered opinion), he insisted. So that was it: he was gone. They were looking for somebody to take his place quickly, and I got put forward to fill the gap, in more senses than one.

This was a big deal because at that point PJ Proby was probably the biggest male pop vocalist in the country. He'd released "I Apologize" and a version of "Somewhere" from *West Side Story* and done well with them. He wasn't doing anything that I particularly got off on. He had a look, though: the sharp features, the jet-black hair over the ears, the pudding-bowl fringe. He had a voice, too—a bit affected on "I Apologize," I thought, but definitely something going on there.

Anyway, he was out of it, and I was in—although not before undergoing a little censorship myself. The promoters were a little bit nervous on the ABC chain's behalf of the lucky rabbit's foot that now routinely dangled from my belt loop while I sang. They reckoned it was suggestive. They may have had a point. So that had to go. And then I was on board.

Which ought to have been the end of it, except that PJ Proby refused to walk away quietly. On the contrary, spotting the opportunity for some attention-getting fuss, which he was never immune to, he continued to turn up at the venues and sit outside the front doors on the hood of his car, mouthing off to the people queuing to get in about how he was the real deal and that I was an impostor. Girls would then take this opportunity to jump all over him and a highly publicity-friendly "riot" would ensue.

I was walking into a minefield here. Many of the people would have bought their tickets before Proby was replaced, and some had bought them specifically to see Proby. Some of them probably didn't even know that he'd been axed until they pitched up on the night. And then they'd had Proby, on the door, getting them worked up by telling them that I was some kind of second-rate stand-in. The girls in the front rows would all have posters of PJ Proby's face, which they would hold up when I came on. I would walk out every night to a sea of PJ Probys.

But then an interesting thing happened. "It's Not Unusual" came out and started getting airplay—Alan Freeman, first and foremost, completely getting it and playing the thing to death on Radio Luxembourg and then everyone else jumping in afterward. And then it began to rise up the charts—all this while I'm out on the tour. And the higher it rose, the smaller PJ's face in the ABC stalls seemed to get. The posters were going down all over Britain. I saw PJ Proby's career get gradually rolled up in front of me.

So, that was one way in which I saw the wave coming before it hit—one way in which I was able to measure the effect that "It's Not Unusual" was having. But there were two other key moments when I caught sight of it from above, as it were. I've spoken about both of them before, but they really were the two points at which I was able to see fame coming, before it broke over me. We were in Bradford for a show, drinking in the pub across the road from the venue during the afternoon. This must have been late January or early February. The pub had just put "It's Not Unusual" on its jukebox. These fellas were playing darts and playing the song, over and over again. They couldn't leave it alone—going back to the jukebox time after time. I heard one of them say, "Who's this Tom Jones guy?"

The other moment occurred in Southampton, on the ABC tour. Again, I was in a pub opposite the venue, having a drink with Chris Slade and Vernon Hopkins. I could hear screaming and commotion outside. I thought it must be something to do with Cilla Black, or maybe the Fourmost had just got out of a car, or some stupid thing. I was heading back to the venue ahead of the others in any case, so I finished my pint, picked up the pork pie which I hadn't finished eating and walked out the door.

Bam! I'm on the pavement under a pile of screaming girls—taken down with a pace and efficiency that a pack of rugby forwards would have been proud to pull off. The people making the commotion outside the pub window were making that noise for me, and I didn't know. Their mission was clearly to gather souvenirs, in the form of lumps of me, my hair, my clothing or really anything that fell within range of their hands. Also to land kisses on my face if possible. I had a raincoat that Gordon had given me—a mock leather thing. It looked cool, I thought. Not after this it didn't. They ripped the shit out of it—left it in strips. I don't know who had the pork pie, but it certainly wasn't me.

Somewhere in the middle of this assault, a policeman got involved. People say the police are never around when you need them, but I disagree. This one grabbed hold of me, somehow pulled me out from under and propelled me down the alley and through the theater's stage door. Once inside, I took a moment to draw breath and gather what was left of my coat. It was my first taste of fan hysteria—or, at any rate, my first taste of it directed at me. It had been, I suppose, an alarming moment. But alarm wasn't what was uppermost in my mind. What I was thinking was, "This is it. It's actually happening." It felt exciting. I was ready.

"It's Not Unusual" reached number one on March 1, 1965—St. David's Day. Back home in Pontypridd, my seven-year-old son, in his homemade St. David's Day outfit, was in a state of tearful confusion because press photographers were camped around his school playground, shouting for his attention and clicking away at him. Meanwhile Linda was doing her best to smile politely into the same lenses, tracked down in her home as the Mrs. Tom Jones whose existence the record company had denied. All this suddenly, and out of nowhere—a sign, though I was too busy to heed it, that when the world changed around me, it changed around the other people in my life, too, people who hadn't necessarily signed up for this deal but were going to get swept along in any case.

THE SPRING OF 1965, and my life is suddenly a blizzard of TV appearances. Gigs, too, because we continue to honor the bookings made for Tom Jones and the Squires before the single hit—small dance halls that don't really expect us to show up once the record has charted. But we see them out. One night in Banbury we play a club so small that the guitarist has to stand in the DJ booth. Afterward, kids are swarming all over the van. In a highway service plaza on the way back from a gig one night, a pack of girls bursts into the gents' and climbs into the cubicle in which I am sitting and minding my own business. That hasn't happened to me before, and it's something to reckon with. Hectic scenes all round. I'm used to working for a reaction. Now people are screaming before I even get to the stage. The power of a hit song. People suddenly make up their minds about you.

But mostly there's TV. I fly to Scotland, my first time in a plane, mime to "It's Not Unusual," fly back. Gordon, who avoids flying whenever he can, declines to come with me, so I fly alone, wondering how it's going to feel, expecting some kind of powerful rush, and not realizing how smooth and gentle it would feel up there. And then coming back at night into London and looking down on the lights . . . I am knocked out by the sight.

I do *Blue Peter* and *Crackerjack* on BBC children's television because those were big "plug shows." The BBC gets letters: "I don't want that man gyrating in front of my young family. And at teatime, too." Apologies to all concerned.

I go on *Top of the Pops*, which is the new BBC chart show, and share a dressing room with Peter Noone from Herman's Hermits—fresh-faced pop boys who have cracked it big with "I'm into Something Good." I go in there with Gordon, hang my suit up on a rail and don't say much. I'll get to know Peter well later on a tour of Australia together, and he'll tell me that he found me scary that day—an intimidating presence in the room. I didn't mean to be. I wasn't saying anything because I didn't know anybody. What I was trying to do was hide the fact that I felt like the new boy at school, where everybody else knows what to do.

I do a show hosted by Frankie Vaughan—a brief interview with him and then my number. They give me a script for the handful of lines that I will have with Frankie before the song. Just before we're about to go on and film it, we're in the makeup room together, and Frankie says, "Come out in the hall with me and let's talk." So I follow him out, thinking, how brilliant that he wants to have a chat. Because I've respected the guy for years—a major entertainer.

So, outside the room, he says, "Thanks for coming on the show, Tom." And I go into a little speech of spontaneous gratitude.

"Oh, no—Mr. Vaughan, really—I've been watching you since I was really small . . ."

There's a look of confusion on his face. He says, "Have they changed something?"

I say, "What do you mean?"

He says, "You're not supposed to say that, are you?"

I say, "Well, I just wanted to tell you . . ."

It dawns on me eventually that when he said, "Let's talk," what he meant was, "Let's step out and rehearse our lines for the show." So now I feel like a total schmuck. Wringing wet behind the ears.

I fly to New York and sing "It's Not Unusual" while walking around between those treacherous white boxes on *The Ed Sullivan Show*. I fly from Heathrow on a kind of real jet plane. I have a few bevvies on the plane, because you can. "Bacardi and Coke, sir?" Is it an option? Why the hell not? "Another one of those, sir?" Well, it would be a shame not to.

I am met by Lloyd Greenfield, the booking agent, at the airport. We pose for a photo. He looks slick and fresh. I look jet-lagged, slightly drunk and have a cigarette in my hand. And then to the Gorham Hotel in Manhattan, with its suite and its private terrace. I send down for some tea. It comes up in a jug with ice in it. Iced tea. Who knew there was such a thing?

I go downtown to the rehearsal warehouse, run through "It's Not Unusual" with the studio band who are working from sheet music. On the recording, there's a moment where the tom-toms double up with the bass guitar—"It happens every day"—bom b'dom—"No matter what they say"—bom b'dom . . . It's a big feature of the arrangement, a hook. But it's just something that occurred on the day in the session, so it's not in the written score. And because it's not in the score, it's not there when we run it through. I explain to the conductor: "It's sounding great. But there's this bit . . . I wonder if we could add it . . ." The conductor looks at me coldly, freezing me out. "Where is it on the score? Point it out to me." And I can't, so that's that. Enough suggestions from the artist, clearly. But the drummer, thank God, quietly says to me, "Show me where it is." So I do, and I get it the way I want it.

In the evenings, the record company wines and dines me. We go to Dick's Steakhouse, which seems to be one of the happening places and where I am introduced around the room. "Hey, man—meet Tom Jones from England." I order an end-cut of roast beef and when it arrives I can't believe it's for one person and not for the entire table. It looks like a Sunday joint for four. This after a shrimp cocktail, with shrimps the size of your forearm and something called Thousand Island dressing, which I have never heard of but which tastes like the elixir of life to me. Being wined and dined by your record company hasn't happened to me in London. But it happens to me in America.

Morecambe and Wise, the great British comedy duo, huge UK stars, are on the show. Even after rehearsals, you aren't guaranteed your spot. You pitch up for recording at the Ed Sullivan Theater on Times Square on the Sunday afternoon and if Ed Sullivan or the producer don't think you're right at the run-through, or they turn out to have too much material, you're struck off. This time, Sid Caesar, the comedian, doesn't make it onto the live bill and walks away disconsolately. Eric Morecambe sees me backstage. "You on, Tom?" I am, and so is he.

No aftershow party. Back to the hotel and then a flight out the next day. I bring back a charm bracelet for Linda, a gold one with a locket on it, and an Omega Speedmaster watch for Mark, as well as that Frisbee. For myself I buy a couple of rings and a Ronson lighter, made of china—one of those big ornamental ones, for the dining table.

I must have done something right that Sunday night because *The Ed Sullivan Show* will have me flying back across the Atlantic four more times in 1965 alone.

And I go up to Birmingham to do ITV's *Thank Your Lucky Stars* in the same week that the Beatles are there, doing "Eight Days a Week"—and that's a thrill because the Beatles are such a big deal at this point (and, of course, forever after). I ask Gordon if we can go and sit out in the auditorium and watch them do their camera rehearsal—even though it's only going to involve them miming to the record—because, though I'm definitely trying not to show it, I'm all eyes and ears about being around them and yearning to be part of this sixties pop thing which they're at the heart of.

Lennon comes out before the others, on his own, and goes to his microphone. He's in tight black jeans and a turtleneck, looking about the place casually and mucking about with his guitar. And then he spots me. And this inspires him to sing.

And what he sings is "It's Not Unusual," except with his own words. "It's not a unicorn, it's an elephant . . ."

Then he nods at me and says, "How you doing, you Welsh poof?"

Wow, a double slap. John Lennon just took the piss out of my song. And then he called me a poof. I'm thrown into confusion: crushed and bristling at the same time. Should I melt into my seat or punch the lippy Scouser in the mouth? I mutter to Gordon, "Why doesn't he come out here and I'll fucking show him." Gordon tries to calm me down: "It's just his sense of humor." I'm thinking, "Fuck that for a sense of humor."

I should be rolling with it, of course, laughing along, cheeking him back, which he'd probably like. But I'm touchy. I'm a novice. I'm working out where I belong here—if I belong here at all.

I watch the Beatles do their song and glower silently all the way through it, stung.

Much later, in April 1975, Lennon and I are both on the bill for a tribute night for Lord Grade—then just humble Sir Lew Grade—in the ballroom of the Hilton Hotel in New York. It's a gala, filmed for television, to mark Lew's contribution to broadcasting and film. It was pretty rare that Lennon played live, after the Beatles stopped. But there he is, for Sir Lew—a measure of how much that guy meant to British entertainment. Peter Sellers is on the bill, too, and Dave Allen, the Irish comedian. Kirk Douglas is in the audience. It's a big deal. I do "I Have Dreamed" and the gospel number "My Soul Is a Witness." Then I go back later and do a duet with Julie Andrews, which I manage to screw up—completely miss a key change and feel like a klutz.

Lennon comes on for his slot that night in a red jumpsuit, round dark shades, long hair combed back, chewing gum, with an acoustic guitar round his neck, and utterly nails Little Richard's "Slippin' and Slidin'"—crushes it with a band with a brass section. You couldn't not be impressed.

That said, when we're backstage after the show, being mingled with by the guests of honor, Lord Mountbatten, the uncle of Prince Philip and the mentor of Prince Charles, comes up to me. I shake his hand, and he says, "My family—we all love what you do." Which is nice to hear. Lennon is right beside me, looking on expectantly, perhaps awaiting a little moment of his own. But Mountbatten just walks past him, utterly blanks him. Lennon shouts after his retreating figure, "Oi! Oi! MBE, me! MBE!"

There was a big finale that night—all the cast on the stage for "Consider Yourself" from the musical *Oliver!* Lennon had got changed by this point into some kind of pale smoking jacket, a scarf and a flat cap. I came on, still in my blue velvet jacket and white frilled shirt, open around my gold crucifix, and took a bow with Peter Sellers and Julie Andrews and then moved upstage, where I ended up standing next to Lennon in the throng. I remember thinking, "My God, he's looking short these days. Has he shrunk?" Then I remembered that I was wearing platform soles.

Anyway, as we stood there, he grabbed hold of my hand. It was just a gesture—the kind of thing you do when you're standing on a stage in a group finale, like linking arms for "Auld Lang Syne" on New Year's Eve or something. But it felt strange, to me. Men holding hands with men . . . I was shy of that. So I shook it off—dropped his hand. Stupid, uptight reaction. I'm sorry now, that I did that.

On the Dick Clark Caravan Tour in the States, by myself.

18

Till My Back Ain't Got No Bone

I have a smash hit record, and it's like night and day. The believers are vindicated, the doubting Thomases are swept aside. A weight comes off my chest, and a dissatisfied nagging in my stomach disappears. I have something to take home in triumph. "Look, it worked out." My mother loves it—visibly swells with it. My son! My son the singing star! On the telly, see? Top of the charts! My father, less so. He's proud, too, I know, and excited—but he's anxious. I'm out there, exposed, unprotected. It worries him at some level—the sheer open exposure of it. The vulnerability to criticism. Like, how could it end well? He's leaping ahead to that a lot of the time.

As for me, I'm full of it—can't get enough of the attention and the praise and the whirling, in-and-out-of-cars glamour of it all, and the ability I suddenly seem to have to change the atmosphere in a room just by walking into it. I get the impression very early on that I'm not going to struggle with this stuff. I know that some people find fame hard to cope with, and that, having longed for it, and gone out of their way to achieve it, they end up wishing it hadn't come to them. And then they spend a lot of time afterward giving interviews in which they make the burden of fame clear in great detail. I sense very quickly that I am not going to be one of those people. I'm confident from the off (and correctly, as it turns out) that fame, in and of itself, will not cause me a minute's lost sleep.

And people will come at me with questions about this down the years. "But don't you wish you could just go into McDonald's or something, without any fuss?"

To which the answer is: no. No, I don't wish that.

I can honestly say this much: it seems to me, as someone who has looked at it from both sides, that being famous is nothing but preferable to the alternative, which is not being famous.

I'm not sure I buy this "fame changes people" stuff, either. Fame doesn't change you. Fame allows you to release things that were already in you, that's all. Character will out. Fame doesn't turn anyone into an arsehole: they were an arsehole beforehand, but they didn't have the opportunity to let it out because someone would give them a slap. Fame turns you into the person you already were but didn't have the outlet to be. It's a bit like drink in that respect.

I'll concede to this much change, in the wake of my first single success: I become less opinionated about other successful pieces of music. Before, when people asked me about something that was a hit that I didn't like, I wouldn't hold back. I'd say, "I think it's a fucking piece of shit." And they'd say, "Well, you don't have to be so strong about it." "Bits and Pieces" by the Dave Clark Five, for instance, which was all over the place in 1964. I fucking hated that. "It's crap." Wouldn't hear any different. And people would say, "What gives you the right to say that, though? You've never had a hit." Well, now I did have a hit, so I did have the right. Yet I didn't want to exercise that right, funnily enough. Having your own hit takes some of that away—takes the meaner edge off it. Okay, not completely: I'll still say, "Fucking hell, how did *that* sell?" But in the main, I start thinking, "Well, good luck to them."

Though I still fucking hate "Bits and Pieces."

I move into Gordon's flat in Campden Hill Towers. It's a time for cigars and champagne because "It's Not Unusual" is going to set us up and make us rich, and we know it. Clearly the time is coming for the longed-for resolution, when I can move Linda and Mark up to London to join me, but in the meantime I become Gordon's lodger, with Linda coming up more frequently. Train fares, no problem now. The phone in the flat rings constantly, all day and all night. I am under heavy manners from Gordon not to answer it because frequently it's the press, and Gordon doesn't want me talking to anybody without him knowing about it first.

I go out. At the end of long days, I hit London and do the clubs, enjoying the thrill of being a singer with a hit record, here in the pop capital. Not that I have money to sling around at this point, because the money, though it's coming, is still a way down the line. One night I have a couple of drinks at the Cromwellian, on the corner of the street opposite the Natural History Museum—a club with a gambling room upstairs, which doesn't interest me, and music room in the basement, which does. As I leave, I bump into Brian Jones of the Rolling Stones and Allan Clarke, the lead singer of the Hollies, who are both pop royalty at this point. They say, "We're going to the Ad Lib. Do you want to come?" So I jump into a cab with them and we head off to the Ad Lib, which stays open later than the Cromwellian. We spend the next couple of hours shooting the breeze, soaking up the attention, ordering drinks, being seen, being seen to order drinks.

Eventually the bill comes. It's enormous. Or it seems enormous to me. And it seems even more enormous when I pat myself down and realize that I am entirely without cash. Sheepishly I ask Allan Clarke to sub me for my share of the bill. He says, "Why don't you write a check?" Even more sheepishly I inform him I don't have a checkbook. (And not just with me: I don't have a checkbook at all.) "I'll pay you back," I say. He says, "But when will I see you?"

Fair point.

However, part of me is thinking: these guys are pop stars, and I've only just come in. Would it really hurt them? But a still greater part of me is thinking: this is really humiliating. Allan Clarke reluctantly pays my share, and we all go our separate ways, though not before I have compounded my humiliation by cadging a share of a taxi.

The next day, back at the flat in Notting Hill, I ask Gordon for some money, which he only reluctantly parts with, and head across to Shepherd's Bush, where, as I found out the previous night, the Hollies are filming something for the BBC. I blag my way in and pay back Allan Clarke. He says, "You didn't need to do that." I say, "Well, it sounded like I did last night."

I realize that I'm sort of in, and I'm sort of not.

But I'm getting further in, and that's for sure. On Easter Sunday, I do the New Musical Express Poll Winners Concert at the Empire Pool (now Wembley Arena) in the afternoon, then get driven into central London to film *Sunday Night at the London Palladium* on ITV that evening. At the Poll show, which is the music paper's annual award-giving extravaganza, is a roster of performers that seems to include just about every heavyweight from the sixties pop and rock scene: the Beatles, the Rolling Stones, the Kinks, the Animals, the Moody Blues, Dusty Springfield, Donovan, the Seekers . . . On and on the list goes. It's the biggest venue I have ever played at: 10,000 people, screaming and shouting in an aircraft hangar. I bounce my vocals off the rafters and hope that something comes across, going off the stage none the wiser. Tony Bennett is there, too, to present an award to the Beatles. I was probably as thrilled to see him as anybody else I saw there. Chris Slade is loving the fact that all these rock drummers are in the same place at the same time, and he is hanging out with Viv Prince from the Pretty Things. Again, though, in this gilded company, I'm self-conscious, withdrawn, drinking the copious bottles of beer provided by the promoters and not saying much. I have the impression that a lot of these guys from the groups are looking at me suspiciously, trying to figure me out: like, who is this guy, and what does he want?

At the Palladium, the show—which is a huge Sunday-night deal at this time—is hosted by Jimmy Tarbuck, who jokes with me backstage and makes me feel welcome. Jimmy will go on to become a great friend and remain one. I am given the choice by the producers between using the Jack Parnell Orchestra in the pit and using the Squires on the stage. I choose the Squires, out of loyalty to them and because it's what I'm used to, feeling the band pounding away behind me. I go on in an open white shirt and tight trousers—the standard stage outfit. The response is muted. Apparently, we're not quite slick enough for the Palladium. This seems to be the verdict of both the critics and the producers afterward. I haven't helped matters by going into an ad lib speech about how happy I am to be on the show, dream come true, etc., and slightly fumbling it.

The next time I appear on that show, just a couple of months on, I will be wearing a tuxedo and sitting on a stool and, with the Jack Parnell Orchestra in full flow, singing "Autumn Leaves," the Johnny Mercer composition. And after that I will be hailed as having "arrived"—a verdict which suggests a gradually solidifying sense, in the world at large, of who I am and what I do.

For now, though, it all seems a bit up for grabs, to me. Deep down, I have been thinking that I can get the door open with "It's Not Unusual" and then, once I've worked my way into the room, throw off my disguise to reveal myself as a rocking blues singer. As far as I'm concerned, I'm the white Wilson Pickett, if only people realized it.

But it isn't everyone's impression. I've started to wonder how much Gordon, even, buys into the vision of me as a proto-rocker or a blues guy. He pays lip service to the idea from time to time but I'm not sure Gordon ever really liked rock'n'roll music all that much in the first place. I know that the Viscounts, Gordon's vocal group, toured with Jerry Lee Lewis for a while, and Gordon hated him. Whereas for me that would have been a big deal. I would have been in heaven. Gordon just thought Jerry was an out-of-control noise merchant. Gordon tends to call rock'n'roll bands "yugger duggers." "You don't want to be one of them yugger duggers," he'll say. Scruffy fucks, in other words. I think he'd rather be aiming me elsewhere.

Constant questions, though. What's the attraction? What are people seeing here, and how can we develop it? What's the best way forward for Tom Jones? What's going to work for me next? Decca don't really know themselves. My first album, *Along Came Jones*, recorded with Peter Sullivan at Decca in between the promotional appearances, has "I Need Your Loving" and Chuck Berry's "Memphis, Tennessee" on it. Both of those are belters. Wilson Pickett's "If You Need Me" is in there, too, and "Spanish Harlem"—soul numbers. But it also has "Autumn Leaves" and "When the World Was Beautiful," by Paul Kaufman and Jerry Harris, both of which are smooth ballads from a calmer, more traditional place. Those songs are there because I love them equally and because I choose to do them. But a sense of confusion is already in evidence. What's my line here? Rocker? Pop star? Variety show crooner and Palladium shoo-in? I seem to be in some place where those things all overlap and blur.

And who's this guy on the album's sleeve, in a red shirt with the collar up and belted jeans, the sideburns and black curls still looking pretty rock'n'roll? Yet he's leaning against a birch tree in a wood, with a stalk of grass in his hand. Urban meets rural? Cool meets . . . uncool? Mixed messages here.

My second single, "Once Upon a Time," is another song of Gordon's and nods very heavily in the direction of "It's Not Unusual," as if to say, "Here's some more of that big pop sound that you evidently liked." But it's like "It's Not Unusual" without the hooks or the snap or the heart or the melodic gift—without everything, frankly, that made "It's Not Unusual" memorable. It only reaches number 32 in the UK chart, so there's a flickering moment of uncertainty there—a chance to wonder whether "It's Not Unusual" might be the extent of it. That one-hit-wonder thing. Maybe people liked the song and could take or leave the singer. Maybe there's no brand loyalty that's been earned here. That's a worry. But things move on so fast, and within only a couple of weeks we have released the song "With These Hands," which does better. It's a Billy Eckstine ballad which Peter Sullivan roughs up a bit, too, putting a big pounding piano thing on the beginning of it. It gets to number 11, restoring some confidence. Be nice to land another killer blow, though—put this thing beyond doubt.

And then, in June 1965, Gordon tells me that Burt Bacharach has a song he wants to play me.

This is exciting. Burt is hot—and also, of course, cool. He's written "Anyone Who Had a Heart" and "(They Long to Be) Close to You" for Dionne Warwick. He has that big-brained, New York songcraft thing about him. Along with Lennon and McCartney, he and Hal David are pretty much defining what pop songwriting means in the 1960s. The B-side of "It's Not Unusual" is a Burt Bacharach song—"To Wait for Love." Which solo singer doesn't want to sing a Burt Bacharach song in 1965?

According to Gordon, Burt is doing the music for a Woody Allen picture and he wants me to try out for the theme tune.

Burt and his partner Angie Dickinson are renting a house in London—in Belgravia, one of the posh parts. He invites me and Gordon and someone from the music publisher over to his house, where he is working on the score for the movie. It's a lovely place, with Persian rugs and a grand piano. And there's Angie Dickinson, who I know from the movies, and who is gorgeous and pregnant, as it happens.

So I'm sitting there with Gordon, and we're all chatting and getting along, and Burt eventually says, "Let me play you the song." And then he goes to the piano.

First up, there's this weird, clanking introduction—like some kind of mad fairground theme. And then there's Burt singing this strange, angular melody, in his flat, sliding voice. This doesn't make the song any easier to get your head around because Burt can't sing and has never pretended that he could.

And next thing he's in what appears to be the chorus:

"What's new pussycat—woah, woah woah."

He sounds like a drunk in a Tube station.

Burt comes to the end, swivels away from the piano, claps his hands together and says, "So. What do you think?"

And what I actually think is: "He's fucking having me on. This is some kind of test. In a moment he's going to say, 'Nah, just kidding—here's the song.'"

There's a long silence. Eventually, I go with my hunch, which sometimes, in life, you have to do.

I say, "That's not really the song, is it? You're pulling my leg."

The color drains out of the music publisher's face. It drains out of Gordon's face, too.

I say, trying to backpedal a little, "It sounds a bit crazy to me, is all I mean."

Burt, to his credit, is entirely unfazed by this reaction and says, "That's exactly what it is. It's a crazy theme, for a crazy film."

He has a projector there. He says, "Let me show you some of this film so you can see how funny and mad it is."

So we look at a couple of clips with Woody Allen in them. They are, as Burt suggested, funny and mad.

I say, "But why would you want me, in particular, to sing this?"

Burt says, "Because you have such a big, demanding, raw voice that if you sing it, you'll make it substantial. Done wrong, it will just be a novelty song."

My instinct is telling me, "No. Don't go there."

I say, "I'm not sure I can pull it off, to be perfectly honest."

Burt urges me not to reach a decision at this point. He says he'll make a demo of the song so that I can live with it a little. And this he duly does. Within the next couple of days, a tape arrives at Gordon's flat—a demo with Burt's voice, again, and Burt's piano, again. And it still sounds as mad-arsed nutty as it did the first time I heard it.

Gordon is saying, "But it's Burt Bacharach. It's a title song. It's a Woody Allen film . . . We have to do this."

I think about it. And what I think about mostly is how it's Burt Bacharach. This is what I keep coming back to. Bacharach is an established artist, a man with a track record. Surely you've got to trust him. There must be something to it if this man is committed to it.

I say I'll take a shot at it.

The vocal session takes place in a studio in central London at midnight at the end of an evening when I have done a show—which is never the best preparation for a studio session. I'm pretty exhausted. Still, Burt's there and he's got the full orchestra, the Breakaways, his backing singers, and no fewer than four upright pianos, for the effect that he's after. It's a proper scene. But I know how efficient these orchestra guys are, and I'm thinking I'll be in and out within an hour, tops, and then home to bed.

We take four hours. I have never taken that long on a song in my life. With me, normally, it's one take, two takes—boom. Not this time. Burt wants the whole thing recorded live, there and then. No going back and fixing mistakes. So until I have nailed it, we have to run at it again and again. Take after take. I actually lose count of the number of times we do it, this mad fuck of a song. And eventually, with the sun already up outside, Burt is happy and, amid whirring milk floats, I go back to Notting Hill and fall into bed.

Even when the single is being pressed, I still don't think I'm going the right way here. I'm still apprehensive about what this is going to mean for me. "It's Not Unusual" was about as pop as I wanted to get, and, for all that it's angular and strange, this "What's New Pussycat?" number is going even further out into the mainstream, to my mind. I'm thinking, it's an out-and-out pop song, a gimmick song, almost. A novelty record. I don't want to be associated with a novelty record. That's career death, isn't it?

I'm not at all convinced. I am more convinced, however, when it comes out and is a hit. The single gets to number 11 in the UK charts. In America, it reaches number 3, which is higher than "It's Not Unusual," which only got to number 10.

And, of course, it grows from there, outlasts its period on the charts, becomes iconic. It's one of those records that comes to speak of its time—seems to contain some irreducible thing which is forever the mid-1960s, turns out to have an appeal which is virtually bombproof. It's truly something to be connected with that, for all that I tried hard not to be.

That's pretty much it for me and Burt, though—frustratingly. I do another song of his later called "Promise Her Anything." But he confesses to me, sometime after, that the number wasn't one of his strongest. Meanwhile he writes "Raindrops Keep Fallin' on My Head" for the movie *Butch Cassidy and the Sundance Kid*—which is a corker—and he gets BJ Thomas to do it. I'm listening to that and thinking, "Why didn't he ask me?" Too soft for me maybe? Couldn't I have managed it? Then there's "This Guy's in Love with You," which he has Herb Alpert do, which seems strange to me, given that Herb's a trumpet player with no real singing voice at all. But, again, Burt must have had a plan. I'm grateful for "What's New Pussycat?," of course—grateful for Burt's persistence and his belief. But I'll be listening to Burt every now and again down the years and wondering why I'm not getting his songs.

Maybe it was something I said.

I WAS RIDING HIGH. But in the summer of 1965, I went back to America for two separate live engagements and had the air let out of my tires a bit.

First, in July, there was a two-week residency at the Brooklyn Fox, a twenties-era play theater on Flatbush Avenue in Brooklyn—tiered seating, boxes, plush seats. I was booked on with the Temptations, Ben E. King, the Ronettes, Gary Lewis and the Playboys—a pretty cool bill, all in all. But the format was lousy: five shows per day, meaning you had to be in the venues all day, from midday to midnight. Nothing to do but sit

around backstage, flirting with Ronnie Bennett of the Ronettes—which
I suppose was no hardship, but time hung heavy even so. And in each of
the shows I only got a three-song slot. The setup—everybody on and off
in no time—felt fake. It wasn't real to me, and I didn't feel I was coming
across, either. I wasn't having an impact there like I was having in
England—or even like I had been having in the clubs in Wales. Something was failing to translate.

Then, in August, I was booked on to a Dick Clark Caravan of Stars
Tour. Clark was the super-smooth presenter of *American Bandstand*, the
big pop music show, and had spun his fame into a promotions business,
sending these pop package tours around the country every year. Interestingly, he didn't seem to travel with them himself and was content to
be a merely peripheral presence, out there on the road. Certainly, on the
Caravan that I was on, if memory serves, Clark popped up at the beginning, showed his face somewhere in the middle for a party and reap-
peared at the end.

I was thrown in with the Shirelles (the girl group who sang "Will
You Love Me Tomorrow" and whom I met with Dionne Warwick in the
Apollo Theater that time), Mel Carter (a Sam Cooke–style ballads guy,
who had a big song at the time called "Hold Me, Thrill Me, Kiss Me"),
Brian Hyland, Billy Joe Royal, Jimmy Ford and the Executives . . .
twelve acts in all. Van Morrison's band, Them, was supposed to be
on the bill, but pulled out at the last minute. Smart move. Peter and
Gordon were the only other British act, and they were the headliners.
They had hit it big in 1964 with "A World Without Love," a Lennon-
McCartney song, and were part of that "British Invasion" thing that I
seemed to be catching the back end of. Nice guys. We clung to each
other a bit for company, in a Brits-together kind of way. Even so, this
was a miserable experience.

There was—just to be clear—no actual caravan. Everybody was
rammed into a shitty bus. No beds or anything as luxurious as that: just
the standard coach seats. The story was that when Chuck Berry was

invited on a Caravan tour, he declined the offer of the bus and drove himself in a pink Cadillac. Again—smart move.

Because, of course, America is not a small place. Boy, did I discover, in the summer of '65, exactly how small America isn't. The National Guard Armory, Sandusky, Ohio; the Memorial Stadium, Terre Haute, Indiana; the Onondaga County War Memorial, Syracuse, New York . . . Seventeen shows in sixteen states in under a month. Sometimes you traveled right through the night, from one city to the next city, and didn't check into a hotel at any point. Just clambered blearily off the coach and into the venue, did the show, and clambered back onto the bus again. "All in Person," the posters said. Yeah, but not necessarily all in one piece.

America was also a racially divided place—which one read about and knew about, yet somehow still didn't expect to see. Because it beggared belief. In the Southern states, there were truck stops where the black performers were not welcome and had to stay on the bus for their own safety. I had never seen anything like this, and it opened my eyes wide. In a hotel lobby once, I sat talking to Shirley Owens of the Shirelles, and she suddenly got up and walked away. I thought I must have upset her, but she explained later that she had noticed white people across the room looking at us. Apparently we were sitting too close to each other, which might not have ended well for either of us.

One night, in the middle of Alabama, at a truck stop where we believed everyone would be safe, we all got off the bus and went in to eat. Big mistake. Some local guy stood up at his table and said, "Who let the niggers in?" Mel Carter couldn't contain himself and went for the guy, and a fight started. When the cops showed up, they arrested Mel and took him out to the car. I tried to remonstrate with one of them. "The guy didn't start it." The cop simply put one hand on my chest, and the other on the handle of his gun in its holster, looked me in the eye and said, "Do you wanna stay out of this, boy?" I was trembling. Is this cop about to pull a gun on me? How far does this escalate from here? Nothing I could do, really. Mel was taken to the cells for a while "to cool down" and rejoined us the next day, looking weary. These scenes didn't exactly endear me to the whole touring process.

I couldn't take the Squires along. I had to use the band on the tour, who were next to useless, in my opinion. Limp. No balls. I was disheartened. It wasn't what I was used to. I'd been spoiled perhaps. In England, I had already started playing theaters. And I had done *Sunday Night at the London Palladium* and all the pop shows. And then New York, *The Ed Sullivan Show*—all great. But then those first live shows on tour in America . . . drudgery.

Jack Nance was the tour manager. He used to be Conway Twitty's drummer. I said to him, "This band is shit." He understood. He sat in on my set a couple of times, just to beef it up and try and make me happier. Great drummer. Didn't make me happier, though. I was on that tour bus with a stiff neck and a bad case of homesickness, watching whole swathes of America go by the window and thinking: is this it? Because if so, maybe I ought to sign out now.

Near the end of the tour, to cheer myself up, during a spare hour in some city or other, I bought a ring which I liked the look of: a big gold number featuring a crescent moon with a sword above it.

Soon after this a fella came up to me and asked, "Are you a traveling man?"

I said, "Well, in a sense, yes, at the moment, because I'm a touring musician. But otherwise no, not really."

The man gave me a hard look. He said, "You shouldn't wear that ring."

"Sorry?"

"That ring. You shouldn't wear it. I just threw a question at you and you came back with the wrong answer. That's a Shriners' ring."

I just thought it was a nice ring, but actually, by wearing it, I was offending against the precepts of the Ancient Arabic Order of the Nobles of the Mystic Shrine—or Freemasons, if you find that easier to remember.

Live and learn.

Altogether I came home from America with my tail between my legs and wasn't fussy about going back.

But, of course, I had to go back, for another *Ed Sullivan Show* appearance in New York. And Dionne Warwick, no less, with whom I had merely exchanged a few words on the set of *Thank Your Lucky Stars*, called up from downstairs at the Gorham Hotel.

"Miss Dionne Warwick is in the lobby for you, sir."

How cool is that?

"I'll be right there."

And then she drove me in a powder-blue Cadillac to Harlem and the legendary Apollo Theater—which, in those days, was a place that a white man needed to have a reason to be, though being the guest of Dionne Warwick would do. It was early evening, still light and summery, and I was in a sky-blue long-sleeve Smedley shirt and sky-blue pants and the black boots from Anello & Davide. And we went backstage, and Dionne introduced me to the Shirelles and Maxine Brown and Chuck Jackson, who recorded "Any Day Now," and there was a lot of surprise and startled expressions because some of these guys only knew me from hearing "It's Not Unusual" on the radio and were clearly surprised to discover that I was white.

To be a white singer whom black singers mistake for a black singer . . . I mean, fucking hell: that was pushing all the buttons as far as I was concerned. The real deal. At the end of the night I went on stage with Chuck Jackson ("Ladies and gentlemen, a soul brother from England—Mr. Tom Jones!"), and we did "What'd I Say," and the place erupted and went nuts. And then I flew home on the highest high.

And then I went back again. And this time I met Elvis Presley.

Passing my driving test.

19

The Jerk

The first time I saw Elvis was on an album cover in Freddie Fey's record shop in Pontypridd. Dressed in black leather, acoustic guitar round his neck. "Fuck me, who's that?"

Then I heard a track of his, without knowing that it was by him—a number called "Salome."

I asked Linda, "Have you heard this song, 'Salome'?"

Linda had to point out that what he was actually singing was, "I feel so lonely."

"Oh. Right."

That would be "Heartbreak Hotel," then.

"Have you heard this song, 'Heartbreak Hotel'?"

Less than ten years later, in an outcome that seems incredible to me, I'm in a hotel room in Los Angeles, getting ready to go and meet him.

It's September 1965. *The Ed Sullivan Show* has now switched from black-and-white to color, which has in turn involved moving the filming from New York across to Los Angeles, where the necessary facilities are. So Lloyd Greenfield, the booking agent, has flown me out to LA, and Linda is along so that we can turn the trip into a mini-holiday. It's my first time there, and I'm grabbed right away by the sunshine, the openness, the cars, the whole vibe. Both of us are. We're staying at the Gene Autry Hotel on Sunset Boulevard, driving through Hollywood, wearing Ray-Bans, looking out at the houses and feeling like we're living the dream.

When I'm done with the show, Lloyd takes us out to Las Vegas for a couple of days—my first time there, as well. By comparison with what it would become, there's not much to it—the Sands, the Flamingo, the Dunes, just that cluster of hotels in a pool of neon—but the place still seems to leap with charisma to me. There's a bit of an edge to it, a touch of sleaze and danger among the glitz.

Linda and I do the shows. We see Kay Starr, who recorded "Wheel of Fortune" and "Come On-a My House." I want to see Frank Sinatra, but he's not in town, so we go to see Mel Torme instead—which isn't exactly a fair exchange, to my mind, because I was never a big fan. However, he knows that we're in the house, and I can't pretend I don't get a kick out of it, partway through the show, when he makes a little nod to "What's New Pussycat?" We also go to see Billy Daniels performing in one of the lounges, but there aren't enough people in the place, so he doesn't go on. That rather shocks me: my thinking is that you always go on, even for two men and a dog. In fact, especially for two men and a dog. The two men and the dog are your best friends in that particular situation. But anyway, when the show doesn't happen, Lloyd Greenfield introduces me to Billy Daniels, and I'm able to tell him how much I liked his version of "That Old Black Magic," which I used to hear booming out of the radio as a kid and which really took that song up a level, I thought.

Vegas feels otherworldly, and yet not. What I see in these big hotel and casino venues in Las Vegas is, essentially, bigger versions of the working men's clubs I have grown up with in Wales. That's what they feel like to me.

Lloyd knows the manager of the Sands, and the manager takes me into the jewelry shop there, where I buy a fourteen-karat gold watch that looks like an identity bracelet—my first gold watch. Then we return to LA.

Where the news from Lloyd is: "Elvis Presley would like to meet you."

Elvis fucking Presley! This is staggering to me. You don't get to meet Elvis. Elvis is untouchable.

He's on the lot at Paramount Film Studios, making a movie, as you do—*Paradise, Hawaiian Style*, in fact. Marty Lacker, one of Elvis's assistants, has been in touch, and we can meet him there tomorrow. That's what Lloyd Greenfield says.

I'm not naive. I know how these things work. Have Elvis's people rung my people (i.e., Lloyd) and said he wants to meet me? Or have my people (i.e., Lloyd) rung Elvis's people and said I want to meet him? Are both of us under the impression that the other one wants to meet us? There's some vagueness here. But who gives a fuck? The point is, I'm getting to meet Elvis.

I say to Linda, "Let's go. We're going to meet Elvis."

Linda says, "No—you're going to meet Elvis. I'm staying here."

Too shy. I try—and fail—to talk her round. "I wouldn't be able to," she says. And I understand that entirely because I'm feeling nervous about it too.

However, I'm going.

I am driven across to Paramount Film Studios in Hollywood, admitted through the famous double-arched Melrose Gate entrance, met, as promised, by Marty Lacker and led on to a closed film set—which itself would be a pretty thrilling thing, even if the set in question didn't contain a mocked-up helicopter from which Elvis Presley is apparently in the middle of singing to a woman in a hula skirt—again, as you do. After a while, when the take is completed, Elvis, still in the helicopter, raises a hand, apparently in my direction. But I'm still motionless and gawping. Marty Lacker nudges me and says, in a helpful tone of voice, "Elvis is waving at you. You could always wave back."

I rather lamely do so.

The next thing, Elvis is climbing out of the helicopter and walking toward me. And as he gets close, he smiles and starts singing "With These Hands."

Elvis Presley in person, singing my fucking song. This is a ridiculous moment.

Then he congratulates me on the song, and I tell him how much I admire and am influenced by him, and we fall to talking briefly, getting along pretty easily, making a connection, it seems to me, until Lloyd Greenfield rather screws the party, to my mind, by butting in to offer Elvis shows in England, whenever he fancies doing them—a little bit of promotional pitching there from Lloyd. Well, you take your opportunities when they arise, I guess, though neither Elvis nor his people seem unduly impressed by this pushiness, and the conversation wraps up soon afterward.

Still, some kind of bond has been made. I won't see Elvis Presley again for three years but, when I do, we take up from where we left off and become friends.

"WHAT DOES 'THUNDERBALL' ACTUALLY MEAN?"

As I stood there in the vocal booth with the headphones on in a recording studio in Cadogan Square in London, it was the only question I had. But nobody seemed to be able to tell me. Or they couldn't be bothered.

"Just sing it, Tom."

"All right, then."

John Barry and Don Black asked me to do that song. They had written it as the title theme for *Thunderball*, the fourth James Bond movie. A big song for a big film. It felt like a major endorsement. Shirley Bassey had done "Goldfinger"; they seemed to like a big Welsh voice. And "Goldfinger" was a massive hit. You weren't going to turn down the chance to follow it.

Shirley Bassey nearly got "Thunderball," too. At least, Barry and Leslie Bricusse had originally written a title theme song for the movie called "Mr. Kiss Kiss Bang Bang," which they got Bassey to sing, and that stayed on there until pretty late in the day, I think. But then, at the last minute, the producers got cold feet about having a song at the top that didn't include the title of the film. So it had to come off, and that's when Barry and Black wrote "Thunderball," and that's when I got the call.

The big feature was the long held note at the end. "Thunder-BAAAAAAALLLL." They wanted that note to set new World and Olympic records for strength and endurance. John Barry said, "Hold it as long as you can, because you'll never hold it to the end—the music is carrying on out for a long time after that. So just get it to go as long as you can."

Well, that started something competitive going in me. All the way through the track, I had a little voice in my head telling me, "Don't forget to take a breath in the middle of that last word"—break the word in the middle and take some air on board ready for the assault on the final peak. And then the moment came round, and, of course, I forgot—just sang on through the word without pausing for supplies. And even as I was going into that note I was thinking to myself, "You cunt." But I held on to it anyway, because this was it—closed my eyes and let it go until my lungs were straining. When I opened my eyes, the room was spinning, and I had to steady myself to stop myself falling forward through the music stand. You can hear me go slightly flat at the end of the note, where the steam ran out. But that was the take they wanted to keep, so that was that.

I went to the premiere of the film at the London Pavilion Cinema in Piccadilly Circus. Chris Ellis drove me up there. I can't remember what the car was that Chris used, but I do recall that it was red, and everybody else was swinging up in black cars. So that was a bit of a sore-thumb moment. There was a huge sign above the doors saying, "The Biggest Bond of All!" A red carpet, flashbulbs—the whole Hollywood-in-London vibe. Honor Blackman was there, looking beyond beautiful in a plunging dress. I sat at the back of the picture house, the end credits rolled, everybody stood and applauded the film, and then we were shown out, and Chris Ellis drove me home. There was no party—or not that I was invited to. It all fell a bit flat. Still, I'd enjoyed the film. I liked Sean Connery as Bond because he looked like he could sort you out if he wanted to—like he could break your neck if it came to it. He meant business; there was something a bit rough in there, and that appealed to me.

The film was huge—the single less so. It only made it to number 35 in the UK. No "Goldfinger" in that sense. Maybe it was just a bit too slick. Whatever. It's on the film for good, long note and everything. Though, yeah, the orchestra won. Just.

MY PROVISIONAL DRIVING LICENSE had been returned to me, following its confiscation after the incident where I'd been pulled over behind the wheel of my brother-in-law's Ford Corsair. And clearly, now that the money was starting to come in, I was about to be able to afford a car of my own. I had my eyes on a red Jaguar E-Type because . . . well, why wouldn't you? It was the star car of the times. But I needed to get my driving test done.

Gordon, fortuitously, was friendly with a driving instructor in Newport in Wales and managed to get me bumped up the waiting list. I went down there and took the test—did all the exaggerated gestures, the big glances into the rearview mirror like a good boy. Then we parked up for the part where he was going to test me on the Highway Code—which is what you did in those days. Not a written test, like now—just a few theory questions tacked on to the end by the instructor, after you'd finished your driving.

The problem was, the guy had pulled us up outside a school, at coming-out time. I was sitting there and in the side mirror I could see all these kids starting to stream out of the school gates. I thought, perhaps I ought to say something, because this could get messy if these kids happen to spot me. But the instructor had already started up with the questions, so I swiveled inward to talk to him, turning myself away from the window as much as I could and hunkering down a bit in the hope of not being seen.

No such luck. There were some screams and the sound of running feet and then the next moment all sorts of clumping noises as the kids started scrambling all over the car. One girl managed to get her hand through the side window and took a hold of my hair, as if in an attempt to pull the whole lot of it out. And the instructor, completely unfazed—like he hadn't noticed anything unusual was going on at all—just carried on asking me about the difference between a triangular sign and a circular sign.

Still, at the end he was pleased to be able to tell me that I had passed. Driving isn't just about having the knowledge, you know. It's about having the ability to apply the knowledge under pressure. And while someone is screaming and pulling your hair off.

EARLY IN 1966 I was booked on to a tour of Australia with Herman's Hermits and again I ran into some anxiety on the part of the authorities about my dancing, and the morality of it. Word had obviously got ahead from some of the first dates on the tour about some of the grinding I was doing and about the effect it was having on the audience. (Essentially, they screamed. Or the female contingent did, anyway. Maybe some of the guys, too. I don't know. I was too busy grinding to pay detailed attention.) By the time we reached Sydney, the police were involved.

A deputation came to the soundcheck, and we were instructed to play a couple of numbers in the manner in which we intended to perform them in that evening's show—the assumption being that the police would stop the show going ahead if they saw anything likely to cause depravity, depravity being something which Sydney wanted nothing to do with, clearly.

I remember a policeman solemnly asking me, "What are you going to be doing?"

I told him, with a completely straight face (and with total honesty), "I'm going to be doing an American dance called the Jerk."

"Are you taking the piss?"

I assured him that I wasn't.

In the end, they found nothing in the rehearsal that they could take particular exception to—though the situation was artificial in the extreme, and I may have been toning it down a bit for the benefit of the lawmen present. Still, it was interesting to me that, clearly, I was felt to be slightly alarming and a potential risk of some kind—certainly by contrast with Herman's Hermits, who were getting screamed at, too, though not as a consequence of anything overt that they did on stage. I was churning people up, it seemed. I was getting across.

For my own part, I didn't think I was doing anything wrong or deliberately subversive: I was doing what I felt. It was coming out of the music. Okay, the tight trousers weren't necessarily coming out of the music. But the dance moves were. I've seen people doing things on a stage in order to be obscene—throwing in a fucking-motion or something—and it's not sexy. It's the opposite of sexy. Mine wasn't a repertoire of moves that I'd deliberately and coldly constructed somewhere in order to prove some kind of point about myself—in order to come over as beyond the law. I simply had a lot of energy and in an instrumental break I thought I had better do something because the spotlight was still on me, and I let the music dictate what then happened.

Herman's Hermits surprised me a bit on that tour. I saw them as a boyish, nice-boy band—a little bit soft, maybe. I was wrong about that, though—certainly offstage. We were on Bondi Beach together one afternoon, checking out the surfers and the sunbathers, and these Australian fellas, sitting up on a wall, were giving Peter Noone and his lot grief, calling them wusses, having a go at their hair. Peter was not one to back down: "Why don't you fucking come down here and we'll see?" The Australian fellas didn't take him up on the offer. But I was impressed. Peter was saying what I was thinking. He didn't take any bullshit.

You saw Peter on the telly—nice face, pretty fringe, clapping his hands to "I'm into Something Good"—and you maybe took a view. But you maybe took the wrong view. Herman's Hermits were around Shepperton one summer, doing some filming, when I was living out that way, so we hung out around the pubs a bit. And one night someone was giving Peter some trouble, for being a pretty boy, and Peter chinned him. Which wasn't what I was expecting to see. I reminded him of that when I saw him not long ago in Los Angeles. He said, "I was just reminding the bloke that I was from Manchester."

My first car, a Jaguar S-Type, outside my first house in Shepperton.

20

Ladder of Excess

It is 1966. Now that the money is coming in, I go house-hunting. Gordon suggests going to look at a new development he has heard about in Shepperton, a village in Surrey, just north of Weybridge, about fifteen miles southwest of London. It's an area to which a lot of stars seem to be gravitating. Lots of nice houses, with privacy, and within striking distance of the action in the city. Most of the Beatles are buying places out there—Cliff Richard, too. Actors and showbiz types, also.

The development is on a long, quiet suburban road called Manygate Lane. It's a block of joined housing around a rectangle of open grass. Designed by a Swiss architect, Edward Schoolheifer. Ultra-modern. Two-story, flat-roofed, white with black trimmings. Aluminum window frames. Linda and I visit together. We love it. The downstairs walls are almost all glass, back and front. Open plan with a beech staircase running up in the center, between the lounge and the kitchen-diner. Polished mahogany floors. Upstairs are three bedrooms and a bathroom. The biggest of the bedrooms—the master bedroom as I must learn to call it—has a washbasin built into it. A washbasin in the bedroom! Who thought of that? There's a small, oblong garden, front and back, with a high, white wall all around it, fairly private. And it's all brand new so you don't need to touch it—just move on in.

The place costs £7,695, which is more than twice the average price of most London houses the same size at this point in time, but I don't mind. According to Gordon, I can afford it, so I dive in. Linda picks out the furniture—G Plan, Scandinavian, good quality. Steel-framed dining chairs. Tall table lamps. Ornaments on the square partitioned shelving unit: china figurines, a ship's bell on a plinth. Record player in the corner. Two crossed ornamental swords on the wall above the television set. *The Avengers* is on the telly, and the telly seems to be sitting on a set from *The Avengers*.

Our first house together after all this time—nearly a decade of marriage.

There's a school for Mark within walking distance. Huge pond in the center of the village. A nice area. Dickie Valentine, the fifties pop singer, lives at one end of our street, which I think is cool because I always liked Dickie Valentine. The only thing you can't do is play music loud, because of the next-door neighbors through the wall—who are Dickie Valentine's mother and father, in fact, and who occasionally have cause to ask, very politely, if I would mind turning it down a bit.

There are some great pubs around, too. Because this is still what I want to do, at the end of the day: go to the pub, play darts. A lot of actors seem to be drinking at the Anchor. Derek Nimmo is knocking about— from the sitcom *All Gas and Gaiters*. Had a bit part in the Beatles movie *A Hard Day's Night*. I get friendly with John Gregson, who has been in Ealing comedies. Ian Hendry, too, who was in *Police Surgeon* and, yes, *The Avengers*; and his wife Janet Munro, who was in the movie *Swiss Family Robinson*.

I'm changing my drinking habits a bit, though. I came to London a beer drinker who smoked cigarettes. Gordon would tell me, "Wait until you crack it. You'll be drinking champagne and smoking cigars."

I'd say, "Fuck off."

But the thing is, I've ended up putting on a bit of weight, so the beer drinking has had to come down a bit. At first I switch to shorts—vodka and lime. But shorts make you too pissed too fast, and I don't really want that. I want to enjoy the night out. It's the landlord in the Anchor who says, "If you like drinking long drinks, social drinks, go to wine and champagne."

So that's that. As for cigarettes, I get full-blown tonsillitis in April 1966, after a bunch of throat problems, and I have to have my tonsils whipped out. Ice cream and jelly afterward: the standard, post-tonsillectomy hospital recovery diet. And while I'm in there, the doctor says, "If you want to help yourself, as a singer, you should probably lose the cigarettes."

I was smoking a lot. I never really counted them. Upward of twenty a day, though. Linda, too. And my father. Smoking was just something you did without thinking too hard about it.

"If you want to smoke," says the doctor, "smoke a cigar."

And that's okay by me. It's never really been about the cigarettes, as far as I'm concerned: more about the paraphernalia around smoking—the lighter, the packet, the things to keep your hands busy. If you're smoking cigars, you've still got the paraphernalia.

Still: it was beer, cigarettes. Now it's champagne, cigars. So Gordon was right.

To go with the new house, I buy a brand-new red Jaguar S-Type. Okay—not the sporty, two-seater E-Type that I've been thinking about. But I need room for Mark and Linda, so I go for the next best thing, the saloon model—long, lots of chrome, hood ornament, wire-spoked sports wheels. Prestigious. Plenty of presence, especially in red. Inside: beige upholstery with red piping on the seats, polished walnut steering wheel. Gordon knew a car dealer—the brother-in-law of Kathy Kirby, the singer. I bought it from him.

Now I've got my wife and my son in a house that I own. And a car. A big leap. A proud time. A brand-new house and a brand-new car. No garage to park it in, but I could hardly care about that. Finally, we are settled—me, Linda and Mark.

Except, of course, there is no settling. I don't seem to be in a business which really allows for settling. Shortly after this I have my second number 1 single, and it all moves on again.

IN 1965, ON A BREAK from one of the *Ed Sullivan Show* recordings, I went to the Colony record store just north of Times Square in New York and asked, "What have you got that's new by Jerry Lee Lewis?" They gave me an album called *Country Songs for City Folk*. Picture of Jerry on the sleeve in a brown suit with big checks, leaning against a tree, but spliced into a shot of a high-rise apartment block, getting the message across.

This was Jerry keeping himself alive, now that rock'n'roll had blown over, by stepping across to country music, and although the hardcore fans might have bridled at it, I absolutely loved that album from the first time I heard it, and played it to death: Willie Nelson's "Funny How Time Slips Away," Hank Thompson's "The Wild Side of Life," a really good take on Johnny Cash's "Ring of Fire" . . . It all sounded solid to me. But the track that really hit me, and had me wondering, was the one that kicked the album off: "Green, Green Grass of Home."

What got me was the melody, obviously, which was sound as a bell, but also, over and above that, the storytelling in the lyric, with the twist and the reveal in the final verse where you realize the singer, longing for home and loved ones, is actually a dreamer, locked away on death row, and will only be going home when they bury him. That got to me right away and kept reeling me back in, every time I listened to it. To take a whole story out and round like that, in only two and a half minutes, and evoke something universal, seemed like something very close to genius to me. The song was written by Claude "Curly" Putman Jr., a Nashville writer. (He later co-wrote "D-I-V-O-R-C-E," which Tammy Wynette had a hit with, and "He Stopped Loving Her Today" for George Jones, so clearly Putnam was no slouch.) A country singer called Porter Wagoner had had a hit with it in the US in 1965, but I didn't know about that. If Jerry Lee Lewis hadn't recorded the song I would never have heard it.

I played it to Gordon, who couldn't hear it at all. "What? You want to record country now?"

"Fucking hell, Gord, there's more to it than that."

Thank God, Les Reed heard something and shared my feeling that there was something in the song that would go far wider than country if it was arranged right—and this despite, I think, not particularly getting off on the song himself. But Les took it away for a couple of days and created that lush setting, pushing it toward pop with the pulse under it— a nod there to "You've Lost That Lovin' Feelin'" in the Phil Spector arrangement for the Righteous Brothers—and with the Mike Sammes Singers rising up through the chorus, like an ethereal choir.

I thought it was a really good song, really well recorded—and an obvious single. But I had no idea of the full impact it would have—the extent to which people would hear something in that version that spoke loudly to them. Not the twist at the end, necessarily—I've often felt that listeners don't really take that part in—but the broader sense in the song of longing to be somewhere your loved ones are and where you are loved. It was released for Christmas in 1966—and of course, people are susceptible to tales of homecoming in that period. But it was also released into the aftermath of the Aberfan Colliery disaster in Wales, the shock of which people in Britain were still struggling to come to terms with. At Aberfan, that October, it had rained unrelentingly for a number of days on a coal-mine landfill and, on a Friday morning at 9:15, the tip became a landslide of slurry which poured off the mountain and engulfed the Pantglas Junior School below. One hundred and forty-four people died. One hundred and sixteen of them were children. The stunned national sorrow was slow to lift, and, amid it all, a Welsh voice singing about the green, green grass of home perhaps felt like a hymn—brought some comfort maybe. I hope so, though, in all honesty, 116 children . . . I don't know how you bring comfort there.

Later on I would hear stories about the song being taken up by American soldiers fighting in Vietnam. It would come over the military radio and reduce people to tears. A rare power that song had, clearly, anywhere people were longing for home or in need of a sense of community, or longing for people to return.

It moved fast—went to number 1 within three weeks of its release, in a period when records tended to take longer to get a hold, stayed there for seven weeks, stayed on the chart for a further fourteen weeks, and has stayed with me ever since.

JUST AS "GREEN, GREEN GRASS OF HOME" is about to hit, I do a piece for a French magazine—a picture story, where I drive back to Pontypridd in my red Jaguar and pose for photos around the place. Singing star Tom goes back to where it all began—that kind of thing. Except in French. I'm not fussy. I never mind going back to Wales. I'll get to see my parents. And I don't mind flashing the car around, either, if people are asking me to do so.

We do various setups. I stick the car outside my parents' house in Laura Street, where it looks pretty incongruous—get a shot from up there of me in a mac looking down over Pontypridd, spread out below in all its glory. We go about the place generally, looking for opportunities. And at one point, as I am coming off the Common in the car, I pass an old van coming toward me, slow enough that I can look across at its driver, and its driver can look across at me, and our eyes can meet.

And blow me down if it isn't the hard case from my days at the paper mill—the bullying bastard with the scarred face and camel overcoat who took against me and gave me grief and made my life a living misery for a while. I haven't set eyes on him since. But here he is plain as day, driving through Pontypridd, in a clapped-out van, looking miserable as fuck.

And here's me, down from London in a brand-new Jaguar.

I am restrained. I don't sound the horn or wave out the window. But I do enjoy the moment.

Maybe this is tempting fate, though. Not long after, I spend a night drinking and hanging out with Vernon Hopkins and some others in the Cromwellian and end up offering to give a couple of air hostesses a lift home. Because, call me Charlie Show Business, but what's a Jaguar S-Type for if you're not going to give a couple of air hostesses a lift home in it? We head north up Park Lane in the direction of Marble Arch, which is a nice, straight, wide piece of road if you want to put your foot down a bit, and we're approaching the Dorchester Hotel at a fair lick when the air hostess in charge of directions suddenly says, "Take a right turn here."

Braking and spinning the wheel at the same time, which is not to be advised, I aim for the turning, miss, and crunch the Jaguar sideways into a metal barrier. Seat belts? Who wears seat belts in 1966? My head jerks upward and smacks against the rearview mirror. My new friends, fortunately, are able to walk away merely shaken, but an ambulance takes me to the Accident and Emergency department, where I receive fourteen stitches inside my hairline. And then I take a taxi home to Shepperton.

I wake in the morning with a headache which only too cleverly combines the effects of a night in the Cromwellian and a car crash. I open my wincing eyes to the sight of my mother—up from Wales and staying with Linda and me, in an unfortunate coincidence. She is unsparing. "Running around with girls, drinking it up, getting carried away with yourself . . . You need to get yourself in order."

The gist is: who do you think you are? Tom Jones?

Gordon, too, thinks I need to slow down. But his solution in this area—a radical one—is to suggest a Rolls-Royce. A Rolls-Royce, he argues, puts you in a different frame of mind, as a driver. Being so big and stately, it's necessarily a more sedate kind of animal. You can't throw it about like you can a Jaguar. You wouldn't crash turning right on Park Lane with a couple of air hostesses in the back because you wouldn't be going so fast in the first place. I think that's the logic. Anyway, Gordon has decided to get himself a Rolls-Royce, and I decide to join him. So he contacts Kathy Kirby's brother-in-law again, and Kathy Kirby's brother-in-law gets hold of a secondhand Rolls-Royce Silver Ghost for me, with a bench-style front seat. I love the shape of the car, and I love the bench seat, but I'm not especially thrilled with the color—it's two-tone, black and green, with green upholstery—but it's available, and there it is, and I now have a Rolls-Royce. I also have nowhere to park it, but never mind. We will soon be moving anyway.

On-stage attire, around 1967.

21

Talk of the Town

"Green, Green Grass of Home" was the start of a run of Top 10 UK singles that would carry on pretty much unbroken through to 1970. "Detroit City" was in there—a country blues, with another big chorus about homecoming. There was "Funny Familiar Forgotten Feelings," a waltz-time ballad by Mike Newbury, the Nashville writer, with the clicked, plectrum-hit bass guitar notes plugging away underneath it. "I'm Coming Home" was in there, too—back to that theme again. And then there was "I'll Never Fall in Love Again"—a Lonnie Donegan song which he had written with a guy called Jim Currie. I had become friendly with Lonnie early on in my time in London, when we did some shows together and he told me he had this number he thought I could do something with. I went over to his house one afternoon—he was living in a nice place in Virginia Water at the time, not so far from Shepperton. Lonnie loved the blues—that's where he was coming from: the blues and old work songs and ballads. He played this song to me, and I recognized the source for it—a song called "I'm Never Going to Cease My Wandering," a Depression-era ballad that I had heard people take a tilt at in the clubs in Wales. So that warmed me up to it right away. Big opportunity to open up in the chorus there, I thought—get some emotion going. Gordon wasn't too keen on it—but Gordon wasn't too keen on Lonnie, for some reason. He said he didn't think the song was strong and was worried that it was going to buckle under my voice and get all bent out of shape. But Peter Sullivan said we should try it and asked me what I was hearing. What I was hearing was "Love Letters," which Elvis had just had a hit with. Chas Blackwell did the arrangement, in waltz time, and he completely nailed it.

I said to Gordon, "What do you think now?"

He said, "It's the way you're singing it."

"Fuck off, it's the structure of the song."

I took the acetate home to Linda. She took it round to Gordon and Jo's, and she and Jo squabbled a bit over who should keep it overnight. And that's when I knew for sure that I was onto something with that song.

IN TERMS OF THE DIRECTION things were going, there was a big moment in 1967 when I was booked to play the Talk of the Town in London. The original booking was for two weeks, but the two weeks got expanded to six—a really big deal at the time. I don't think any other British artist had played a run in that venue for so long. What happened there over those weeks, and what then followed from it, did a lot to set my course from that point on.

The Talk stood on the corner of Charing Cross Road and Leicester Square. It had once been the Hippodrome theater. Bernard Delfont turned it into a nightclub in 1958. Ethel Merman sang there. Frank Sinatra, Judy Garland, Sammy Davis Jr., Tony Bennett—the big acts in from America. It had a ritzy glamour to it. Smart choice of name. The Talk of the Town. Spoke for itself. And it worked, because that's how people thought of it—as the center of a certain kind of show business world. Backstage, it still felt like a theater—a warren of corridors with tight little dressing rooms off them. The auditorium was tiered, with a balcony, and had a thrust stage that could be lowered flat for dancing and raised up for the entertainer. You came down, forward of the band, into this lower area where the audience was on chairs and tables, dragged right up to the sides of the stage. So it was a dining room within a theater, a huge difference from the dance halls and clubs I was used to. I was going into a different scene. One show per night, starting about ten o'clock. Proper orchestra: four trumpets, four trombones and five saxes, a full brass complement, conducted and arranged by Johnny Harris—my first big dates with him. Johnny was great: a long-haired Scot, a former big-band trumpet player who would eventually come out to work with me for a while in Vegas. Johnny wore an iron boot, on account of the polio he had suffered in childhood, but that didn't stop him jumping around at the podium during shows, hair swinging. Gordon took exception to that a bit—would have a word with him about it from time to time—"Look, there's only one star here" kind of thing. But I didn't mind it. I loved what he brought to the music and to the gig.

The Talk was the first time I wore a tuxedo. Dougie Millings, whose shop was round the corner from the venue, in Old Compton Street in Soho, made it for me. Dougie dressed all the pop stars—Adam Faith, Tommy Steele. He made those collarless jackets for the Beatles, and hundreds of other bits and pieces for them. And he made me this beautiful, midnight-blue tux with a low-fastening, double-breasted waistcoat that doubled as a cummerbund. So I went from the tight pants and open shirt into designer evening dress. That said, in the heat and the exertion, the tie would come off pretty early in the show. And so would Dougie's beautiful jacket and the waistcoat. Never mind the surroundings, it would get down to open-neck shirt and pants again fairly fast. I reverted to type.

I would open with "Good News," a Sam Cooke song, up tempo, a fantastic thing to stride out to, through the band, on to that thrust stage—like: "Have some of this." There would be "Shake," which I could leap all over the fucking place with. And we would end with "Land of a Thousand Dances," the Wilson Pickett stormer: "You've got to know how to pony"—all that. But in between I'd have done "That Lucky Old Sun," "I Believe" and "My Yiddishe Momme," stripping it right back—the big, yearning, sentimental ballads that I'd grown up with. On account of the last of those, a lot of people who came to see me in London thought I must be Jewish, but I was just singing the song my father loved and sang to me.

The album that we recorded there—*Tom Jones, Live at the Talk of the Town*—was the first time that I had been recorded in concert with a band, and it just flowed. I get a proper hold of the songs on there, really get down to the business of trying to make them mine. Like "Hello Young Lovers." I don't care if Andy Williams or Perry Como or some other fucker has got that song tattooed on his chest; I'm singing it as though it had never been sung before that particular moment, in that particular room, on that particular stage. But there's light and shade there, too. I'm not just trying to blow the wall down. If you're lucky as a singer, you'll find yourself sometimes with the right combination, and this was one of those times: Johnny Harris conducting; a shit-hot orches-tra; the Squires all punchy, at their best; Peter Sullivan and Bill Price looking after the recording; the right room, filled with the right people, who totally get it. It's the right combination. And the right combination lets you be yourself. And it's not there always, sadly. It's not something you can necessarily will. You can't bring that about—nor always put it back together again once you've happened on it. Bits come away. It slips and slides. But in that room in the Talk of the Town in 1967, it was there, for sure. I think *Live at the Talk* is maybe the best record I ever made.

It was an older crowd, for sure. But this whole dinner-theater thing seemed to be as new to a lot of the people in the audience as it was to me. How did you behave in this setting? What were the rules? How did you respond? What kind of good time was available? People were still work-ing it out. But I was getting a kind of pop show reaction in a nightclub setting, where there was an extra intimacy to it, on account of the closeness—more heat under it. No question, a lot of the most excited people in the room were female. That was becoming par for the course for me. But one night, the place was entirely booked out to some kind of all-male convention. There was less screaming that night, it's true. But the atmosphere wasn't any less intense. Fellas seemed to get off on it, too.

Altogether there was a stir. People wanted to check the show out. Other entertainers were piling in to get a look and coming backstage afterward—not just musicians, but actors from the West End shows, film people, television personalities. Ava Gardner came to the show. George Raft, the Hollywood star, wanted to come one night and couldn't get a ticket. Okay, I was in evening dress; I'd stepped away from that Carnaby Street pop thing; but it felt like the big time. London, 1967, the Talk of the Town—you felt like you were at the center of something.

An American agent, Buddy Howe, called Shell Talmay, an American producer working in London, and asked him what was new. He said, "Tom Jones is at the Talk of the Town."

Howe came to talk to me backstage. He said, "You should be in America." I was a bit hurt. I said, "I've been in America. I've done five *Ed Sullivan Shows*, a couple of tours . . ."

He said, "Well, okay. But maybe you were playing the wrong venues." I noticed that he wasn't talking now about the National Guard Armory, Sandusky, Ohio, or the Onondaga County War Memorial, Syracuse, or any of those other places I'd shuffled around on the Caravan of Stars. Nor even the Brooklyn Fox. He suggested the Copacabana in New York. And after that, why not Miami, why not Las Vegas? Not theaters— nightclubs. He was saying, "This is where your future is." And Gordon was seeing dollar signs and nodding and agreeing with him. Maybe they were right. Maybe it really was pointing that way at this point. Either way, the nightclub thing was about to take over for me.

Buddy Howe booked me into the Copacabana in New York for a week in 1968, just trying me out. And beyond that would lie some nights at the Flamingo in Vegas and the Deauville Hotel in Miami. Those were the three hot nightclubs for entertainers in America at that time. I would essentially be on trial in each of them.

SOMEWHERE OUT THERE, PJ Proby was still being annoying. He was still cracking on like a stuck record in interviews, saying it was only because he busted his pants that time on the Cilla Black tour that I made it. His view was, if it wasn't for him, Tom Jones would still be singing in working men's clubs. His mistake in the seam department was the making of me—according to him. And he was sounding like he was ready to make it physical, too. "I could beat him in a sing-off," he told some newspaper or other, "or I could beat him in the street."

I had some dates at the London Palladium around this time—in 1967. After finishing up there one night, I went to a club called the Bag O'Nails, a big musicians' hangout with live music in Kingly Street in Soho where you were likely to see members of the Beatles and the Who and the Animals and where, on this particular evening, I found Proby sitting at the bottom of the stairs with his back to me as I came in. So I put my hand on his shoulder and I bent over and said, very quietly, just for him to know, "You've been bad-mouthing me. There's no press around, and it's quiet outside. Why don't we step out and sort it out?"

Fair play to him—he didn't look intimidated. Well, not much. But he simply said, "Well, what's the point, if it's quiet outside? If nobody's going to see it, what's the point? I'm only doing it for the publicity. I've got nothing against you really."

I gave him a look and left him to it.

The next day, George, the doorman at the Palladium, came into my dressing room when I was getting ready before the show and said that PJ Proby was outside, asking if it was okay to come in. I said, "Why not?," wondering what was going to happen this time. He arrived with a bottle of bourbon under his coat, said hello and good luck and then stayed in the wings for the whole show. And afterward we sat down in the dressing room and worked our way through his bourbon, getting on well, straightening things out. Chris Ellis was driving me home in my Rolls, so we gave PJ a lift to Notting Hill on our way back out to Shepperton. The good vibes continued in the car. A lot of bourbon had been drunk, and forgiveness and friendship were well and truly in the air.

At Notting Hill, just before PJ got out of the car, I said to him, "Mind when you close the door, won't you?" The blacked-out windows in the back of that secondhand Rolls were brittle, and you had to be careful about slamming the doors because the glass was liable to crack.

"Oh, sure," said PJ Proby.

He hauled himself out of the car and onto the pavement and then leaned back in, a little unsteadily, to offer his final wishes.

"A great night, Tom. Forget all the bullshit. We are the *two* greatest singers in the world."

And with that he slammed the door as hard as he fucking could, and the window cracked.

Chris Ellis floored the accelerator before anything else could develop. Our paths have not crossed since.

Moving into Springfield House in Sunbury-on-Thames.

22

The Copacabana Hit

In 1968, I have another huge hit: "Delilah," a Les Reed song with lyrics by Barry Mason and Sylvan Whittingham. Big, loud, orchestral setting, triple-time, traces of flamenco . . . what is this music? It doesn't seem possible to fit it to a category, squeeze it into the usual boxes. It's clearly a great story-song: the ballad of the spurned and vengeful lover, a melodrama with some real emotion at the core of it. When I get to the line about the knife in my hand, I'm really seeing it and feeling it. In some ways, it's also a nut-busting rock number waiting to happen; a piece of stadium rock before stadium rock had been invented. (The Sensational Alex Harvey Band will get to that aspect of the number in 1975.) But then it's also a pub song, a folk song, a drinking song—or, at any rate, a song for people who have partaken of drink; that massive, sing-along, sway-along chorus. Again, though, as with "What's New Pussycat," at the back of my mind there's the question: whatever else this is, is it a novelty record? Where does singing this take me? Where does this land me up?

And, of course, where it lands me up is the charts. Number 2 in the

UK, number 15 in the US. Top 5 in Canada and Austria and Norway. Number 1 in Ireland, Germany, Switzerland, Finland . . . A truly international hit.

There's no shortage of money, so we move house. Good-bye Manygate Lane, hello Springfield House on Springfield Grove in Sunbury, just a couple of miles north. Fairly congested suburban area. Construction work underway on the new M3 motorway. But our house is the big one at the top of a quiet cul-de-sac. Trees around it. An acre of land. Belonged to Eddie Jarrett, the manager of the Seekers, who's moving on. The owner before that, funnily enough: Dickie Valentine. Other houses stand fairly close on each side, but the twin gates and the driveway sell it to me almost as soon as we get there. Big gates, big drive. It feels like another step.

Inside: a huge living room, for which I buy a baby grand piano. Records brought back from America, from my raids on the Colony record store, stacked deep on the floor by the record player. A separate dining room with a dining table for twelve. Upstairs, not just a sink in the master bedroom now, but an actual en-suite bathroom. Plus three other bedrooms and what they call a "family bathroom," though we know now that our family will grow no bigger than the three of us. We have tried for another child, but Linda has miscarried and, although it was very early in the term, the doctors say there's damage, which means she won't conceive again. Which is sad. But we have our son and we know we are lucky in that.

Meals out for the three of us now, at the Indian restaurant in the High Street in Lower Sunbury.

Also decent pubs: the Three Fishes, the Magpie Hotel.

I talk to my father about retiring from the coal mine. He's fifty-seven going on fifty-eight, and, as far as I'm concerned, for the sake of his health, and his lungs in particular, the sooner I can get him out of there the better. He doesn't mind the idea of stopping, but he's anxious about taking the step. What about the years to come? Sure, I'm doing well

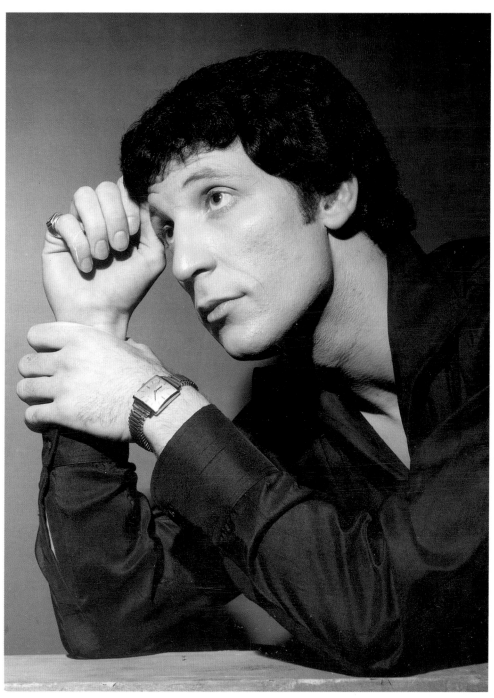

In my early twenties as Tommy Scott.

Me and my portable record player in Manygate Lane.

Performing in the early days with the Squires.

Still a Teddy boy.

With Linda, up from Wales, checking out London.

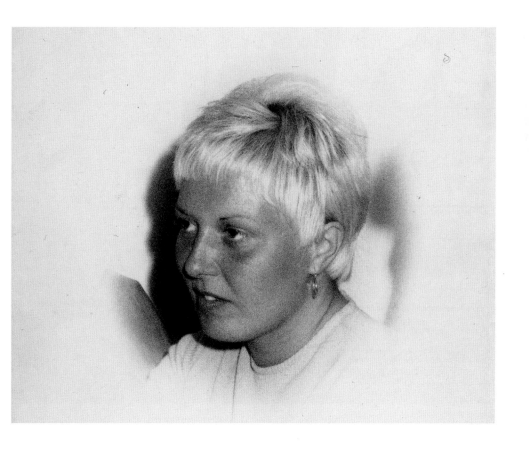

St. David's Day, 1965. Mark is at school in fancy dress when "It's Not Unusual" hits number 1 and photographers turn up.

A happy day, too, for my mother and sister.

Performing at the Paget Rooms in Penarth, July 1965.

On *The Ed Sullivan Show*, in New York, December 1965.

Having a peaceful moment.

Up on a London roof.

This Is Tom Jones—can you spot me in the background?

A beautiful moment with Jerry Lee Lewis and Chet Atkins.

Rockin' with Ella Fitzgerald.

I had to pinch myself—singing with Stevie Wonder and Aretha Franklin.

now, and there's money about, but what if it all goes tits up? It's a fickle business. There are no guarantees.

As it happens, I'm more confident than that. Will pop music survive? Is it just a temporary craze? People are asking the question. But as far as I'm concerned, I'm in it now. I'm not a fad singer. Maybe I won't ever again have hits as big as the ones I've had. But I'll always be able to sing *something*. I feel sure about that.

But also, my father doesn't really know how much money I've already made.

I say to him, "Well, why don't you work out what you would earn between now and retirement and I'll write you a check for that now."

My father retires. He uses some of his new free time to learn to drive, taught by my cousin Idris. I buy him a red Hillman Hunter, and then my parents move out of Laura Street and into the vacated house in Manygate Lane, which they have always loved.

I change my car, too. My Rolls-Royce Silver Cloud has single headlights, but they bring out a new one with double headlights. I see one when I'm driving past the showroom of Weybridge Autos, in silver, with red upholstery. And I think, "Wow." So I put the green one in for the later model and trade up.

New big car, proper family house with gates and a driveway and an acre of land, really putting down roots.

We'll be moving on again inside a year.

I KNEW WHAT THE COPACABANA in New York was like because I had been to see Peggy Lee there one time, and also the Supremes, when I was getting to know Mary Wilson, who was a good friend in this period. The Copa, as everybody called it, stood on East 60th Street in midtown Manhattan, between Fifth Avenue and Madison Avenue. Brazilian décor, Chinese food. Seats for 150. It had been there since the forties. Sinatra, Dean Martin, Jackie Gleason—they'd all worked the place.

Norby Walters' bar was next door. On one of those trips—it could have been the Peggy Lee one—I was in that bar with a friend of mine and some other people, talking and drinking. Suddenly a thick-set, middle-aged man in a pinstripe suit came over to our table and, without any introduction, sat down, busting in on our group. I was in the middle of saying something, and he interrupted me, saying, "Hey, kid, I'm talking to you." Which kind of irritated me. I didn't mind fans coming up—I liked it, in fact. But being interrupted by a fan while I was having a conversation with friends was something I was less thrilled about. The next thing, though, this guy in the suit fixed me across the table and said, "What kind of a man are you?"

My friend was suddenly kicking me under the table. I shot him a glance and noticed that all the color had drained out of his face. He was startle-eyed and battleship-gray. Which ought to have alerted me that something was up, but somehow didn't. I turned back to the guy and answered his question.

"Well, I think I'm man enough for you."

We looked at each other for a couple more beats. My friend had stopped kicking me now and was rock still. And then our visitor grinned and got up and walked away.

My friend, still breathing with some difficulty, said, "Don't you know who that was?"

"No idea. Wasn't it a fan?"

"That's Sonny Franzese."

I said, "So?"

My friend said, "From the Colombo crime family."

"Ahh . . . Well, why didn't you fucking tell me?"

"I was kicking you under the table . . ."

The Copa was a big place for gangsters. Its owner was a man called Jules Podell. The story was he had been given the Copa in 1940 as a favor by the Mob, for keeping his mouth shut and taking a prison stretch, or some such. That was the story, but there were many.

Jules was a large character who imposed himself on the atmosphere. The Copa was so small that the dressing room was actually part of the hotel next door, accessed by a lift up from the club's kitchen. You'd descend on your way to the stage, and Jules would sit outside the kitchen in a sharp suit and highly polished shoes, on a stool by a little table with the cash box on it. He had a thick silver signet ring that he would knock on the table any time he wanted a drink—rap, rap, rap—and a drink would be there, served by Carmine, his right-hand man. Vodka martini mostly, it seemed to be. I didn't ask. Everybody told you, "Don't talk to Mr. Podell unless he talks to you." So, except to say "Good evening," I didn't.

He had a loud, harsh voice—a voice like a bread knife on steel. Some nights as I came by, he'd say, "Hey, Tommy. C'mere." And then he'd shout through to the kitchen staff, "Say hello to Tom Jones." And the kitchen staff would drop what they were doing and clap me furiously, in obedience to Jules Podell's command. It was something out of a movie.

When I was there for that first week, in 1968, the audience was a bit thin on the ground some nights—a bit of a comedown from the Talk. But a nightclub crowd isn't straightforwardly a pop singer's crowd, so I wasn't a special draw as far as the usual Copa-goers were concerned. I was as young and as poppy an act as they had had in there. Bobby Darin had been there, but he was at the slick end of pop. I was more raucous, despite the tux—jumping about the place and ripping into soul numbers. But I knew that I was there to prove a point—to get in there and show them what I could do. Then maybe people would start showing up.

One night, with the room not particularly full, I was singing "Danny Boy" in a version modeled on the one that Jackie Wilson did—a great, great version with a fabulous arrangement which has a big dramatic ending, featuring lots of stops and teasing repeats of the Latin word "Ave." Now obviously, in a supper club, you got used to a bit of conversation going on in the background now and again. But this time, there had been a woman at the front, talking to this guy almost nonstop, right from the kickoff, not taking a lot of notice of me. And she certainly wasn't taking a lot of notice of me in these poignant gaps in my big build-up at the end of "Danny Boy." She was gabbing right through them.

I paused between "Aves," turned to the woman and, in the silence, said, "'Scuse me, sweetheart, could you speak up?"

At that point, I noticed that the guy who was sitting next to her was of a considerable size. Indeed, he seemed to be as tall sitting down as I was standing up. I thought, "Ooh shit, this fella could take umbrage here, and he looks like he could punch me back into the kitchen if he took a shine to the idea."

There were a couple of seconds in which this very large man stared at me blankly—seconds in which the night, and possibly my entire career at the Copa, and beyond that in America, could have gone either way. And then he turned to the woman and said, "Yeah, why don't you shut the fuck up?"

I completed my "Aves" and finished the song to an ovation.

One night, in the Copa dressing room, I received a visit from a familiar face, accompanied by two other faces, not familiar. Chris Ellis was with me, working as a personal assistant now, in the absence of any driving to do, looking after me and my clothes. He was putting my suit in the closet when these three guys entered without having taken the trouble to knock. Chris obviously felt a little protective.

"Who the fuck let you in here?"

"Tell the kid to relax," said Sonny Franzese.

I recognized him. You couldn't miss him because he looked exactly like a Mafia guy is meant to look.

"Remember me?" he said.

"Hey, Sonny, how are you doing?"

It turned out that Sonny Franzese was a big fan, and he just wanted to say as much. Which was a bit of a relief. He was around the place again when I went back and did the second series of shows in 1969. By that time, the word was out about me, and it was bedlam. The band was on risers, but where you sang was on the floor, in a tiny square area which had shrunk right down because they brought the tables and chairs right up to it. I was very accessible down there, and many members of the audience duly accessed me. Women were literally climbing across the tables to get to the stage to grab me for a moment and kiss me. You'd get about two or three flying in per number. The Copa had fellas working there in red coats, who would kneel by the tables, and act as bouncers, which worked up to a point. But nevertheless, Sonny Franzese had obviously observed all this going on and had become concerned about the situation.

"You don't have a bodyguard?" he said to me.

"No," I said.

The next night when I came in and went to the dressing room, there was this monster standing outside the door—a guy who looked like he'd been made out of a mixture of steak and granite and then wrapped in a suit. Serious, unflinching face.

"Who are you?"

"Sonny sent me."

"Oh. Okay."

Years later, I see the great Francis Ford Coppola movie *The Godfather*, and my jaw drops. There's a character in that film, Luca Brasi, a mean, murderous motherfucker who is Vito Corleone's personal enforcer. Brasi was played by Lenny Montana, an ex-wrestler—and Lenny Montana was the guy that Sonny Franzese sent me that night in 1968 to be my bodyguard, the guy I found blocking the door. Essentially, for the rest of that week at the Copa, I had Luca Brasi looking after me. And even Don Corleone thought twice about picking a fight with Luca Brasi.

Lenny would walk me to the floor, going ahead of me, ensuring a clear path, pushing down the outstretched hands. And then he would kneel down at the side for the duration of the show and make sure I didn't get swamped. He didn't say a lot, but he didn't really have to. He was what you might call a reassuring presence.

There were a lot of gangsters and their wives and girlfriends in the audience. Gangsters got to like me. And far better that than gangsters not liking me. Sonny Franzese, in particular, continued to take me up as a cause. He seemed to be intrigued by my Welshness, was keen to get his head around the distinction between English and Welsh. He once told me that he had some Scottish guy that he was doing business with—and that the guy was crazy. "So I asked him about the Welsh," said Sonny. "And he told me the Welsh are even more fucking crazy than the Scots." I didn't tell him otherwise.

Sonny once slipped me a card with a phone number on it and told me if I ever needed anybody, I should call the number. Didn't matter where it was in the world, he said. "Can even be fucking China. Just call." I never did. I never had any cause to. But I guess it was reassuring to know the option was there.

Gordon wasn't too keen on me having these wise-guy buddies knocking about. It got him frightened a bit. His worry was that somebody, at some point, might want something—might lean on us for a piece of what we had and turn it all sour. He warned me, "You've got to be careful around these guys." Well, I think I definitely was careful, apart from that very first night with Sonny. Certainly nobody came after me for anything. They just seemed to like the singing. It has rung down the years. "Wise guys love you from the Copa." I liked that, that I got respect from those guys. If their wives liked me and their girlfriends liked me, it seemed to be okay with them. I think that's because they saw me as a man, a stand-up guy. It wasn't like their wives were going crazy for some wishy-washy pop-kid with a waspy waist, and they didn't get it.

It was in the Copa that I was seen by Phil Miller, who was the booker for the Flamingo in Las Vegas. So that whole route opened up right there. I was on a nightclub path, for better or worse. Probably for better *and* worse, the way it worked out. But at this stage it was exciting to me. Why wouldn't it be? In Vegas, Sammy Davis Jr. would say to me, "I heard what happened at the Copa. What did you do to those people?" And Sammy had had his own huge run at the Copa in 1964. Suddenly I was impressing Sammy Davis Jr. And I can't deny that the fact I could impress Sammy Davis Jr. seemed pretty fucking impressive to me.

Ready to rehearse in LA.

23

Made My Bed

It happens for the first time on one of those nights in the Copa in 1969. I'm drenched with sweat. Just occasionally someone on a table near the stage will reach out with a white linen napkin for me. I'll dab at my brow with it and then hand it back. Not this one woman, though. This one woman has something else in mind. She stands, flips her dress up, steps out of her panties and hands them up to me.

This is, I am immediately aware, a sharp step-up from table napkins.

What to do about it, though? What to do or say about this intimate, and rather thrillingly warm, item of clothing, currently in my hand? I have years of experience in theaters and dance halls and now nightclubs. I've not come in for much abuse in that time, but I still like to think I've had most things thrown at me that an audience is likely to throw. It's a fairly limited repertoire of objects, after all. Mostly glassware. And you learn the techniques. If someone chucks a bottle, you try and catch it, or you pick it up and drink from it, or you say, "Are you sure you'd finished with that?"—something to defuse the situation, maybe even turn the moment to your advantage.

But if someone throws their underpants? The underpants that, until that very moment, they had been using as . . . underpants?

There is nothing from the stagecraft handbook that I can pull out here. This is all new. I'm thinking on my feet here.

What I do with the panties is, I dab my brow with them. And then I say, "You want to watch you don't catch cold."

Which I think is pretty bright, considering.

And then I hand them back.

Not knowing what I have just inadvertently started.

How could I have known? Who could have seen how big these panties would get? As it were. Who knew that by dabbing my brow and playing along at the Copa that night, I was creating a monster? A monster made of underpants.

I mean, you don't want to sound ungrateful. God knows, you never want to sound ungrateful. You certainly don't want to sound ungrateful about women handing you their panties—because what man who likes women wouldn't find something to hold his attention there?

It's just that the panty thing . . . expands. An American columnist writes about what he saw at the Copa. Word gets out. The gesture gets taken up and repeated. The underpants, and my reaction to the underpants, become a moment in the show—and then a number of moments in the show. For a while the panties continue to be recently removed panties—apparently a spontaneous reaction. But very soon, people are bringing panties to throw—packing a spare pair for the occasion. It becomes a thing. It becomes what you do at a Tom Jones show. Bring Tom the gift of underpants.

Within a couple of years, wherever I play, the stage by the end of the night will have grown a carpet of donated underwear. When the venue has emptied and the house lights are back up and the clear-up has begun, some janitor with a wide broom will be out there sweeping the stage clear of underwear.

Who could have predicted this? And beyond that, who could have seen that it would end up getting in the way? That it would dominate to the point of becoming almost my entire image, or certainly, for a while there, the first thing people thought about. Tom Jones: panty magnet. And yes, I know: there's no limit to the things you can grow tired of. But even so, who could have foretold, when that solitary woman in New York paid tribute to me with the most intimate gift that she happened to have about her person at the time, that I would one day, a number of years afterward, have cause to be a bit pissed off about all the underpants?

AUTUMN 1968. I'm in the Scotch of St. James in Masons Yard, which, there being a fast turnover in these things, seems to have become the swinging-London hangout of choice since the Ad Lib Club closed down in 1966. A couple of girls are making a fuss of me, and from behind them I hear this voice say, "Excuse me—leave him alone."

It's Paul McCartney. He sits down, and we talk properly for the first time. I tell him it would be nice if he wrote me a song. He says he's got something I might like that he has just demo'd up and he'll get it across to me.

I don't really know how serious he is, but, sure enough, a day or so later, Gordon tells me that Paul McCartney has come through with a song. "The only catch is, he wants it done now. If you don't take it now, he'll do something else with it. But if you want it now, he's giving it to you."

I listen to the demo. It's just McCartney's voice and a piano. It doesn't hit me as being anything all that special, to be perfectly honest. At least I can't quite hear what's in it for me.

In any case, I've got plans for other things at this point. I'm all geared up to release an old Clyde McPhatter song, "Without Love"—on which I have fought Peter Sullivan to let me do the spoken-word introduction. Speaking on records kind of went out of fashion after Jolson, but, for me, Elvis brought it back with "Are You Lonesome Tonight." You can pull it off if there's belief there in what you're saying.

Anyway, that's in the pipeline, along with another potential single called "Love Me Tonight," a Latin-inflected dance thing. So we phone McCartney and say, "Thanks, but no thanks."

Which is how I came to turn my back on "The Long and Winding Road." Much later I hear Ray Charles do a version of it and get right to the soulful heart of the thing.

My regret doesn't in any sense decrease.

Schmuck.

Maybe if he'd sent me "Let It Be" . . .

On the set of This Is Tom Jones.

24

Everything's Got a Price

Among the people who came to see me at the Talk of the Town in 1967 was Sir Lew Grade, the chairman of ATV, later Lord Grade. I liked Sir Lew. And later I liked Lord Grade. Most people did. He was loud and funny and he seemed to be on the side of the right things: popular entertainment, cigar smoking, to name only those. He showed up at the Talk with a fella called Martin Starger, who was Sir Lew's equivalent at ABC television in America. Ever since then the idea had been floating about of me doing my own television series—meetings, backward and forward, between Gordon and Sir Lew, with me sitting in on some of them, and, as usual, not saying much—until eventually some kind of deal was struck for a pilot to be made. And after that everyone would take a view.

"What am I supposed to be doing, then?" I asked Gordon.

"You introduce guests, you chat a bit, you sing."

"Really?"

This was late 1968. Lulu was doing TV shows, but the only variety shows on British television that were hosted by male popular singers were imports from America: Perry Como doing specials like *Perry Como Comes to London* and the Christmas ones, Andy Williams with *The Andy*

Williams Show. Cliff Richard had had some TV series, but those weren't variety; they were all about Cliff and the Shadows. Andy Williams was in his early forties, Perry Como in his fifties. Seasoned performers, safe pairs of hands. I was twenty-eight and had been famous for just three years. The thought of doing telly hadn't really occurred to me along the way, except as it arose from promoting the records. Did going on *Ready Steady Go* a few times qualify you for your own series? It didn't seem to be qualifying many other people. I could see myself landing flat on my arse, or worse. Which meant I wasn't jumping up and down to get in the studio and get cracking.

On the other hand: your own TV show? In some respects, that was the star prize, the gold medal. They weren't handing television series out to just anybody. In terms of putting yourself in front of people, that would have to be an arrival of some kind, wouldn't it?

Plus, the way the deal was structured, Grade would go into business with ABC in America, and the show would go out in both places at once. So I'd be taking a shot at British television and American television with the one stone. I'd be a singer with his own show on both sides of the Atlantic. Assuming the pilot worked. And assuming the show worked after the pilot.

So I did the pilot, driving out to Elstree Studios in Borehamwood, north of London, one of the main homes of the British film industry but also where ATV had a setup for program making—turning up in the parking lot with my driver in my Rolls-Royce, already Charlie Show Business, you'd think, though wary as fuck, deep down inside.

The producer was Jon Scoffield—nice guy, in his late thirties, given to wearing cardigans and, occasionally, a string of beads. He'd worked on Cliff's shows, and also on *Sunday Night at the London Palladium*, and he did *Spotlight*, another variety show which I had been on the previous year, so I knew him a bit and trusted him. The format for the show had already been thrashed out: an opening number for me; a guest slot with some chat and a duet; a sketch or song-and-dance number; and then, to finish, a "concert spot"—me and the band hammering through two or three songs in front of a studio audience, which was the bit I most liked the sound of.

The guests booked for the pilot were Dick Cavett, the American comedian; Juliet Prowse, the actress and dancer; and the Fifth Dimension, who did "The Age of Aquarius." I would later hear that the presence of the Fifth Dimension had caused flutters with potential sponsors of the show in America—the reason being, they were black. Incredible, but this kind of thing would become a persistent theme as the program developed. Apparently, in the recent past, Petula Clark had touched Harry Belafonte in full view of some cameras, and the balloon had gone up. American television, permanently paranoid about how things might be going over in the Midwest, was twitchy as hell over black and white interactions on screen, as I was to discover.

I didn't know what to think about the pilot when it was done. I liked the concert slot, certainly—was worried that some of the other stuff might have come off a bit clunky. It seemed to play well, though, and the show got commissioned, by ATV and ABC together. The plan was to shoot at Elstree in the first instance and then, later in the year, over in Los Angeles. The deal for three series of *This Is Tom Jones* was worth £9 million. It was the biggest deal that had ever been struck for a singer-led variety show—and it seemed large enough to me to merit getting my nose fixed, which I now duly did, reshaping the section which had been battered flat in various collisions on the streets of Pontypridd.

Before filming began, they put me in a room with a speech and drama coach. I didn't like her. She was like a schoolteacher, and I was very hopeful that I was finally beyond all that. I've never been one for taking instruction at the best of times—and not because I think I already know it all, but the opposite in fact: because of the danger of being instructed to do something that I can't and then getting shown up. Here I was, though—back at school and getting all hot about it. There was a lot of quick clapping of hands. "You want to go UP at the end of your

SENTENCES." Really? I thought she was making me sound like a twat. So I asked if I could be freed from that.

Each show took six days to shoot, driving over to Elstree for a 10:00 a.m. start, which meant leaving home at nine—the first time I had been forced to get up early in the morning consistently since the days of working on the building sites. I would carry on sleeping in the back of the car and get the main part of my waking-up done at Elstree, where, on the more difficult days, a jug of Bucks Fizz could often be used to speed up the process. The days were long and often highly inactive, in keeping with the traditional film-set instruction: "hurry up and wait." Double the agony in this case. American television used a different line format from British television, so, for the first series, we were shooting each episode twice—once for British use, once for American use. It was a lot of stopping and starting and going again.

Fortunately, for my comfort during downtime, they stuck a giant caravan in the hangar at the back of the studios, the kind of "static home" you see parked up at the seaside. Bedroom, bathroom, kitchenette with a dining table, daily supply of cut flowers and fruit. My own trailer. Hollywood in Borehamwood.

The ABC connection meant that a lot of the guests were coming out from America. They were flying them in first class, putting them up at Claridge's or the Dorchester, chauffeuring them around in a black Daimler. No hardship. Even so, in that first series, before the show had any traction, some of these guys must have been puzzled.

"You're doing an ABC TV show . . . in England."

"Huh?"

"With Tom Jones."

"Who?"

"In Borehamwood."

"Where?"

So that was the advantage of the ABC connection. The disadvantage was that the show had to meet America's far stricter rules on broadcasting propriety. A censor from ABC would be sitting there in the corner, during rehearsals, looking out for anything wayward. In the first series, the censor was a spinsterly looking woman who, at any break in the proceedings, would take out her knitting and start clicking away. First hint of immorality, though, and she'd be out of her corner like a train. I was doing the Rolling Stones' "Satisfaction" at one point, for one of the concert slots, and the number was halted.

"You can't sing those words while moving like that," said the censor. "You're making it look as though the song is about *sexual* satisfaction."

"Well, isn't it?"

We went again, and I toned it down, and the censor went back to her knitting.

When I did "Somewhere" from *West Side Story* with Leslie Uggams, the censor asked the director if we could look at each other less longingly—like looking at each other longingly wasn't what "Somewhere" was about. We were instructed to look away and into the camera a couple of times to break the "intensity." Apparently we were looking like we wanted to devour one another. And maybe we did. But if you are going to sing "Somewhere," you might as well sing it like you mean it.

On another occasion, Nancy Wilson, the American jazz singer, and I were going to do "Passing Strangers," a beautiful song that we both liked and which sounded really good, traded between the two of us. The censor went bustling up to Jon Scoffield and told him he had to change the song. There was nothing suggestive in it, but apparently if we seemed like passing strangers now, then that meant we had once been lovers, and that was unacceptable, what with her being black and me being white. This was the kind of craziness you were up against. So we junked the idea of doing the song and then went backstage sheepishly to break it to Nancy. Nancy was, like, "Oh, but it was working so well, wasn't it?" We were too embarrassed to tell her the reason why the song had been pulled. We said it was about a problem getting clearance from the publisher.

I should have been ready. On *The Ed Sullivan Show* in 1967 I had been asked to change some words in "Delilah." I thought they were about to come at me about the bit with the knife and the stabbing, but no. The problematic line was: "At break of day, when the man drove away." "That implies that the man was there all night," the censor explained. So instead I had to sing: "At break of day I was still 'cross the way." Such bullshit.

In Elstree, we had the Jack Parnell Orchestra for the in-house music, beefed up with Big Jim Sullivan on guitar and Ronnie Verrell on the drums—players who could give it a bit of a push. So I never had any problem with the music. But I was getting into some other areas here: the scripted "casual" exchanges, the corny sketches and mainstream dance numbers. In some of the setups, I found myself sitting down to sing. When had sitting down to sing ever been a part of what I did or who I was? I'd always been up in front of a band, getting that propulsion from there. Now I was sitting in an armchair, singing to piped music. Quite a change there. Like Val Doonican, I guess. But Val was forty-one at this point, and I was twenty-eight and not particularly feeling the need to take a load off.

Also, up to this point I'd been dancing the way I felt it. But now, for the special dance numbers, I was in with a choreographer, Norman Mayne, putting steps together. And I wasn't sold on that. Plus the in-shot audience for the concert spots, gathered close to an illuminated thrust stage, was made up entirely of women—the show playing on that aspect of things. Why no men in that crowd? Wasn't I playing to men, too? There was plenty, clearly, that I could have thought harder about. But in television, you surrender control. What you say, how you say it. What you sing, how you sing it. You do what you're told to do. Wear this. Stand here. Walk over there. Say that. Now sing. Now dance. Now stop. Instinct, which might have been serving you well up to this point, no longer operates. Suddenly you're looking to communicate with a camera, rather than an audience, and that's another thing altogether. It stands to reason that some of the edges are going to come off here. This is television. Television is exposure like you couldn't dream of—but it's exposure that comes with conformity, exposure mostly on other people's terms.

But I was largely oblivious to all this at the time. The way I saw it, there was a trade-off. Yes, I might have to put on a space suit and sing "Fly Me to the Moon." Or I might have to sit down with Sergio Mendes and sing a song in Portuguese, which put me right out on the limit of my comfort zone. But at the same time, I could get to perform with all these people I liked: Jerry Lee Lewis, Little Richard, Wilson Pickett. I got to sing "See Saw" and "Spirit in the Dark" with Aretha Franklin, and you don't forget that in a hurry. We never got to Chuck Berry, alas. But we were very quickly getting to Stevie Wonder, Ella Fitzgerald, Johnny Cash, Tony Bennett . . . I was getting my rocks off. I could do the ballads, rip the shit out of the rock'n'roll numbers and meet and sing with these great people. And I didn't seem to be afraid of it. I thought I could do it all. Why not? Why should there be a limit? Why not be versatile?

Well, maybe because, in the end, versatility ends up confusing people, and they lose sight of what you are—and maybe you lose sight of what you are, too. But that thought wasn't in my mind a lot at this time. I was having too much fun.

For fuck's sake, *Jerry Lee Lewis* was on the show, sitting almost side-on to the keyboard, mic stand between his legs, rumbling and roaring through "Great Balls of Fire," "Move On Down the Line," "Long Tall Sally," "Whole Lotta Shakin' Going On," while I stood right there, in a crewneck sweater, leaning on the piano, trading lines. And forget the wooden scripted dialog and the goofball gags at the start, because what that segment opens out into is without question seven of the most exciting minutes of my life.

Yet, on that very same episode, I'm singing a soft ballad with Barbara Eden, the singer and actress from the American sitcom *I Dream of Jeannie*. And that's a contrast worth mulling in terms of the range of the show. But I didn't mind singing with Barbara Eden if it meant I could sing with Jerry Lee—just as I didn't mind singing with a Broadway singer like Robert Goulet if it meant I got to sing with Wilson Pickett. Fair play to Robert Goulet, though—he could handle his champagne. He came back into the caravan for a session afterward. Jesus, that man could drink. He was more rock'n'roll than the rock'n'rollers.

The biggest mistake I made with Wilson Pickett, however, was to go out drinking with him after the show. We got in my Rolls and we went to see Ben E. King at a show in London and then on to the hotel where Pickett was staying, where we settled down in the bar. We had done this blistering duet on "Hey Jude" for the show, pushing each other all the way, having a great time, ending up in each other's arms at the end of it—one of those duets where it feels so good you just have to laugh. And so, after this night out, our friendship was pretty cemented, I thought. But then, in the hotel bar, I said something about how much I liked the version of "Midnight Hour" that he had done for his solo spot, and the whole thing suddenly turned. Pickett started dismissing it: "That wasn't really rhythm and blues, that was an excuse for rhythm and blues." It wasn't authentic enough for him, apparently. It was too mainstream. He began to imply that he had sold himself out just by appearing with me.

"One day, we won't need you white fucks," he said. "We'll have our own networks and our own TV shows."

I thought, fuck me: I've gone out of my way to get this guy on the show, and he's coming right at me like I'm some kind of redneck. Chris Ellis was with us and he chipped in, telling Pickett, "You think you're on this show by public demand? The only reason you're on there is because he asked for you."

Pickett said, "Who the fuck are you? You're not even a fucking entertainer."

At this point I considered it prudent to leave, taking Chris with me. "TV Host in Brawl with Guest" wasn't a headline any of us particularly needed.

The Rolling Stones wouldn't come on because they wouldn't do "variety." Well, fuck 'em, then. We'll have Little Richard instead. That was the attitude. And he'll come on in a gold cassock with his hair greased high and his upper lip leaking sweat, and we'll do "Send Me Some Lovin'" and "Good Golly Miss Molly" and floor the place. Or we'll have Dusty Springfield—twice. I thought so highly of Dusty Springfield. She showed you how close country is to soul. We were on the same wavelength. I've got a great picture with Paul, Ringo, her and myself at the Melody Maker Awards in 1966: the Beatles had won best group, she had won best female artist, and I had won best male. Dusty was the real deal.

But, of course, the show varied. And I guess they wouldn't have been able to call it a variety show if it hadn't. At any rate, Raquel Welch was on. We did a Western-themed song-and-dance routine to "Along Came Jones"—me flinging a tumbling stunt man out of the way and rescuing her from mock railway tracks in front of a cardboard train. Pure Saturday night primetime. I got the impression that if this wasn't actually the worst time Raquel had ever had in her life, it was at least one of them. At one point she got in a snit because she thought the floor manager was staring at her—which, being Raquel Welch, you thought she might have grown used to, though maybe you never do.

She said, "What's the matter? You haven't seen a pair of tits before?"

The floor manager said, "I haven't seen yours."

It was in the press that Raquel and I were having an affair, which was bollocks. There was a publicity shot done of the two of us with a chess board. I don't actually play chess, but never mind. Next thing, the story was that we were on the phone to each other for hours on end, playing chess. Brilliant. But that kind of shit was always flying around.

Shirley Bassey, too, had a bit of a stormy time getting her number together. Something wasn't right with her arrangement or her costume or the lighting—I forget which now. Maybe all of those things. Anyway, she abruptly announced, "I'm not happy. I want to leave."

To my surprise, Jon Scoffield attempted to call her bluff. He came down onto the studio floor and said, "Your car will be ready in five minutes, Miss Bassey."

So Shirley swept out, only pausing to add some graffiti to the *This Is Tom Jones* sign hanging in reception. There it was, in bright red lipstick: "Tom Jones is a poof."

With some guests I was aware of fighting preconceptions about myself, suspicions looming large. Janis Joplin came on and she clearly didn't want to be there any more than she wanted to be spending the day stubbing her toe on a chair leg. She was someone from the sixties counter-culture who took no shit, and she was on *This Is Tom Jones*, and that was something for her to be chewing on, right there. Like, who was I to her? Fair enough. She hated the set, too. "What are these fucking plastic rain-drops? I'm not singing with those." They had to be taken down. But then we sang, and it all melted away. We did this belting version of "Raise Your Hand," studio dancers pulling shapes behind us—her in purple loon pants, hair and necklaces swinging, me in a black shirt with puffed sleeves and a lace-up neck, the original odd couple. But it took off and soared. We reached an accommodation with each other by singing it out. And that was great.

Same thing, to a lesser extent, with Mama Cass Elliot, coming from that folk-rock thing, which was somewhere I didn't much go, yet blend-ing together okay—duetting on a medley with "One Night with You," "Do Right Woman," "Love Me" . . .

After filming, Cass told me she was throwing a party in her suite at the Dorchester and said, "If you're in town . . ." The suite was stuffed with people when I arrived and already cloudy with richly perfumed smoke. Cass Elliot said, "What would you like?"

I said, "I'll have some champagne, if you've got it."

"Sure, I'll send down for a bottle."

I said, "Well, a bottle isn't going to go far in this crowd . . ."

She said, "You'll be the only person drinking it."

She was right. I sat down on the couch next to a girl with long straight hair, poured myself some of the champagne, lit a cigar. Chris Ellis was there with me, having a beer. We were both looking around a bit awkwardly. Everybody in the room was smoking pot, passing round these steaming great joints the size of policemen's truncheons.

"Want some?"

"I'm fine with the champagne, thanks."

I was probably getting high anyway, just breathing. I turned to the girl with the long hair who'd been sitting next to me and found her on the floor.

"What are you doing down there?"

"I don't really know." Very giggly.

Before long everyone was sliding off the furniture and lying on the carpet, giggling. Everyone except me, bolt upright on the couch with my champagne and cigar, wondering, "Where did everyone go?"

So I talked to Chris Ellis. And then we went home.

Drugs were really coming through strongly in this period, but they were never my thing. I thought they were anti-social. I saw people smoking pot, and they were inhaling it and holding it in their lungs, which didn't appeal to me, for the same reason that I'd stopped smoking cigarettes. And cocaine, I knew, would get up your nose and then dry out your throat—and dryness is the worst thing for your vocal cords. And then I saw where people were doing it, and it just didn't look attractive to me. I'd see all the bending over in toilets in nightclubs—like Fagin counting his money. I'd be in the toilets because I wanted a shit—and it seemed to surprise people, like they'd forgotten by then that that's what the place was really for. There was nothing there that I couldn't get from wine and champagne and a Cuban cigar. Drinking out of a nice glass, if at all possible. I'm not keen on drinking from the bottle, unless there's no alternative. I'd rather have a glass.

And, yeah, maybe I was a bit frightened of it, too. Maybe I didn't want to find out what it felt like to be high on cocaine because I was scared of it. That, too.

One party, someone was trying to get me to have some dope and they said, "I've got some great Colombian red." I said, "No thanks. Cuba is as far south as I go."

I thought, what a fucking great line! And it just popped out! I was very impressed with myself for quite a long time there.

THE BIGGEST CASUALTY of the TV show was my relationship with the Squires. Discontent had been brewing up in the band for a while. They were on a retainer but Gordon was running a tight ship, even when success hit. The band wanted more money. Getting money out of Gordon, though, wasn't the world's easiest job. There was a crisis point a couple of times. Vernon Hopkins said, "If we don't get a raise, Tom, I'm sorry, we're off." I told him to talk to Gordon, because Gordon was running the show. Vernon clearly thought I should have been campaigning harder on the band's behalf. Vernon may have overestimated my influence in that respect. I did ask Gordon about the band's situation plenty of times, asking him if he could bung them some more. But asking him about it and getting him to part with the money were different things.

Gordon's attitude was, "You can always get musicians." My attitude was, "But they're my mates." It was a constant battle between us. We did the Talk of the Town album, and then the TV show came up. Jack Parnell had the music covered for that, but Gordon got the Squires to do the concert spot. At that point Gordon warned Vernon that, if the series came along, the band would have to be learning arrangements fast and would need to be able to read music.

This wasn't the first time that Gordon had started on to the band about learning to read. While I was away in America in 1965, he urged them to get on and do it. They didn't, though. Reading music didn't feel like a very rock'n'roll thing to be doing. Not a very pop thing to be doing, either. You didn't read music: you listened to it and then you did it. I could relate to that: I didn't read music either. However, for a band, doing telly, when you've got to be slamming the arrangements together and turning it around fast, on the studio's clock, that's different. When the TV show got commissioned, it meant that there would be six months of 1969 when I wasn't doing live work and therefore wouldn't be in need of a band. Gordon took the Squires off the books.

Mickey Gee had already gone. Bill Parkinson took his place when we played the Talk of the Town, which Mickey had decided wasn't going to be his scene. Vernon was the one I was most concerned about. He was the one who dragged me out of the pub to go and sing in the YMCA with the Senators. We'd done thousands of miles in the backs of crappy vans together, set out for London, crawled upward from there. He'd been along for the journey up to this point and now it had ended for him, while it was still raging on for me. That wasn't going to be easy for him.

Vernon was still around, living in Shepperton. He'd taken up with a singer called Myra Lewis, and they were performing as a double act. My recollection is that we were still friendly after the layoff. But the less I saw him, the more bitter he seemed to become about what had happened. I once asked him to come round because I had a load of clothes I wasn't wearing and me and him were about the same size, so I figured he might want to take some of them off my hands. Did that feel patronizing to him? It wasn't meant to be. I just thought he might like some of these clothes. He came up to the house and picked a few things out. Then, later, I saw him give a television interview in which he said I'd charged him for the things. Why would I need to do that? And he said I didn't even invite him in for a cup of tea—like I'd just slung them out the door at him.

Then he built it up a bit about the old days, saying that I moved out of the Ladbroke Grove flat after "It's Not Unusual," leaving the band down there in the Black Hole of Calcutta, and that I was driving a Jag around while he was still kicking mice away from the door. Well, for one thing I really don't remember seeing any mice in Ladbroke Grove. And for another, none of us was living in that flat by the time of "It's Not Unusual," because Gordon had moved us up to Shepherd's Bush. And there were definitely no mice there.

"Tom let the boys down" was basically his line. But the fact is, Peter Sullivan didn't want to sign the Squires to Decca, he only wanted to do a solo deal for me. People had stopped seeing a unit. They had started seeing a singer and a backing band. Should I have done more to resist that? Would I even have had the power to? It was me who insisted on keeping them on, making sure they were a part of it. I felt sorry for Vernon when it ended for him because he did kick the ball off. But then the game changed, and we got swept apart.

Chris Slade stayed on for a while. He always wanted to be a rock drummer, and he forged on and made it—Manfred Mann, AC/DC. And I caught up with him a few times in California. Chris told me, "Vernon took it badly." I said I realized that. But I don't know what else I could have done. It was all moving forward so fast, and it was hard for me to keep my eye on what was coming apart behind me. I like Vernon, and we were close, and I wish that it had ended better. But the way it ended doesn't undo everything that happened up to that point, and Vernon's part in it. I listen to the Squires on *Live at the Talk of the Town* and I listen to Vernon's bass and I think, fucking great. Nobody's taking that away.

Doing a sketch.

25

Convenience Is the Devil

It is now 1969. With the television deal in place, I decide to go house-hunting again. Linda, Mark and I drive in the Rolls-Royce to meet an estate agent on the St. George's Hill estate, near Weybridge, where the roads are thickly tree-lined, azaleas bloom along the gravel driveways and the houses don't seem to have gardens so much as parks. English turf. Old money—but also new money. Increasingly, new money. The estate agent shows us a place called Brambletye, and we're immediately in love with it. Gatehouse, long drive, farmhouse. Astonishing view to the rear across rolling countryside—and a swimming pool, which the owners let Mark jump into while we're looking around. I'm sold on it, ready to put the money down right there—until the agent takes me aside and says he thinks we should look at just one other place before we commit.

So, leaving Mark in the pool with the people at Brambletye, because we're sure we'll be back in a short while to offer them a deal, we drive on across the estate, up Tor Lane to a house called Tor Point.

And this one feels even better. Circular drive. Huge, seventeen-room brick mansion. White columns on the porch. High ceilings, huge, broad polished-wood staircase. Separate guest wing. Vast terrace over-looking a seven-acre garden, which rolls down to the golf course. Even more astonishing view than Brambletye. Present owners: Sir Hugh and Lady Tett, Sir Hugh being the chairman of Esso, the oil company, who, a little uneasily, now offers us sherry on the terrace. I think he's in a state of shock that a pop singer is about to buy his house. A Welsh pop singer, too. I do my best to mind my manners. Sir Hugh tells us that the house was originally built, around the turn of the century, for Sir Robert McAlpine, the house-building magnate—Concrete Bob, as they called him. I'm thinking to myself, if Concrete Bob doesn't know how to put a house together, then who does?

We go back to Brambletye to pull Mark out of the pool and sheep-ishly let the owners there know that we've had a change of heart.

Tor Point is the dream house. Seven bedrooms with en-suite bath-rooms. Chintz sofas picked out by Linda. Crystal chandeliers. Thick, cream-colored shag-pile carpets. Antiques in copper and brass—bed warmers and kettles and coal tongs and bellows. A gold-leaf telephone on an anthracite base. A gym, a sauna. A bar, with a dart board and a billiards table. A Welsh dragon in tiles on the floor of the indoor swim-ming pool.

We can't imagine it getting any better.

My parents love the house and love the area, so, in due course, I buy another place on the estate for them to live in—Fernwood House, which Sir Hugh and Lady Tett had set aside on a plot of land for themselves when they left Tor Point but decided not to use. Maybe they were think-ing, "Oops, there goes the neighborhood." I don't know. All I know is, my parents are very happy with Fernwood House, moving across from Shepperton. My sister Sheila and her husband Ken have been sharing the house in Laura Street with my mother and father, and they come too, moving into the Tor Point gatehouse. Ken packs in his job at the golf course in Pontypridd and becomes the groundsman at my place instead.

The family reunited. Transplanted from south Wales and reassembled in nicer houses with lawns on St. George's Hill. But still the same people. Taking up where we left off. My local becomes the Flintgate in Weybridge. Sunday lunchtimes, Saturday nights, I'm in there with my father and my brother-in-law and, in due course, Mark, fifteen going on sixteen. The men of the family, going out to drink.

Landlord and landlady at the Flintgate: Bruce Reid and his wife, Davina. Bruce has a voice like a high-pitched foghorn, all treble and no bass. He's frequently keen to remind you that you're not up to much. "Haven't you got any fucking homes to go to?" But he'll do a lock-in after closing time on a Saturday night, and we'll settle in until the early hours. Mixed crowd: millionaires and minicab drivers, businessmen and ex-cons. Not always easy to tell the two apart, in both cases. A piece of Britain, caught somewhere between the sixties and the seventies and not quite knowing yet which way to face. Fella often in called the Rev—a former sign painter, now with unsteady hands, who speaks like Terry-Thomas. One night the Rev eats the flower arrangement on the bar and is sick on the hood of someone else's car in the parking lot. The paintwork never recovers.

Gordon, who has also bought a huge house for himself and Jo and their children on St. George's Hill and called it Little Rhondda, can't understand my interest in the Flintgate. "What do you have in common with those people?"

I tell him, "I like them." And I like pubs. When I've been away, I like to get back to that. It's got nothing to do with wanting to keep my feet on the ground, either, in some kind of thought-through way. I'm going there because it's where I want to go.

Gordon likes bettering himself, though. That's important to him. That's the way he's headed. Fine restaurants. High-end gambling joints in Mayfair. Nights with John Aspinall at the Clermont Club in Berkeley Square. He has learned about wines—takes me along in that interest a bit, educates me. Fine dining, too. At the beginning, restaurants and food weren't important to me. I'd eat pretty much anything, pretty much anywhere. Food was a substance: get it eaten and go to the pub. But under Gordon's influence I start to get into it. I learn to spend time over a meal, enjoying the fine food, enjoying the fine wine.

But I still prefer the Flintgate.

Bruce the landlord marshals the pub rugby team. Three hours of drinking over Saturday lunchtime and then up to the rec to take on Staines Metropolitan Police Second XV, or some such. Whoever's available and willing, in whatever kit they can scramble together. The team in the matching kit will be the opposition; the team in everything else is the Flintgate.

The Rev becomes the ref. And even then the Flintgate never wins.

One weekend, Frankie Stevens is around—successful singer from New Zealand, won *Opportunity Knocks* in the seventies.

"Played any rugby, Frankie?"

"Junior All Black, mate."

The Flintgate still doesn't win.

Do I play? Don't be daft. I watch. Mark plays. But not me, thank you. I'm happy where I am: on the touchline, in the darkening winter afternoons, in a sheepskin bomber jacket, courtesy of my friend Jukie Schreyer from Montreal, who can get you any kind of coat you like, as long as it's a sheepskin coat.

Happy on the touchline in a sheepskin bomber jacket, smoking a cigar, pissing myself laughing as the Flintgate's half-cut first XV gets pummeled yet again.

Not just happy. Truly content.

IN THE AUTUMN OF 1969, I fly out to Los Angeles to film a second set of shows for *This Is Tom Jones*, with the first set already having been broadcast and then rerun through the summer. And here's how you really crack open a place as big as America, of course. Not pushing from state to state on a Dick Clark Caravan Tour, but by the electrical wonder of television. I can feel it almost as soon as I step off the plane. The air has changed for me here. A police guard around the studio. Queues around the block for tickets to the recordings. I'm in American households now. I'm on American television, with its commercial breaks—five in an hour. I'm singing soul and I'm selling soap suds. I'm a TV star in America.

In LA this time, I rent Paul Newman's house off Coldwater Canyon, a beautifully furnished, cool, open place with its own reel-and-projector cinema. And here's a contrast that I find myself thinking about as I wend my way to the ABC studios on Talmadge Avenue each day: on the one hand, those mornings pushing round the North Circular for an hour, under gray skies, to Elstree; on the other, these new mornings here, slipping on a T-shirt and driving up through the canyons for twenty minutes to Burbank, with the palm trees waving and the sun beaming down. The daily grind does seem a little less . . . grinding here.

On another trip here to film the show, when Paul Newman's house proves unavailable, I will rent a property belonging to Peter Lawford on the beach at Santa Monica (which, unbeknown to me at the time, was somewhere Kennedy quietly entertained Marilyn Monroe, or the other way around). And that feeling about the contrast with Borehamwood won't change.

Then again, you can see LA rubbing off on the shows—and not in an entirely positive way. The English-made ones had a bit more edge to them, a bit more grit. The LA ones are softer somehow. Yet it's the same director—Jon Scoffield, who flies out to make them. It's just something about the environment they're being cooked in that takes the spice out of them slightly. And you can see it in me, too: a little more relaxed, a little more professional. Getting used to this. Fewer edges.

Until the singing starts, anyway. Still edges there. Crosby, Stills, Nash & Young come on the show. They're not long back from playing Woodstock—getting on for half a million people at the definitive hippie love-in. I sing "Long Time Gone" with them, and it sounds huge—rock, gospel, soul and country all rolled into this giant ball.

We're chatting afterward. Graham Nash asks me, "How come you didn't play Woodstock, Tom?"

I have a moment's pause here. Is he taking the piss? He doesn't seem to be.

I say, "Er, well, I don't know. I guess it had come and gone before I knew it."

In truth, that California flower power thing—kids sitting in fields . . . I'm not getting that at all. Jim Morrison and the Doors doing "Light My Fire." My feeling is, that's one of the dreariest things I've ever heard. All sung flat. Who's lighting a fire in that song? Nobody that I can hear. And that organ, twiddling away—I'm not fussy on that.

But it's 1969, and that's the way it's going in some places at this time, and you just have to accept that you aren't quite going with it.

Outside Elstree Studios, showing off the Rollers.

26
___

Working for the Man

As the sixties become the seventies, I'm a singer, a television star and then, almost by accident, a company director. Gordon and our accountant, Bill Smith, decide to set us all up as a limited company. There are good tax reasons for doing so, apparently, none of which I particularly take the trouble to study. The company is called Management & Agency Music Ltd. Drab name, but MAM sounds pretty good, when you say the initials. Little tribute to our Welsh mothers in there, too, Gordon points out.

MAM is a talent management agency, a bookings agency, a record company, a publishing house—the whole music industry under one roof. A one-stop shop, a 360 deal, as you'd say these days. And there lie the seeds of its demise, perhaps—for MAM is clearly a giant potential conflict-of-interests case, built almost in kit form. But that is years away at this point. For now everything is golden and shiny. In 1969, MAM goes public. I am apportioned 863,750 shares, whatever that means. All I know is that the share price is soaring, and that those shares will be worth millions in a few months. I also have two Rolls-Royce company cars for my pleasure—a brand-new Phantom 6 and a Corniche drop-head coupe. Gordon snaps up a personalized number plate for me:

TJ BIG. I'm not sold on it. It seems a bit over the top, not to mention subject to misinterpretation, and I can foresee it creating some potentially uncomfortable situations while I'm behind the wheel. So Gordon happily takes the plate himself. One day, finishing up at Elstree Studios, Gordon goes out to the parking lot to find his pristine white Corniche, now marked TJ BIG, has mistakenly come under bizarre bombardment from fans and is almost entirely smothered in weird messages written in red lipstick, saying things like, "WE LOVE YOU TOM!"

All three of MAM's directors are issued with a pair of Rolls-Royces—me, Gordon and Engelbert Humperdinck.

I knew Humperdinck when he was Gerry Dorsey. That was in 1964, when I first came to London. Gerry was an old friend of Gordon's, trying to get going as a singer. Nice man. Good voice. I was dimly aware of having seen him singing on the telly when I was down in Wales. Not a rock'n'roll singer or a blues singer. More of a Dean Martin than an Elvis Presley. But he could sing a ballad, no question—get it right across. Gerry had made some headway in the early sixties, but he'd had a bout of TB, coincidentally enough, which forced him out for a while and set him back. Now he was trying to get his career back on track, living in a flat above a furniture store in Hammersmith, with a wife and a kid to fend for. I could relate to all that. Gerry could drive, and I couldn't at the time, and he would give me a lift to gigs around London every now and again. He got a gig in the Astor Club, but he didn't have any musicians, so Gordon hooked him up with the Squires. We all got on well.

The song that changed things for Gerry forever was called "Release Me." It was an American country number from the forties that knocked about pretty much unrecorded until Kitty Wells sang it in the fifties, after which Esther Phillips had an R&B/pop crossover hit with it in 1962. I recorded the song, but in a poor version—a version that Peter Sullivan had come up with, doing it like Ray Charles had done "I Can't Stop Loving You," the choir carrying the first line, and then the singer coming in on the second line. A kind of call and response thing, with a gospel flavor to it. When I listened to it, I thought it was an album track—and never thought about singing it straight ahead, without the choir. And this despite the fact that I used to do "I Can't Stop Loving You" in my live set— and sang it through, without the call and response. Why we didn't do that with "Release Me," I have no idea. We should have persevered with it, like we did with "It's Not Unusual." But I guess there was other stuff going on.

Gordon then got Gerry to have a go at it. And then he played the demo of Gerry to Peter Sullivan at Decca without telling him who it was, because Gerry had been around the block a bit, and the idea of trying again with Gerry Dorsey wasn't going to set Peter Sullivan's heart pumping, to Gordon's way of thinking. So Gordon's question to Peter was, "Would you record this voice?" And when Peter said he definitely would, Gordon made him shake hands on it.

"So, who is it?" said Peter.

"Gerry Dorsey."

"Oh, no . . ."

Gordon realized that Gerry would need a new name, to give him a clean slate. I remember Gordon telling me about it, all excited.

"I've got it. I've got a new name for Gerry."

"What is it?"

"Engelbert Humperdinck."

"Fucking hell, you've got to be joking."

"No. It's the name of an old German composer. It's perfect."

"That's a horrible name. How could you expect anyone to say, 'Ladies and gentlemen, Engelbert Humperdinck'? And then the guy's got to walk on the stage . . ."

"No, that's the point. It's hard to say—but once you've said it, you want to keep saying it. And it's so outrageous you won't forget it."

I couldn't see it for the life of me. And I'd never have worn it myself. But Gordon was right. Absolutely right. Humperdinck did the song, straight, and "Release Me" turned out great. Huge hit in 1967. Kept the

Beatles' "Strawberry Fields Forever/Penny Lane" single off the top. Sold more than a million copies. Stayed on the chart for over a year. I thought, fuck—I wish I'd done that. "Release Me" was a great record, sung fucking well, and fair play to him.

Once Engelbert became Engelbert, though, he seemed to leave Gerry Dorsey behind. Maybe he had to do that to make the name stick—buy into the whole thing entirely. But you certainly didn't want to go calling him Gerry anymore. My brother-in-law, Ken, made that mistake one Christmas over at Gordon's house, when Engelbert was playing the piano.

"Hey, Gerry, congratulations on your new record."

No reaction. So Ken tried again.

"Gerry—congratulations, you know, on the record."

At which point Humperdinck spun round.

"My name is Engelbert Humperdinck, and don't you ever call me anything else."

My mother, who was also among those in the armchairs that day, wasn't impressed: "If you were wearing a hat right now, it wouldn't fit you."

My father bristled about it, too. "For two pins, I'd have knocked him down."

Still, relations, though lastingly wary, were patched up. Certainly I recall another Christmas, later on, around Weybridge, when Engelbert joined me and my father and Ken in the great Welsh Christmas-morning tradition of heading to the pub. Sadly it turned out that it wasn't a tradition so widely shared in Surrey, and we had to drive around for some time before we found a pub that was open, eventually landing up in the Three Fishes in Sunbury. Jimmy Tarbuck was with us, too, and he, bless him, absolutely refused to go along with the Engelbert thing and continued to call him Gerry. But he was the only one, and, for some reason, Humperdinck seemed to take it from him. The rest of us stuck to Engelbert, although we were permitted to shorten it to "Enge"—as in "Stonehenge."

That particular Christmas morning, incidentally, Humperdinck got royally drunk, and I ended up carrying him up the steps to his new house on St. George's Hill. I don't think Humperdinck's family was too impressed ("Happy Christmas—and you might want to get some strong coffee on . . .") and I was bollocked for it by Gordon afterward, though why the blame was mine specifically I never worked out.

As the seventies went on, people would inevitably link me and Humperdinck. The sideburns, the cross and chain, the pinkie rings . . . there were some obvious points of comparison, some details where you saw the guiding hand of Gordon Mills over both of us. For all the similarities, though, I never felt we were on the same page, in terms of what our voices were about. If I had felt that Gordon was paying more attention to Humperdinck than he was paying to me, or that Humperdinck was getting great material that I wasn't getting, it would have bothered me. But I never did feel that. Sure, I had some twinges about "Release Me"—that "it could have been me" feeling. But that was partly my own fault. And in those early years, before it all went tits up between Gordon and Humperdinck—which was when I ended up taking a stronger view— there was a lot of solidarity between the pair of us, me and Enge. We were on the same team—MAM—and bowling along together.

Gordon's other major asset at this time was a kid called Ray O'Sullivan. I was round at Gordon's house, Little Rhondda, the Sunday afternoon when he turned up at the door. He had arrived on a bicycle. Gordon didn't have any gates fixed at that point, and this guy just came up the drive and rang the bell. Shy young fella, didn't seem to have anything about him at all. But he wanted to play Gordon some songs and he sat down at the piano—and Jesus, straightaway you saw the talent. Gordon's eyes and mouth were circular. And this kid has just walked in off the street! He'd been playing his songs around the place, and nobody wanted anything to do with them. No manager, no publisher, no record company. I don't know how Gordon kept his jaw off the floor.

Gordon took him in—put him up at the house, gave him a new

name, signed him into the whole MAM deal. This, too, would go tits up eventually, but it was all roses at first. The artist now known as Gilbert O'Sullivan hit it—went global with his first record, which was the song he'd played to me and Gordon that afternoon: "Alone Again (Naturally)." Great, great song. It was a number one in America. I thought the flat cap and shorts in which O'Sullivan so memorably propelled himself into the limelight were one of Gordon's brain waves—and a fucking stupid one, at that, if I'm being honest. But apparently they were Gilbert's own plan. Again, whoever knows what's going to work and why?

Everything at this time seemed to turn big, though. The Midas years for Gordon. MAM acquired Paul Anka's publishing, as he was down on his luck at the time. Anka had written "My Way," which was a French melody that he put fresh words to and which nearly ended up being mine. Anka told me I could have the song if Sinatra didn't want it, but he was obliged to submit it to him first. Within days we heard that Frank wanted the tune, so that was that. But the Spanka catalog was a nice little earner for the company, and Anka didn't exactly let anybody down later when he wrote "Puppy Love," which was a huge hit for him and later again for Donny Osmond.

When Gordon was trying to persuade Anka to part with his publishing, we both visited him in his apartment in uptown New York. Very smart place. I think his wife was an interior designer. Certainly the apartment looked like it. We watched a movie and drank a great deal of champagne. Anka claims that in the morning his wife asked where the potpourri was from the ornamental bowls in their sitting room. The night before, those bowls had been full of colorful and fragrant dried leaves. Now they were empty. Anka reckoned that, in the dark, during the movie, Gordon and I must have eaten it all in mistake for potato chips.

I don't think that's very likely. On the other hand, we were very drunk.

Anka also claims that, on another occasion, Gordon and I took him to an obscure club in London where people were watching a woman having sex with a sheep. I don't remember that, either. And how drunk would you have to be not to remember that?

Anyway, the upshot was that Anka signed his publishing over to MAM. Altogether the company was flying. Me and Humperdinck were selling records and creaming it in America. Gilbert O'Sullivan was also huge. We had Lynsey de Paul, a big star—though she fell out with Gordon over wanting to produce her own records, an idea which caused Gordon to come over a bit Welsh ("Can you fucking believe it?"). We had a huge amalgamated agency division, cornering the concert market. There were major stakes in jukeboxes and slot machines. There was interest in a private airline, running businessmen in and out of suddenly oil-rich Nigeria. There was the opportunity to be in at the beginning of a proposed fast-food franchise for the UK—something called Burger King, although, actually, the company walked away from that one. And why not? It was never going to catch on.

Even so . . . Hit records, important publishing holdings, major tour promotions, five-story office in Mayfair overlooking New Bond Street and called MAM House . . . At this point MAM was arguably the biggest thing in the music industry outside the major record companies. The money was pouring through the windows.

Little Rhondda, Gordon's house in St. George's Hill, Surrey.

27

Hold That Tiger

"I'm going to build a zoo in my garden."

So Gordon Mills said to me, at some point early in the seventies.

Interesting.

Gordon had never mentioned a passion for wildlife during the emerging years of our friendship. But he had been hanging out with John Aspinall, one of his gambling chums at Aspinall's Clermont Club in Mayfair, and Aspinall was an animal collector who had built a couple of zoos in his time, so something there must have got Gordon going.

In fact Gordon was suddenly interested in the environment altogether. He would go at me from time to time about colored toilet paper.

"Don't buy that. It's bad for the environment. Only use the white stuff."

"Okay."

And he got passionate about endangered species. Suddenly I was getting lectures from him on the future of the panda. He thought I needed educating on that.

I've never liked zoos. I'm not keen on seeing animals locked up. I'm not all that keen on seeing them in the wild, either, to be honest—not face to face. I'd rather watch them on telly, given the choice. Nothing against them: I'm just not keen to go onto their turf, or for them to come onto mine.

But Gordon felt differently. He built a primate house in the grounds of Little Rhondda, on St. George's Hill. I called it a monkey house once, and he didn't like that. I said, "But it's where you keep your monkeys." He said, "They're not fucking monkeys." You needed to know these things. It was a serious piece of construction, though—like you would find in a public zoo: a brick building with an outside pen attached to it, and a walk-along viewing area. Proper stuff.

First up, Gordon acquired a gorilla—Ollie, his name was. Ollie only had one eye. He had been mistreated, and Gordon had saved him. The way Gordon saw it, he was giving back to the less fortunate—the one-eyed of the gorilla world. There were also gibbons, an orangutan called Louis—five or six species in their own spaces. It was quite a big deal for something in your garden.

Then came the tigers. A pair of them. Bengal. The tigers, understandably, needed a big enclosure. It took up most of the five acres of the garden.

And then there was the giraffe. It was a giraffe that couldn't get up at one point, I think—but again, Gordon came to its rescue, got it sorted out. Got it back on its feet. Organized some apparatus that lifted it and allowed it to stand. There's documentary film of this moment. Linda and I caught it out of the blue at home in the middle of a nature program on PBS one night, not really all that long ago. "Fuck me—there's Gordon, saving a giraffe." He was saving animals that would otherwise have been destroyed—from zoos and circuses and people that had had them and couldn't look after them. He was doing good works.

Gordon wanted me to go on safari with him, to Africa, but I didn't fancy it. I said, "I don't really like seeing them in your primate house, let alone on their own territory." He had decided to go into Cameroon in order to witness gorillas in their natural habitat. So he took Johnnie Spence, the musical arranger, who would do anything for Gordon.

Johnnie Spence was terrified by the experience. I asked him afterward what it was like. He said, "The guide was always saying, 'They won't hurt you.' But the guide didn't have a nose. I said to him, 'What happened to your nose?' The guide said, 'I accidentally got between a mother and a baby. But they won't hurt you normally.'"

Johnnie had a machete to help him cut through the undergrowth but, slashing away, he mistakenly got it stuck in the trunk of a tree and couldn't get it out, so he had to leave it there. He told me he carried white wine in the plastic water bottle, clipped to his belt.

Gordon had a touch of malaria on that trip. I didn't hear anything that made me think I'd been wrong not to go.

There would be parties and gatherings at Little Rhondda, and, at some point in the evening, Gordon would say, "Come and see my primates." Which is quite a good line. And then you'd troop out, with your glass in your hand, and check out the giraffe and the one-eyed gorilla. One night, Ollie was lying on the ground with his hand through the gap at the bottom of the bars. To my surprise, Linda bent down and put her hand in Ollie's hand. "Oh, look—he's lovely." Ollie was looking up at my wife with a loving expression on his face. But I panicked: in my mind I was thinking, "This is an animal, and animals can't be trusted, which means that any minute now he's going to rip her arm off." I shouted "Hey!" and banged on the cage. Ollie immediately let go of Linda's hand. But then he jumped up and, I swear, ran his fist along the bars, at me, as if to say, "Don't spoil my evening or you'll get yours."

Later on Barry Mason, the lyricist on "Delilah," took his girlfriend into the primate house, and she got close to the bars. When she went in she was wearing a maxi dress, and when she came out, it was a mini. Ollie had reached through and ripped half her dress off—took fashion back about five years.

And then there was Louis the orangutan. Now, he was a horny fucker. Maybe orangutans are like that, I don't know. But they've basically got four hands. Pair of droppy eyes, slow . . . I thought, this is harmless. It's not Ollie, I'll be all right near the bars. But Louis grabbed my hand and tried to put it on his cock. I managed to free myself. But then his foot came out and pulled me up against the cage. So I had to wriggle out of that. And every time I shook off a hand, a foot would get me, and every time I shook off the foot, it would be a hand. And all the time he's got a hard-on. Once I realized what he was all about, I never went close to him again.

Gordon, especially when he'd had a drink or two, would offer people money to go in the cage with Ollie the gorilla. He'd bet them a sum that they wouldn't go in there for a minute. Terry Downes, the former world middleweight boxing champion, the famous "Paddington Express," was at a party one night, and he was up for it. I thought, I know Terry Downes is handy, but maybe not against a gorilla. I helped talk him out of it.

I didn't follow my own advice, though. Gordon had an idea for a picture: me with one of his two Bengal tigers, with the tiger standing up, with its paws on my shoulders, both of us staring at each other. In Spain, they were calling me "El Tigre." Gordon could see a publicity shot here.

I couldn't. I said, "Gordon, I don't think that's a good idea."

Gordon had this madman called Tiger George as his gamekeeper. Tiger George wasn't averse to wrestling with the animals if he had to—and sometimes when he didn't have to. Gordon said, "Tiger George will be there, he'll handle this fucker if he needs to. And I'll be in there with you, too."

There was a photographer we used, called David Stein. Gordon had somehow bullshitted him into going in there. I remained uneasy about it.

"He'll be well fed and watered," said Gordon.

"But what about if he wants to play? Wild animals play with things, and I don't want to be the toy."

We went in. David Stein was carrying his cameras, looking anxious. So was I. I knew that I was out of my depth. I knew that I'd got no fucking chance with this tiger.

"Don't show him any fear," says Gordon, helpfully. "Animals can sense fear."

I don't know what the tiger was sensing, but it went for David Stein. There was a pond in the middle of the enclosure, specially built for the tigers to splash around in, and the tiger grabs a hold of Stein's jacket with his teeth and starts to drag him toward the water—which, as Gordon explains later, is what they do with their food. I was frozen. Tiger George got involved and kicked the tiger up the arse to distract it. The tiger spun, which caused David Stein's camera to flip up and cut his lip, but at least left him free to run away. But the tiger was now staring at me—right in the eyes.

The eye of the tiger, well before Survivor knew anything about it.

"Don't panic," said Gordon. "Animals don't . . ."

Fuck the lecture. I grabbed Gordon by the back of his jacket and held him in front of me, like a shield. Because what's a manager for? Then, like that, with Gordon held between me and the tiger, I backed away to the gate, only releasing him when I was outside the enclosure.

Back at the house, Gordon sloshed some brandy down David Stein. "That was fucking close," I said—quite angry, really, not yet ready to see the funny side.

"We'll calm the tiger down and try again," said Gordon.

"You're kidding. I'm not going back in there."

And I didn't.

Amazingly, Gordon never got hurt. But he had a leather jacket that was covered in scratches.

Extraordinary times, though, looking back. They say cocaine is God's way of telling you you've got too much money. I'm not questioning Gordon's good intentions. But maybe having your own zoo is another one of those ways.

With Elvis, just before his comeback.

28

Elvis Presley Blues

I went into Las Vegas at the right time. When I did my first shows at the Flamingo in 1968, the place was going into a major phase of expansion. There had been a switch in the Nevada State gambling laws in 1967, and corporate money was flooding into town. Casinos were going up, resorts growing outward, and the Strip getting longer, and the race was on to find big-ticket entertainers who could reliably draw in the crowds and their money. Boom time. The place felt seductive to me in any case. Vegas! I know what the word evokes now—glitter and glitz and superficial razzamatazz and cheesy grins and "taking in a show." Dolphins jumping through hoops. But you have to strip some of that away to get back to the Vegas that I flew into at the end of the sixties. Frank Sinatra was there, Sammy Davis Jr. was there. Soon Elvis would be there. It was a scene. There was a strong sense at the time that playing Las Vegas was something you earned the right to do—that it was something you had to qualify for. The rock'n'roll and the soul acts were in the lounges, the smaller places—Fats Domino, Gladys Knight and the Pips. Whereas at the Flamingo, and later at Caesars Palace, I was getting booked to play in the main room. I didn't see too many downsides to it. I was thinking,

"Hey. This is all right." The massive hotel suites, the restaurants, the bars and clubs, the otherworldly atmosphere of a place that was running to its own clock—it didn't feel like a step down, I have to say.

A high-pressure gig, though, that first time. Screw it up and you weren't likely to be given a second chance.

Unless you were Elvis Presley. Elvis came to see me play at the Flamingo, right at the beginning of it all, in '68. He was driven up with Priscilla in a limo from LA, because he wasn't flying anywhere at that time. The pair of them came backstage after the show, Elvis wearing a jacket with buttoned pocket flaps over a white turtleneck, Priscilla with jet-black lashes and her black hair piled up high, in a dark evening gown. They congratulated me, and we posed for a few pictures. I didn't know what was in Elvis's mind at the time, but it emerged he was planning a comeback in Vegas. Elvis played Vegas in the fifties, did the Frontier and flopped there. It was the wrong place for him to go at that time. But this noise around the show that I was doing made him come and check it out.

And there was serious noise. I didn't screw up at the Flamingo, as it happened. I picked up from where I had left off in the Copa—wearing a tux, but not for long, pounding it out, women going nuts and flinging themselves at the stage. Underwear flying—and room keys now. Room keys were Vegas's little twist on the hysteria—hotel fobs lobbed with a clunk onto the stage as if to say, "You know where to find me." Well, okay. But they got swept up afterward and returned to reception.

The Flamingo billed the show under the heading "Tom Jones Fever" and sold the place out. The *Live at the Flamingo* album that was recorded and released in 1969 is pretty much the show Elvis came to see in 1968, in my first year there—and that album is steaming, if I say so myself. Johnny Harris was the arranger again, as with the *Live at the Talk of the Town* album. Looking back, the show softened up slightly when I went over to Caesars Palace in 1971—lost a bit of rawness when Gordon got rid of Johnny (finally fed up with him throwing himself around in front of the band) and brought in Johnnie Spence. But in the meantime it was pumping. And Elvis could see and hear a possibility for himself in the way that show of mine at the Flamingo was coming across. He saw something in it that was close to what he did himself, and it persuaded him to go back and give Vegas another shot.

Elvis and I were only together for a few minutes backstage that night. But in May 1969 I was playing a season at the Paradise Lounge at the Ilikai Hotel in Hawaii, a new high-rise luxury development, and I got the message: "Elvis is trying to call you." I rang the number, and Elvis said, "Man, you're a hard person to reach." He was on holiday in Hawaii and evidently he'd been calling the suite and saying, "It's Elvis Presley" and people had been thinking, "Yeah, right," and hanging up on him. I had to tell the people who were with me: "If somebody calls and says he's Elvis Presley, put him on to me because it *is* Elvis Presley."

Joe Esposito, who was Elvis's road manager, came to pick me up at the hotel and took me out to the beach house that Elvis was renting outside Honolulu. When I arrived, though, Elvis wasn't there. Priscilla was in the house, and various members of Elvis's entourage, the "Memphis Mafia," but not Elvis.

But then, almost immediately, he came in the front door.

"I got the guitars!"

He was holding a pair of them aloft, one in each hand.

Charlie Hodge, another of Elvis's assistants, told me, "We realized you were coming today and we hadn't got any instruments in the house. So Elvis said we had to drive downtown to the music store."

We sat down on couches in the living room, me with one guitar and Elvis with the other, and we picked and jammed a bit, and I struggled along gamely with the handful of chords that I knew. But I soon gave my guitar to Charlie Hodge, because he was a better player than me, to put it mildly. A couple of hours then passed very easily, all of us talking and singing fifties rock'n'roll songs together—bits of Jerry Lee, Chuck Berry, Little Richard.

Elvis used to like to make a statement and would want some silence from the room while he made it. He'd suddenly announce, "I wanna say something." And everybody had to shut up. And then he'd say what he had to say, normally underlining it by pointing in that way he had, with the forefinger slightly crooked and the rest of the fingers quite open—a sort of uncurled point. On that occasion in the sitting room in Hawaii, he said, "I wanna say something." And then to the silent and attentive audience he declared: "Tom Jones is not only a great singer, he's a great man."

At this point, Lamar Fike, a rotund guy who had been with Elvis for years, said, "Why don't you two just get married then?"

A crisp white frost descended on the room at this point, and there were a few intakes of breath, because clearly coming out with a smart remark on the tail of one of Elvis's proclamations wasn't quite the done thing—especially for the staff. Lamar looked immediately embarrassed and apologized, saying he was only trying to make a joke. I didn't mind. I thought it was funny. The atmosphere quickly recovered.

We talked about the Beatles. They were a threat to Elvis in some sense, because they were so big. But I think what troubled him more about them was that he just didn't get it. *How* were they so big? They weren't sexy to him. There was no threat—no balls. There was nothing that he could relate to. He said that when he'd met the Beatles they had sat there in awe. They hadn't come at him with anything, and he'd been surprised by that.

He was curious about my singing—couldn't quite put me together with my voice. He had questions: does everyone sing like that in Wales? Where are you getting it from? Is Wales different from England, then? Are there lots of black people in Pontypridd? (I told him there was a small Afro-Caribbean community in Tiger Bay in Cardiff. But I had to confess to him that the only black person I saw as a young kid was my father coming home from the mine.)

We went outside and larked around on the grass, compared stage moves—pulling shapes, me giving it this, him giving it that—while Priscilla filmed us on a movie camera. Holiday stuff. And then we went in the sea. Elvis couldn't swim, though. So we stayed where it was shallow and mucked about on little mini body-boards.

In 1969, when his comeback shows started at the Hilton, I saw a lot of him. We would both be booked in for month-long stints and, where we overlapped, we would stay on for a few extra days and go and see each other's shows and hang out. He would come into Caesars with his people and always sit out on the end of the half-moon-shaped booth. Then when I introduced him from the stage, he could get up and stand in the aisle to take the applause, rather than get trapped in by the booth's table. People thought these things through.

Sometimes, though, Elvis would show up unannounced and simply walk out onto the stage while I was in the middle of a song. The audience would suddenly go up and I'd think, "Christ, I've bust my pants or something." And then I'd see him walking out of the wings with a grin on his face, pointing at me, or stopping to pull a karate move. But he'd never sing. I'd often offer him the mic, but he said Colonel Parker, his manager, wouldn't let him—that his deal at the Hilton prevented it. Elvis used to love to joke around, and Parker sat very tight on that. So there would be no impromptu singing on stage.

I saw his comeback shows early on, and he started off strong. He'd slimmed down for it and he'd never looked better. But as time went on, it wore him down. A month straight, two shows per night—that'll do it to you. I was still pounding the shit out of it, vocally, and it was getting to me, too. But Elvis at least knew how to do it, vocally, without wrecking himself. He was better with pacing. He told me, "You need more singers on stage. That's why I've got the fellas. When I go up at the end, they go up with me. I could virtually pull out, and the note will still be there. I'm covered. You should get yourself covered."

I said, "I don't want to be covered."

I paid the penalty a few years later in polyps on my throat.

Linda had ducked out of meeting Elvis that time in Hollywood in 1965, but she couldn't avoid meeting him when she was with me in Vegas and she quickly found out that he was easy to be around. Elvis liked Linda. He would tell Mark, "Always look after your momma." He gave Linda two necklaces, on separate occasions, and told me how lucky I was to have married my childhood sweetheart. He said he was sure that he had never loved anyone as much as he loved his childhood sweetheart, and I could understand if that were true.

One night when I came off the stage he was already in the dressing room. Somebody had been pitching a song to him, but he thought it would be better for me. He said, "Tom, I've got this number . . ."

I had just come off stage and was dripping with sweat. I said, "Elvis, I'm going to jump in the shower, I'll be right with you."

He said, "No, but this song, man . . ."

I said, "Really, just give me five minutes here."

I went through into the shower—a big walk-in shower that they had put in for me—and I was washing my hair, eyes closed against the soap. Through the rush of the water I heard Elvis singing. I thought, I'm going nuts; I've been in Vegas too long—I'm hearing Elvis Presley in the shower. But no. I rinsed out the shampoo, opened my eyes, and there he was. He had opened the shower door and was standing there, singing the song to me.

I was looking at him and, even at that moment, I was thinking, if I tell this story, who's going to believe it?

I said, "Elvis, seriously—I'll be right there."

Maybe he was checking me out—I don't know. But I closed the door and finished in the shower and then I stepped out to towel down in the main part of the bathroom—only to find that Elvis was still there and that, moreover, he had clearly taken advantage of his time alone to avail himself of the facilities and take a dump in the toilet. He was wearing, on this particular evening, a North Beach leather suit. A lot of us had them at that time—natural leather with a lot of give in it, and stitching all along the edges. But unlined, so a bit of a struggle to put on. Therefore, when I emerged from the shower, the exact sight that greeted me was of

Elvis, leaning against the sink, washing his hands, with his back to me and with his leather North Beach trousers and his underwear still around his ankles. Without any further ceremony, he picked up a washcloth and proceeded to wash his arse with it. Which I'd never seen done before. He then slung the washcloth on the floor, took a towel off the rack and dried the rest of himself off.

What I'm saying is, he must have felt quite comfortable, all in all.

Actually, there are married couples that don't go to the toilet in front of each other. So he must have felt extremely comfortable.

Anyway, now there was me naked, and Elvis half naked, and he was still on about this song. We moved out of the bathroom and into the dressing room area, with the mirror in it. I was still trying to get myself together, pull on some clothes. He was looking at himself in the mirror, apparently oblivious to the fact that his trousers were still at floor-level.

I said, "Elvis, your pants . . ."

He called out, "Red!"

Red West, Elvis's bodyguard, came bursting in from the room next door, all tensed up and ready to go as though there was something major going down.

Elvis said, "My pants, man. My pants."

Red got down on his knees and hauled Elvis's tight, hard-to-shift, unlined leather trousers back up where they needed to be and relaced them.

The song? I can't say I concentrated on the song. I do know that the idea evaporated. Elvis never mentioned it again.

That wasn't quite the end of it, though. Red took Elvis back out to where everyone was sitting. I paused to have a piss—and found that Elvis had left a .45 automatic pistol on the back of the toilet. Loaded, too, because I checked it out. Elvis, as I now discovered, was given to carrying a gun in the small of his back, just in case . . . well, I don't know. Just in case, I guess.

I put a towel over it and quietly handed the weapon back to him in the room. Elvis didn't miss a beat. "Thank you very much," he said, unwrapped it in plain view and slipped it back behind him.

That was my first real glimpse of the paranoia that Elvis lived with as a matter of course. But it was there, too, in the way that, generally, after a short time in my dressing room at Caesars, he'd want us to head back to his place at the Hilton, rather than anywhere else—presumably because he felt safer there, more in control, in his own environment. A lot of the time I was able to think that Elvis enjoyed being Elvis. He once complained to me that he couldn't go into restaurants and not be noticed—the traditional lament of the famous man. I had to point out that the rhinestone suits, which he wore off stage as well as on stage, the massive hair and sideburns and the huge dark glasses were not necessarily helping him in this area. But that didn't convince him to change any of it. So I assumed he didn't want to. My assumption was that Elvis wanted to be Elvis more than he wanted to be anything else, and, if he gave voice to any regrets about it, it was only because he thought he ought to.

Yet there was a question that he asked me one time, which would come to haunt me in the light of what eventually happened to Elvis and which I have thought about a lot down the years.

"What do you take to keep sane? What drug do you use?"

And it clearly puzzled him that I wasn't using anything, because, as far as he was concerned, how could you not be?

ONE TIME IN 1971 I was following Frank Sinatra into Caesars Palace, so I went in a few days early to catch his show. Linda and my mother and father were with me. People said, "With Frank, don't be surprised if he doesn't acknowledge you from the stage." I didn't care one way or the other, I just wanted to see him sing.

But he did pick me out.

"Ladies and gentlemen, I want to introduce you to the number one singer in the world right now. Right now."

He said "right now" twice. I don't know whether he meant to imply, "He's number one right now, but give it a week or so . . ." Anyway, I wasn't going to ask questions. I'd just been acknowledged by Frank Sinatra. And in front of my parents. A major moment.

Afterward we all went to the Galleria, the big bar in Caesars, and I went back to pay my respects. He was in his dressing room with a few of his people, but no other guests. He said, "Are you by yourself?"

I said, "No, I've got my family with me."

He said, "Where are they?"

I said, "Well, I didn't want to bring them all back—I've got my mother, my father, my wife, a couple of friends . . ."

He said, "Your mother and father's here? I want to meet them."

I said, "They're in the Galleria bar."

He said, "Well, let's go."

He told one of his fellas to go over to the Galleria, clear an area around my parents and put the rope up. And then the fella came back and got us, and we went over, to find my mother and father and Linda all sat tight behind a velvet rope, wondering what was up. We must have been in there for two hours, talking. And Sinatra spent far more of that two hours talking to my mother and father than talking to me—was genuinely interested in them, full of questions, asking my father about his job and my mother about her childhood and both of them about raising me. They were pretty much his age, working-class—he related to them. But he was also plainly curious, and I was deeply impressed by that because, with the famous, curiosity about other people tends to be one of the first things to go.

Occasionally after that I'd be walking through the Galleria and hear his voice. "Thomas!" And there he would be, on a stool, bourbon in hand. He told me, "You know, it's the truth: the only reason I drink is because I hurt my hand years ago and the ice numbs the pain."

I was taking him seriously until he winked.

Sinatra thought I should sing standards. "That's what I hear for you."

Meanwhile I've got Elvis saying, "Don't go there. Not standards. Leave that to Sinatra. We don't do that."

Elvis telling me one thing, Sinatra telling me another. And in the middle, me, trying not to be too dizzied by it all.

MY ROUTINE IN VEGAS was pretty set. Eight hours of sleep from about 5 or 6 a.m., which was when I would eventually turn in, then up in the afternoon and into the gym for a steam bath and a two-hour massage. The fella that ran the health club at Caesars, Mike Caplin, was an ex-pro fighter with a flattened nose and a blunt voice, and he said, "You train like a boxer—with the rub-downs and the steam." Maybe. Quite a bit less road-running and sparring, though, if I'm being honest. But the shows were keeping me in trim. And I was keeping in trim for the shows. It was a virtuous circle, give or take the drinking, deep into the night.

I would sweat out the drink in the steam room. The room that they had there wasn't a conventional one—it was more like a sauna, really, than a steam room, but if you threw a lot of water about, you could generate some moisture. Fellas would go in there to read their newspapers and they would get the hell out when they saw me coming because they knew I was about to steam the place up, and their papers would be a ball of wet tissue within moments. Mike Caplin would be in there, chucking the water on the coals for me and clearing the place out, saying, "If he don't go on tonight, I don't work tomorrow."

The dressing room at Caesars wasn't especially big. They said, "Anything we could do?" I said, "Well, I'd like to have a bigger dressing room if I could." So they built me one, at the back of the stage—a full suite of rooms with a bar and a dartboard, and with the separate changing room and the walk-in shower, the one that Elvis would eventually come barging into. The other entertainers used to thank me for it—but Frank persisted with the old one. It was closer to the stage, and

I think he liked the smaller dimensions of it. He'd got used to it that way. And maybe he didn't want a lot of people in there, and that was the best way to guarantee that.

I liked the people coming back afterward. It was a big tradition for a performer to go back after a show and pay his respects. When we were first at the Flamingo, we didn't quite realize that, and Chris Ellis would be on the door turning everybody away. People would expectantly make their way round at the end of the show and there would be this Welshman telling them to fuck off. But we soon worked it out.

Or almost. One night, Chris banged on the bathroom door and said, "Edward G. Robinson is here to see you."

I shouted, "Fuck off, he's dead."

And then walked out to find Edward G. Robinson in the dressing room. I wanted to shrivel into the carpet, but Edward G. Robinson simply said, "It's okay—everyone thinks I'm dead."

At Caesars, I'd come off stage, take a shower, get into a robe and hold court. Invariably people would want photographs, so I had a pair of white clogs that I would put on after showering, in preference to the usual slippers. The clogs had a bit of height in them and made me look taller in the pictures.

Little tip there.

This was Vegas in the early seventies, and I was in a toweling bathrobe and clogs and feeling like the king of the Strip.

IN 1973 OR THEREABOUTS, back in England, I go to a fireworks party at Lulu's house. She's married to Maurice Gibb of the Bee Gees, and the rooms teem with the major players of early seventies British rock and pop. Rod Stewart is there. Marc Bolan. Robert Plant. Elton John. Various Bee Gees. The new blood-type. The current players. Everybody seems to be wearing satin jumpsuits. There's a decent spread of platform heels. Orange is among the preferred colors of the day, for both shirts and slacks. Yellow gets a good showing, too. And there's much excitement about what's in the kitchen.

"You've got to see what's in the kitchen, Tom."

What's in the kitchen, on the table, is a mound of cocaine, reaching toward the ceiling—virtually a slag heap of cocaine, with straws sticking out of it.

I don't have any. In fact, I'm tempted to go in there and blow very hard, just to get a reaction. But I don't want to spoil anyone's evening.

Elton John comes over. "Hey, Tom. I was going to come and see you in Houston not long ago. But I didn't have my tuxedo with me."

And I'm thinking, Christ, how do I weigh this remark? Is that where I stand with these people? Am I the butt of the joke now? Mr. Tuxedo?

It's been a handful of years since I broke big, and I'm already fair game.

On stage at Madison Square Garden.

29

What Was I Thinking?

When the TV show is a hit, the concerts around America move on to another level. That side of it all explodes in a way that I could never have predicted, and by no means just in Vegas. In the summer of 1970, I begin a US tour that will take in Madison Square Garden in New York, the Forum in Los Angeles and the Cow Palace in Daly City, near San Francisco. The Stones and the Faces are playing Madison Square Garden but at this point, at the dawn of the arena rock show, no solo pop singer is going into those 12,000-seater-plus halls. I'm blazing a trail.

Limousines and five-star hotel suites. A privately chartered United Airlines 727 whisking the show from city to city. Me normally asleep up front from takeoff to landing. The Blossoms on backing vocals—Darlene Love, Jean King, Fanita James, all right on it. Punchy orchestra with Big Jim Sullivan on guitar. Gladys Knight and the Pips as support act. Also, for a portion of the tour, Count Basie and His Orchestra, the Count himself apparently none too keen on interacting with anyone and simply losing himself in card games all the way around.

And in between those big dates, we're doing theaters in the round. Playing to two or three thousand people from a plain white stage in the center of the floor, with the band down below in the pit—just me on a bare set in the spotlights. Sound business for the promoters: stick the singer in the middle of the hall, get more people close to the stage, expand the premium-dollar seating area.

But sound business for me, too, because, the whole setup is a huge kick. Some entertainers don't like the crowd at their backs. It makes them anxious or they find it hard to work. And I've always thought of myself as someone who needs a band punching away behind him, needs to thrive off that. But, hell, I'm loving it up there on my own, in a blousy white shirt and tight black trousers made for me by Robbie Stanford in Shepherd's Bush, with the zip up the side to smooth out the front. Phil Solomon, one of Gordon's business acquaintances, says to me, "You come across as raw sex, so don't wear underwear." So I go out like that one night, in my flat-fronted Robbie Stanford trousers, leaving less than nothing to the imagination. And afterward Phil says, "Second thoughts . . ."

But hallelujah, these times see a major breakthrough in male underwear. Briefs come in, the more cumbersome Y-fronts go out. Great timing. So you can hold it all together and be wearing pants without looking like you are. Perfect for my purposes.

Standard joke cracked by Pat Henry, the comedian, who does the warm-up slot before I come on: "You people in the front row here— you'll be able to tell whether Tom's Jewish or not."

Some of these venues offer a rotating stage, but I decline it on principle. My notion is, if anything is going to rotate up there, it's going to be me. No radio mics in those days—the microphone is on the end of a mile of cabling which sometimes gets bundled up around your feet. But then you can make like a whip with it—give it a crack, make a statement with it.

And the scene in the hall is madness from the moment I get on until the moment I come off. To get to the stage, I enter through the auditorium, picked out by the follow-spot, like a boxer on his walk to the ring. Pandemonium guaranteed at this point. I have to be forced through the crowd by security staff at the start and then forced back out again at the end, with women, stirred right up and cutting loose, hurling themselves out of their seats at me and hands coming in to clutch whatever can be got a hold of.

I'm in my oils, frankly. I'm in good shape—fit as fuck at this point, and proud of it. And there's nothing else for anyone to look at, so I go nuts and dance.

THERE WAS SEX IN THE SHOWS, and there was sex around the shows. The air seemed to crackle with it.

In Las Vegas, they talk about "the drop"—the money spent in the casinos and restaurants and bars by gamblers after a show. If you run a big joint in Vegas, you're looking for performers who can boost the drop. It's a monetary measure of how the good feeling generated by the entertainer—or merely by the entertainer's presence in the building—spreads outward through the resort. Sinatra was the undisputed king of the drop. When Frank was in the house, people gambled that little bit more loosely, lived that little bit higher, parted with their money that little bit more willingly.

I was good for the drop, too—especially in those early Vegas years, but beyond that, too. When I played, the drop went up at the tables, the tips were bigger, the waiters and the taxi drivers went home happier. And part of that elated energy, for sure, was an active sense of sex around the scene—a pervasive sexual charge.

Same thing at those big seventies tour dates. Best clothes. Perfume in the air. People getting revved up. A willingness to cut loose and let go. A general horniness in the crowd. The atmosphere alive with the possibility of sex—in a way that was definitely going to play out to the advantage of the band and the crew, and beyond. The story was that even the stage doorman would get some when I was around.

As somebody once said, I was the Pied Piper of pussy. To use another rejected title for this book.

And the chances were that, in the early part of the evening, while this erotic charge was building, the Pied Piper would be in his dressing room, in a bathrobe or an unflattering velour one-piece leisure suit, throwing darts.

But then it was showtime and the stage clothes would go on, and the lights would go down, and it would all ignite. Attraction comes pretty easily to a singer on a stage—the magnetism that arises from simply being that person up there. One of the comedians who worked with me used to say, "When I go out there, I'm the ugly little Jewish guy. When I come off, I'm Errol Flynn." And just to prove it, in the intermission, almost invariably, this comedian would be somewhere getting blown.

So I've got the singer-on-a-stage thing going for me, and then television comes along and adds a whole other layer. Never underestimate the extent to which people want to have sex with people who are on television.

At those early seventies live shows, it was graphic—and, to some extent, would remain so, even after the decade wore on and it tipped over and became a parody of itself. My shows were getting to women. And I knew exactly how much the show was getting to some of them because I had undeniable evidence in the form of their underwear, which they were handing up to me so that I could mop my brow and which I was therefore bringing up to my face.

When you're a performer and you find something that works, you work it—so it grew and it built. When I stooped, mid-song, to kiss the women who had forced their way to the edge of the stage, it wasn't just a peck on the cheek. It was full-on, mouth-to-mouth.

I was going over as some kind of love god, and I was going over so strongly that occasionally I was even persuaded of it myself. The road will set temptations in front of you that are hard to resist.

Coming out of Heathrow with Dai Perry.

30

He Was a Friend of Mine

With all this frantic stuff going on in the American arenas and theaters, it was increasingly obvious that I needed a bodyguard. My first thought for the job was a guy called Rocky Seddon. I had met Rocky when he was working as a bouncer at a theater in Liverpool, and I really liked him. He was a former middleweight boxer, but not a particularly distinguished one, I think. The word on Rocky was that he should have rented advertising space on the soles of his shoes—that kind of boxer. But he'd worked around the place a bit—he'd been with the Ryan twins, Paul and Barry, when they were having hits. So he wasn't entirely a novice.

Rocky came in for an interview when I was in the recording studio, and I was slightly disturbed to see him walk in with a limp. A limp isn't necessarily a great asset for a bodyguard. But Rocky assured me that he'd got it in a car crash and that it would heal soon enough. So Gordon took him on.

Somehow Rocky's limp never seemed to leave him. To my recollection, he continued to limp the whole time he was with me. My limping bodyguard.

Then, in 1971, I went to Cardiff to do a show at the Capitol Theatre, and the photographer Terry O'Neill came with me, and, during the day, we drove over to Pontypridd to take some pictures—turned the Rolls across the width of Laura Street outside my parents' old house. We were trying to get in and out without being seen, but my old friend Dai Perry's mother spotted us and came to her front door in her house coat.

I said, "Where's Dai?"

She said, "He's downstairs in the kitchen."

One of my oldest friends, too shy to show his face. I hated how fame could do that.

I said, "Well, why doesn't he come up?"

A few years had gone by. It was good to see him. I got him to come to the show in Cardiff, and then we went out and had some drinks afterward and caught up. He was going through a divorce and wasn't in a particularly happy place. So I offered him a job with me. My thinking was, he's a rugby player and he's handy. He's used to a scrum-down—he'll be good on tour in America.

Dai started coming out with me in about 1971, when I still had Rocky Seddon on the go. So, for a while there I had two permanent bodyguards. Chris Ellis was still with me as my driver and personal assistant. Elvis had his "Memphis Mafia." Chris Hutchins, a former journalist on the *New Musical Express* who was my publicist at this time, called my bunch "the Taffia."

And Dai was great. He stuck to me like glue and he was my mate, and I loved having him there. But he didn't think too much of Rocky. "That fucking Rocky Seddon is getting in my way. He's a waste of space. You might as well not have anyone."

One night, in Los Angeles for a show, we went to dinner in Beverly Hills, and the two of them set off at each other.

Dai was saying, "You couldn't fucking hit a cow's arse with a banjo."

Rocky was coming back at him, "Well, let's get in the ring, then."

And Dai was saying, "Fuck the ring, let's do it here."

My bodyguards were spoiling for a fight with each other. Pontypridd in Beverly Hills.

"Fellas, fellas—you're supposed to be looking after *me*."

Rocky's leg continued not to get better and so, unfortunately, we had to agree to a parting of the ways. So now the job was Dai's. He was coming in at a big time—those American tours of the early seventies. He saw the bedlam at its peak. But he was good at it. He had the right skills. He would protect me on the way down the aisle to the stage and then he would sit on the steps and keep an eye out for invaders. And if anybody tried it, Dai was up there like a rocket, taking them off their feet like he was playing rugby. They would be back in the audience before their feet had touched the stage. And then he'd disappear as fast as he had got up. He was dead quick. Fast on his feet and he could tackle. Perfect.

On the way out, we would go like hell. Dai would be in front of me, and I would grab hold of the back of his belt, and he would set off up the aisle, barreling through. The only thing missing was the ball under his arm.

One time, at a soundcheck in Memphis, our tour manager was briefing the chief of police—pointing out that when I come down the aisle, the balloon goes up, so he should get a line of men along there, good and tight.

The chief of police said, "Hey, these townspeople, these are my people. They're good people."

"Yes, but, trust me, this is something like you haven't seen."

And still the chief of police wasn't impressed. "Listen, I know what shows are like . . ."

Dai is getting involved, with his thick Welsh accent: "You'd better listen to what the guy is telling you, because when Mr. Jones comes out . . ."

That night I got to the stage okay, with the police holding everyone back, but it was pretty wild. So, at the end of the show, the chief of police decided he would lead us back up the aisle, going ahead of Dai, with me clinging on to Dai's belt as usual. But the chief of police didn't move fast enough for Dai. Dai was straight into the small of his back, he went down on the floor, and we ran right over the top of him, left him face down, as if flattened by a steamroller in a cartoon.

And then out into the waiting limo, the door closing, sinking back into the seat, out of breath, soaked with sweat, towels on the backseat ready, and the car wafting you out of there, into the night, while the audience is still inside screaming.

What a thrill. Never tired of that.

That's how it was. Bedlam. When I was hotter than hot.

SADLY, DAI CAME TO A STICKY END in Caracas, Venezuela, in 1974. I was flying in to do a couple of shows at the Hotel Tamanaco. Chris Hutchins said there would be reporters at the airport when we landed, but there was a scheduled press conference at the hotel, so we were to walk right through.

We came off the plane and, sure enough, there was a crowd of reporters. They came right around us and started to jostle. All Dai had on his mind was getting me through and out, so he was pressing me forward and doing some fending-off. One of the journalists got round behind Dai and was kicking him in the back of the legs, which I could sense Dai becoming a bit disconsolate about. We were almost out of the airport when Dai's patience finally snapped, and he spun round and smacked the bloke. Full on. The blow would have put the guy on the ground, I'm sure, but the throng of people held him up.

We got in the car. Dai, perhaps not yet fully appreciating the gravity of the situation, said, "Why the fuck didn't he drop?"

I mumbled something like, "Well, I don't think he had anywhere to go."

The fact was, of course, that Dai had hit a journalist, and this would all turn sour pretty quickly if the journalist decided to press charges. In

Venezuela, Dai would most likely be imprisoned while awaiting trial, and who knew how long that might drag on?

Three years prior to this, Dai hadn't even been abroad. Now here he was on the verge of a jail sentence in South America. Funny how quickly a life can change.

Jackie Green, my agent from New York, was there, and Lloyd Greenfield, and also Mark, my son, then seventeen. The decision was taken to get Dai out of the country the next morning, preferably before the courts opened. The options seemed to be an early flight to Miami, or a boat out to Barbados. We settled on the flight.

That evening we had dinner in the suite, and Dai was in tears. He said, "I've let you down. I should have been more professional. I shouldn't have let the fella rile me."

I said, "We'll get you out, and I'll see you in Vegas."

Dai flew out to Miami early the following morning without being detained at the airport. We'd got away with it.

I did the two shows, and, the day after that, soon after lunch, we got ready to leave.

We got to the airport and waited in the first class lounge while the tour manager went to get the passports stamped. When he came back he had everybody's passport but mine.

"They've confiscated it. They're holding you responsible for the incident on the way in."

Nobody had mentioned it the whole time we'd been there.

I said, "What's it got to do with me?"

"You can't leave the country."

The newsman that Dai had decked was called Manuel Olalquiaga, and apparently he was pressing for a criminal charge of assault and a $65,000 civil claim—proof that it was quite a hard punch. We were instructed to return to our hotel and not to leave our room. So we trooped back and sat mournfully in the suite, trying to figure out how we could resolve this.

First of all, Chris Hutchins called the British Consulate. He said, "Guess where they are? They're out to tea."

You see it in movies . . .

Eventually, two young fellas arrived at the hotel, in shorts and flip-flops. These were the guys from the British Consulate. I thought someone from the Consulate would look like a schoolteacher—someone who might know something I didn't know. But here were these young blokes. In flip-flops.

"Nothing we can do about it," they said. "We don't really throw much weight here."

Thanks for everything.

Chris Hutchins then had the bright idea of calling Harold Wilson, the British prime minister. Chris knew him—or so he claimed. And why not go to the top? Nothing the prime minister could do, though, apparently. Or nothing he wanted to do. Maybe he wasn't a fan. "Tom Jones? Venezuela can have him."

I was in that hotel suite for three days in all. Time hung very heavy. There was a fella standing outside the door all day with a machine gun. I said, "Look, I'm not going anywhere. They don't need to put a bloke on the door with a gun." Someone said, "No, he's with us. He's stopping people coming in here to get a hold of you."

Finally, on the morning of day four, I was taken in a taxi to see a judge in his office on the top floor of a dingy, under-furnished administrative block, somewhere downtown. We spoke through an interpreter. The judge seemed at one point to be showing me the gun holstered under his linen jacket, getting a lot of pleasure out of that. He asked me if the man who had struck the journalist was working for me or whether he was working for my company. I explained that the man in question was employed by my company, MAM, not me. That seemed to be the critical detail. The judge signed a piece of paper, handed it to me and said, "*Vamos pronto.*" I said, "I don't understand Spanish, but I understand that."

I didn't relax until the plane was in the air. Chris Ellis was so relieved to touch down in Miami that he got on his knees and kissed the tarmac.

Sadly there was no reunion in Vegas. As far as Gordon was concerned, Dai had acted beyond his remit and had cost MAM a lot of money into the bargain. So he sacked him, and Dai went back to Wales.

But our friendship continued. Dai came out to America for a holiday with us in 1996, with his girlfriend, Glynis. It was two years since he'd had a triple heart bypass and he was in good shape. In January 1997 I spoke to him on the phone, and he was sounding great. It was the last conversation we had. Two days later, Dai had a heart attack while out walking alone on Graig Mountain above Pontypridd. I was so upset about it. My old buddy. At his funeral at the Court Chapel of Rest in Treforest we sang "The Old Rugged Cross," and I laid a wreath. The card on it said: "Friends forever."

Linda in Majorca in the sixties.

31

Honey Honey

It is 1972. I'm driving through South Kensington with Mark, and a song that I haven't heard comes on the radio. Long, long intro. Really long. Long as most songs. Bass figure and a hi-hat ticking away. Other instruments coming in, and the whole thing building, but not lifting, staying grounded—all on one chord. Broody. And then finally it breaks like a storm and the voice comes in.

"It was the third of September . . ."

And at that point my hands actually tighten on the steering wheel, and the hair goes right up on the back of my neck.

It's the Temptations, doing "Papa Was a Rollin' Stone." A seven-minute single edited down from a twelve-minute album track.

I'm entirely sold on it. But my reaction, there in the car, is a mix of two things: intense admiration and, along with that, deep, deep longing, bordering on envy.

"Fuck me. If I'd have had that . . ."

It becomes a refrain as the decade moves on and the distance between me and my last hit record grows.

In 1973, when Al Wilson releases "Show and Tell," which goes to number 1 and sells over a million copies: "Fuck me. If I'd have had that . . ."

In 1974, when Johnny Bristol releases "Hang on in There Baby" and goes Top 10 all over the place: "Fuck me. If I'd have had that . . ."

I've had a big hit in 1971 with "She's a Lady," which Paul Anka wrote specially for me, scribbling the lyrics on the back of a TWA menu, somewhere between New York and London, and adding the tune in an hour and a half at a piano later. Afterwards he'll declare that he hates the song—will claim that it's his least favorite number of any that he wrote and that he thinks it's chauvinistic. Maybe he's right. Actually, definitely he's right. But it was a hit for me—a dance floor number in the earliest days of disco and the last significant hit I would have in America for a number of years.

It was also the last record of mine that Peter Sullivan worked on. Peter left Decca to join George Martin, the Beatles' producer, and form their own company, Associated Independent Recording. Gordon tried to persuade them to bring the business into MAM, but they wouldn't go for it, wanting to be out on their own. Gordon told me, "Peter won't be doing your records anymore." And I thought, this is a bad sign. He was behind so much that was good that I had done—always first-class recordings, whatever we were doing. He and Gordon would have fights about things, but they would tend to agree in the end, and it would come out right. After Peter, things started to come unhinged for me as far as recording was concerned, and that was no coincidence, the way I saw it.

In the UK, after "She's a Lady," I would have another hit with the Percy Faith ballad "Till" and with "The Young New Mexican Puppeteer," both produced by Gordon. But then I begin firing a succession of blanks. "Golden Days," "Today I Started Loving You Again," "La La La," "Pledging My Love," "Ain't No Love," "I Got Your Number"—records that don't even make a dent, don't make it onto the charts at all, but simply get released and die.

I'm saying to Gordon, "Why aren't I getting the songs? Where is the material?" And Gordon doesn't seem to have any answers. He'll say, "Well, the live shows are going great." And they are. But what about getting hits? Isn't that what it's about? Isn't that what keeps you afloat?

In the mid-seventies, I'll look and see that Leo Sayer is having hit records, and it's confusing to me. How? How does that work? I bump into Adam Faith in the lobby of the Bel-Air Hotel one day. He's managing Sayer. And Faith says, "Got the new Tom Jones now."

Really? This must have been 1974. And Leo Sayer is the new Tom Jones? So what happened to the old Tom Jones?

And Barry Manilow is having hits. I mean, fair play to him: the fella can write a song. But how the hell has that come about? That nasal voice. Surely not even Barry Manilow could like the way that Barry Manilow sounds.

In 1972, "Papa Was a Rollin' Stone" goes to number 1 in America. Fuck me. If I'd have had that . . .

MEANWHILE, BACK AT TOR POINT . . . well, how would I know? I'm hardly ever there. Three months of the year at best. Constantly touring, constantly working. My dream home on St. George's Hill. My family all around. It would be nice to live there one day.

One thing I know is that Mark is not happy. Linda says, "He's missing you. You're not seeing enough of him." Tricky road for Mark. In some senses he's a privileged kid and in other senses he's had a hard time of it: set fair in Wales until the age of eight, when his dad suddenly turns into Tom Jones and he's abruptly transplanted to Shepperton to become the only kid in school with a Welsh accent. Two more house-moves later and now he's an adolescent boy rattling around in a huge mansion with his mother, in the near-permanent absence of his father.

If I had been more educated myself, would I have made sure my son got an education? Would I have packed him off to boarding school?

I'd have rather shot myself than packed him off to boarding school.

But something needs to happen. In 1973, Mark turns sixteen. Linda goes to see Mark's headmaster and talks to him about withdrawing him from school. Mark leaves education and comes with me, on the road.

On the question of whether it's a smart idea to expose a sixteen-year-old to the lifestyle of a touring musician—whether this is the smart educational move—only time will tell. But I do know that I want him to see what I do and I want him to be proud of me, and I'm thrilled that he's there, and thrilled, more than that, that he *wants* to be there.

But now Linda is alone at Tor Point. And my parents are wondering why they left Wales to be near their son, if their son was hardly ever going to be around. And, on top of all this, we're about to discover that I can't come back at all.

IN 1974, WHEN I WAS about to set out to America for a tour, Bill Smith, who was the financial adviser at MAM, said something about a tax situation that was brewing. He told me, "If a Labor government gets in at the next election, you might want to think very seriously about not returning."

I laughed and said, "Nah, that won't happen."

In October 1974, Labor, under the leadership of Harold Wilson, won the general election with a majority of three seats.

Which meant, on that narrowest of margins, that the top rate of income tax went up to 83 percent on earned income, and to 98 percent on unearned income. Which, as Bill Smith explained, also meant that virtually everything I had earned in the preceding year I would be kissing good-bye to, just by setting foot overnight in the UK. And, of course, it wasn't just about me. I was a cog in a corporate wheel here. When I kissed good-bye to money, so did MAM. What was bad for me was bad for the company.

I said to Bill Smith, "But I'm barely ever in England. Couldn't we do a deal?" I was ready to negotiate. I would happily have paid 50 percent.

Not possible, though. And not entirely a matter of what I wanted or didn't want, in any case, with the MAM machinery beginning to click into action behind me. The result being that, for two years, between 1974 and 1976, Britain became somewhere I couldn't go. I was effectively homeless—in limbo. I was biding my time, waiting to put in a green card application which would enable me to live in America permanently, if that's what it came to, but still wondering whether, if I hung on long enough, deferred the decision, this whole situation might somehow blow over and leave me free to go back to Britain, where my wife, my house and my family were.

People were leaving Britain in droves at this point. "The brain drain," they were calling it, although it also included rock musicians. Rod Stewart, Eric Clapton, Joe Cocker—they all abandoned ship in this period and flew off to exile in America. And I'm not sure how many of them felt they had a choice in it, or whether they were simply getting steered around by managers and financial advisers, like I was.

The way it worked was, I was free to come and go in America in this period, but only for a certain number of days in any year, beyond which I would become liable for tax again. My schedule was carefully constructed to allow me to save those precious days wherever possible. For instance, if I was on the West Coast, and a couple of days opened up between shows, I would get outside American waters by going down to San Diego and renting a boat called the *Wild Goose*, which apparently belonged to John Wayne—not that I ever bumped into him on it. It was a converted minesweeper. Not a pretty boat. An ugly iron tub, frankly, but nicely fitted out inside, with its own crew, and more than capable of taking me twelve miles off the coast, which is where I needed to be in order to be technically outside the US for the night.

Or, if there was a bigger gap in the schedule, I might head down to Acapulco on the Pacific coast of Mexico for a while. Acapulco was great in those days, in the mid-seventies—no armed guards patrolling the beaches, a jet-set destination, a lot of Hollywood people. The clubs were buzzing. We were there for Christmas at one stage. I flew out Linda, my parents and my sister. I think that time in Acapulco might have been technically my father's last hurrah. After a lifetime of mining and, more particularly, a lifetime of heavy smoking, he was beginning to suffer with his lungs, but it hadn't reached the point, as it would later, where it would prevent him doing things. Out at a restaurant one night, my mother was on at him about his smoking—about lighting one off the end of another, which he liked to do. At one point, after she'd had a go at him, he turned away from her, put a fresh cigarette between each of the fingers on one hand, lit them all up and turned back to her, attempting to puff on them all at the same time. Which was what you might call defiant. We would go to dinner every night and then hit the clubs.

If I was on the East Coast, I would fly out to Bermuda, spend some time on the beach there. Or maybe down to Barbados, where, again, I managed to congregate the family and spend a month. Hardly a hardship, but a strange way to be with your loved ones: hooking up in remote places after months apart, and then going our separate ways. I caused Linda a lot of anxiety in this period: "When are we seeing each other next? Where are we going to live? When is this going to end?" It got to me, too. Sunshine and holidays, yes. But that sense of being on the run lost its glamour pretty quickly. I was fed up quite a lot of the time—rootless, missing Linda, worried about my parents, wanting to feel settled somewhere. Also lastingly bitter at the government, and the set of circumstances, that had (as I saw it) locked me out of my own home.

Somewhere in the middle of this strangeness, in early 1975, I was invited to attend the Friars Club roast of George Raft at the Beverly Hilton in LA. Raft, the Hollywood actor, was seventy-four at that point and ripe for the honor—which is to say a dinner and speeches from your peers in which the shit is ruthlessly ripped from you.

I wore a light-tan safari jacket and matching pants, a chunky brown knitted tie, a giant gold belt buckle. Gold ring, gold bracelet, cigar. I found myself seated next to Cary Grant, who was seventy-one and stylish as hell in black tie and who made a great play at the start of the evening of putting large clumps of cotton wool in his ears, in a mock attempt to protect himself against the bad language and close-to-the-bone gags for which these Friars Club roasts are renowned.

Milton Berle was there, Don Rickles. Incredibly, Mae West, rarely seen in public, and now aged eighty-one and wearing a mountainous blond wig, made an appearance—prompting a gag from the comedian Buddy Hackett, who was the night's emcee: "Remember Mae, George? Remember when you first fucked Mae and the sparks were flying— because you forgot to take off your tap shoes?"

Hackett then turned his attention to Cary Grant and me: "Look at these guys: the old fuck and the new fuck. Between them, these two have stretched more tunnel than the guys who built the New York subway."

I was thirty-five years old—half the age of most of the legends in this room—at a dinner for George Raft, getting teased in the company of Cary Grant while Mae West looked on. I thought of my father, for whom Raft was always the ultimate Hollywood idol, and how little he would believe this.

And yet I was still technically homeless and utterly frustrated by it. The closest I would get to Britain in these two years would be in transit at Heathrow Airport—changing planes between, say, America and France, which was somewhere else I brought the family together for a while. Once, the press was at Heathrow to talk to me, and one of the journalists asked, "Don't you wish you could just head off up the road to a pub?"

"No," I said, "not a bit of it."

But I lied. At that point, there was nothing I wanted to do more.

IN 1976, I QUALIFIED for a green card and took up permanent residence in the US. I needed to be somewhere, and it couldn't be Britain, so it might as well be Los Angeles.

I saw a house on Copa de Oro Road in Bel-Air that I really liked—a copy of an Adams house, very similar in style to Tor Point. Circular drive with an Italianate fountain in the center of it. High ceilings, grand staircase, beautiful marble bathrooms, big swimming pool. Not one but two bars and a cinema. It belonged to Dean Martin (which explained the two bars), but Martin was going through a divorce and shedding some property, so it was for sale.

The three of us from MAM all moved to LA at this time. Gordon found himself a place in Holmby Hills. Engelbert Humperdinck bought a house just above Sunset that used to belong to Jayne Mansfield. And I bought Dean Martin's house.

So that was the end of Tor Point. I put it on the market for £350,000. Dean Martin's house was costing about a million, so I wasn't exactly up on the deal. I was extremely sad to sell up, too. Again, it was what I was advised to do: sell up and get out completely. Gordon, by contrast, kept his house on St. George's Hill even after he moved to America—a fact that maybe should have given me more pause at the time than it did. Once I had the green card and formal American residency, I had the right to be in the UK for three months of the year. Maybe I could have kept Tor Point, and had it there to move back into when the tax situation lifted, which it pretty quickly did. But that discussion was never had.

Linda and I loved Tor Point and, even though I had been spending less time there, being forced out of it was a heartbreak. Linda was terribly homesick at first—longed to be back. We both did, but she had it far worse than me. Another tough period of adjustment. Another period in which Linda was asking herself the question: would I be happier if my husband had never been successful? If none of this had happened? If life had gone on in Pontypridd and we had stayed put? And I didn't know how to answer that question because I felt the answer ought to be "no," but it's a double-edged sword, clearly. It was cutting two ways. What I did know was that I didn't want it all to stop and disappear, even assuming

I was in a position to make that happen. It was up and running now, for good and bad.

We fought the homesickness by trying to create in Bel-Air what we had in St. George's Hill. We thought, we'll take Tor Point and plonk it down in America. If we're not allowed in Britain then we'll have our piece of Britain right here. We shipped out the furniture from Weybridge and reassembled Tor Point on Copa de Oro Road.

I swore that I wouldn't lose my Welshness—that I wasn't going to go transatlantic. It felt important to me. I watched myself with the American terms—elevator for lift, sidewalk for pavement, trashcan for dustbin. I still do.

Soon I was adding a British phone box to the decor. One of my cousins had tipped me off that British Telecom was about to get rid of the old red box from the top of Laura Street—where Linda and I did our teenage kissing, the one from which I rang the maternity ward in Cardiff that Saturday morning and was told I was a father. I didn't like the thought of anyone destroying that, so I arranged to buy the box and shipped it to LA, where it turned up one afternoon, roped to the back of a truck. And I had it put up beside the swimming pool, with a working phone plumbed into it.

One day, years later, in 1984, I was by the pool and the phone rang in the phone box, and Mark's voice at the other end said, "You've got a grandson." That's where I heard that Alexander was born. So the phone box in which, at seventeen, I became a father is also the phone box in which, at forty-four, I became a grandfather.

Early on in Bel-Air, I walked out one morning to the mailbox in my dressing gown and I heard somebody cry, "Yoo-hoo!" and there was a bus full of people pointing movie cameras. Because it had belonged to Dean Martin, the house was already on the tourist trail. I put up a wall and some gates to get in the face of that a bit. And the sun shone, and it was always warm by the pool, and I had a wine cellar stocked with very nice French wine, and very soon I discovered that I wasn't missing St. George's Hill quite so much.

True, I missed pubs. I used to drive over to the King's Head in Santa Monica, which was the big ex-pat hangout for people who missed pubs. But there were professional British people in there moaning about the beer, and it just didn't feel the same to me. In the end, I thought: fuck it, I don't need it. I've got the Bel-Air Hotel around the corner. I can go in there and moan about the beer if I need to.

When they realized I wasn't coming back to Tor Point, my parents decided they wanted to go back to Wales, so I bought them a place at Pentyrch in the Vale of Glamorgan. They would come out to LA frequently to visit us, but my father's lungs weren't getting any stronger, and it was clear that traveling any distance was soon going to be beyond him. So at that point, I found my parents a house in Bel-Air a couple of miles up the hill from mine, and they came out to live. They loved the life there, relaxed into it. They loved the house—the Villa Fontante, a modern, architect-designed place, which my mother filled with brass and copper ornaments, a tin of Brasso ready to go at any time. I think they felt less vulnerable and less self-conscious in LA than they had in Surrey, and even in the Vale of Glamorgan—less exposed to the press, or just to people making comments. My father, always so strict about clothes, loosened up and began to wear some of the things that I was able to pass on to him—a few striped shirts, some brightly colored trousers, some zippered boots. It was great to see.

They both loved coming up to Vegas for shows, too—especially my mother, who exploded onto the scene there. "Good evening, ladies," I would say, somewhere near the top of a show. "Good evening, Tom," my mother would shout from her booth, louder than the rest, clear as a bell. My father didn't go much on the gambling, though. He had always loved to gamble, back when he didn't have any money to gamble with. In Vegas, I would offer to give him some money to play with, but he always turned it down. He said it wouldn't be any fun because it wouldn't be his money. There wouldn't have been any edge. Fair enough.

My sister Sheila came to live in LA, too, around this time. She had been through a divorce, which upset her very badly. Her husband, Ken, took up with a barmaid in Weybridge. For which I felt partly responsible, because it was me that was forever picking Ken up and sweeping him off round the pubs. I hadn't realized he was going to take it seriously. I was in America on tour when that particular balloon went up.

So I found a house for Sheila, too, and she came out and joined us, and once again I had my family around me and could begin to feel settled again.

Other relatives would come out for holidays—aunts, uncles, cousins—and their jaws would fall open. I loved showing them the house. They were so impressed. All except my Aunty Alice, my mother's older sister. It was her seventieth birthday, and she had never been anywhere outside Wales, so we thought it would be nice to fly her out to Bel-Air for a celebration.

The limo pulled up from the airport with my mother and father and my Aunty Alice, fresh in from Pontypridd. She stood on the driveway looking up at the house. I gave her a kiss and said, "What do you think, then, Aunty Alice?"

"Awful long way away, Tom."

And that was it.

She came to Vegas. We went to the Japanese restaurant, the Ah So, in Caesars Palace. Not a sushi place, one of those Japanese steak houses where they chop it up in front of you. It was straight-ahead food, really, and you could see what they were doing with it: steak, bit of shrimp. I thought Aunty Alice would go along with that.

"No, I can't, Tom."

"Why's that?"

"I don't like foreign food, Tom."

I said, "Well, it's pretty regular food—beef and prawns . . ."

"No, I can't eat Chinese food," she said.

"No, it's Japanese."

She said, "There was a lovely man in Treforest who wanted to open an English tea shop, and the council wouldn't give him permission. What do you think is there now? A Chinese restaurant."

"No, but . . . Oh, never mind."

She had some rice.

We went to see Siegfried and Roy. They were working in the main room in the Riviera, with tigers. Aunty Alice liked that.

So I was living in LA, family around me, coming home to Dean Martin's old house, and, when I was there, it was almost like I could feel the tension going out of my shoulders—could feel myself unwinding. I got comfortable. If you've got money, LA will do that for you. It's an easy place to be—for better and worse. The harder questions fall away. You stop asking them.

Feeling like a twat in a hat.

32

Opportunity to Cry

As the 1970s become the 1980s, I'm out on the road, churning out the live shows. Okay, not on the scale of those huge tours at the beginning of the decade. The TV show is gone, and the hits have dried up. And the UK doesn't seem even remotely interested in what I'm up to. But that doesn't mean I'm not in demand. Up to 200 nights a year. Working my butt off. Selling out across America.

People still want to see Tom Jones in the eighties.

Tight pants and wide-open shirt with gold cross and chain, of course. Hair natural, in a huge "afro," platform shoes and brightly colored suits, I looked more like a Temptation than TJ.

No Madison Square Garden in these years, maybe, but I'm the king of the multi-night circuit, and no dispute about it. Put me in there, I'll fill it for a week, a fortnight—a month if you need it. At the O'Keefe Centre in Toronto, Canada, I'm the unionized stagehands' best friend. No better time to threaten a strike than when I'm about to roll into town—like firemen threatening to walk out on Guy Fawkes night. Pay and conditions bettered on the leverage of a sold-out sixteen-night Tom Jones run.

"Welcome back, Tom."

Fourteen-night runs in the Circus Maximus in Caesars Palace—two shows a night. And then, when that deal comes to an end in the mid-eighties, over the road at Bally's, who offer a one show per night, two on the weekend deal, so slightly easier on the voice. It's a less prestigious room, but it's still Vegas, isn't it? And I'm still filling it. Plus Atlantic City opens up—which is big news as it's the first major casino town outside Nevada, which was never going to happen because gambling always was and always would be Nevada. Yet here it is and I'm here all week if you want to catch me, offered a very sweet deal at Resorts International, bankrolled by Meyer Lansky and fronted by Frank Sinatra.

Or I'm up at the Circle Star near Oakland—big, boozed-up theater-in-the-round crowd there, where I reckon the manager is charging more for a glass of champagne than it costs him for a case, but they're still buying when I'm in town.

I come, bringing fun and sex—Tom Jones, International Singing Superstar.

I'm tearing my voice up, to be honest. Ripping it to shreds. A run of two shows a night, every night for an entire month in the same venue—which happens at one point—will *really* do that to you. I can feel it. It's like I'm losing touch with the voice. I'm losing lightness, losing agility, losing control. I'm struggling to make the voice float. And it's a vicious circle because, after a while, I'm having to push the voice to get through the show, and the harder I push, the more damage I do, and the more damage I do, the harder I have to push. I'm overworking it. And the product is that I'm working with a lesser voice than I know I have.

When I complain to Gordon about this, he says, "Talk more, then. Entertain more. Goof about. Give the voice a break during the show." But it's not enough. And also, what am I becoming while I'm talking and entertaining and goofing? Where's the emphasis falling? What's the priority here? This is not what I envisaged, coming in. This is not the way I saw it going.

On holiday with Linda in the late sixties.

My Rolls-Royce.

At the London Palladium with the Squires.

Whipping up the band at the Copacabana.

Treasured times with my father in Acapulco.

Singing a duet on *The Bob Hope Special* in 1970.

Performing with Kirk Douglas in
The London Bridge Special.

A superb example of the seventies look.

Russian Olympians Vasily Alekseyev and Sultan Rakhmanov give me a lift.

Belt-buckle competition with Elvis.

A little bird told me in Barbados . . .

Conical hat and cardigan in Japan.

Fun at an LA Dodgers baseball game with Mark and my father.

Poolside tea in Bel-Air with Mam, Dad, and Sheila.

With Ali at the fights in Las Vegas.

A few laughs with Michael Caine and Dudley Moore.

It's a Royal Knockout with (clockwise from left): Walter Payton, Emlyn Hughes, Sheena Easton, Debbie Flintoff, Jenny Agutter, Anthony Andrews, Virginia Leng, Cliff Richard, Kevin Kline, Jackie Stewart, me, the Princess Royal, and Sunil Gavaskar.

Four generations: me, my mother, my son, and my grandson.

Dancing with Linda.

End of the night with Mark and Gordon.

Something else Gordon will say: "You have everything you want. You have the lifestyle you dreamed of. You should be thankful for what you've got." And I can't argue with that. The house, the cars, the things I set my sights on—all there. That, and the repeated validation of sing-ing for an audience, which is enormously important to me, and seductive—a kind of drug, in a way.

So this is what I'll do because this is what people want from me and this is what makes me money to sustain my lifestyle and the lifestyles of everyone associated with me—agent, promoter, management, MAM, the people for whom I am, essentially, a golden turn: put him on the road and watch him earn. I'm the coal for the money-train. This is what I'll do because I'm keeping everyone happy and ensuring the machine remains oiled.

Although, how much am I actually earning in this period? Me, per-sonally, I mean, rather than the machine. How much am I walking away with, if we do the sums? It's not a question I'm really asking. My atti-tude, as ever: turn your back on that stuff and trust that it's okay. Leave the sums to the others. But just supposing we do those sums . . . These are fairly well-paid gigs, aren't they? Once the commissions are taken, once the agent, manager and the promoter have deducted their percent-ages, once the equipment is settled for, and once the band is paid, then all the travel and accommodation and food is taken care of, what am I clearing?

The truth is, by the time the seventies roll into the eighties, I am working as hard as I have ever worked, or even harder—and operating, personally, at a loss.

Which is why it's better that I don't think about it.

No income from songwriting, of course. And no new income from singles and albums. If only. Dropped by Decca and picked up by EMI, I'm still making records, but mostly recorded in a hurry, in a month away from touring, nominally in the diary as my "holiday period," working in Gordon's new LA facility, Britannia Recording Studios, in a stucco building on Cahuenga Boulevard, next door to George Barris's auto-customizing garage—the place where Barris built the Batmobile for the TV series and turned around Elvis's Cadillac Limousine. The place also (I might as well mention) where George once did a grand job on my replica Auburn Speedster, originally a left-hand-drive car which I had exported to Weybridge and switched to right-hand-drive for British roads, and which I then got George to switch back again. Back when I had money to sling around.

But George Barris's magical powers of transformation don't seep through the walls into the studio next door, and the hits don't flow. I get some success with my first single for EMI, "Say You'll Stay Until Tomorrow," a country song written for me by Roger Greenaway and Barry Mason. But it turns out not to be the beginning of anything other than a long string of misses. "No One Gave Me Love," "Have You Ever Been Lonely," "Do You Take This Man" . . . Miss after miss after miss.

No matter. There's time, isn't there? I'll get back to that. A song will come. My voice is still there. And for as long as my voice is still there, I can never feel entirely out of the running. I still know I have the ability, with the right song, to start over, kick it all off again.

With the right song. Whatever the right song is. Wherever the right song is.

And so what if the shows are getting smaller? For afterward we dine. At the best restaurants available. For somehow the meal after the show has come to take on an absolute importance. Sometimes, in the wings between the last number and the first encore, I'll already be asking: "Where are we eating? Is the restaurant sorted?" It's how I remind myself that all is well, that I'm still a figure of consequence here, that I'm still top drawer. Good food, in a world-class restaurant. Good food as a high-class vehicle for the consumption of lots of equally good alcohol. Mark and me together. The post-show champagne in the limo. The bottle of white wine with the plate of smoked salmon starter. The bottle of red with the steak main course. The cognac with the coffee. The Cuban cigar. The champagne for the rest of the night in the club.

And then, eventually, the five-star bed in the five-star hotel. I'm playing the Westbury Theater in Long Island, but I'm staying at the Waldorf Towers in Manhattan and hitting Regine's and Studio 54 until sun-up. I'm playing the Westbury Theater in Long Island, but by the end of the night, and the champagne and the wine and the cognac and the champagne, it might as well have been Madison Square Garden.

The world-class restaurant, the five-star hotel, the A-list club. These are the things that keep me afloat—even though, in financial terms, they are the things which are sinking me. These are the things that help me ignore the fact that I'm well into the Maintenance Years at this point. That, just turned forty, I'm touring my reputation. A heritage act before my time.

And making no money.

The restaurant, the hotel, the club—these are the things that help me ignore the fact that I'm in a long, slow freefall, heading for the dressing room at the Chateau de Ville Dinner Theater in Framingham, Massachusetts.

Heading for the bottom, where this book began.

AT THE BEGINNING of the eighties, to nobody's particular surprise, after four barren years, EMI passed on the opportunity to renew my recording contract. Gordon got me signed to a record deal with Polygram, but the question was still, as it so often had been: "What are we going to do with him?" By now this wasn't a question to which Gordon or myself had any clear answer. The prompting came from Polygram. Looking backward, the last record of mine that had been anything like a hit—"Say You'll Stay Until Tomorrow" in 1976—had been a country number. So Polygram figured: let's pursue that further. Let's get him to go country.

I wasn't opposed to the idea. I had always liked country music, after all, even if it wasn't where I was coming from. Jerry Lee sang country songs without sounding like a country singer: maybe I could go that way with it. And "Green, Green Grass of Home" was a country record, albeit that we made it country-pop, so it crossed over. I was thinking, maybe we'll get another "Green, Green Grass" out of this, and it'll all come back.

I was also thinking: fuck me, I've got to try *something*.

The first album was *Darlin'*. On the sleeve, I was in a tasseled shirt and a Stetson, but still with the visible chest hair and necklace. "Country music," it seemed to be saying, "but still Tom Jones, obviously." On later album sleeves in this sequence, I would upgrade to a suede Civil War outfit in tan and, at one point, climb on a horse.

I should have been diving right in. I should have been making my version of Ray Charles's *Modern Sounds in Country and Western Music* from 1962—a cracking record, thought through at every point: Hank Williams's "Hey, Good Lookin'," Floyd Tillman's "I Love You So Much It Hurts"; Charles putting his stamp on the material, and not wearing a cowboy hat on the cover, still himself, if not more so. Instead it was coming off like a box-ticking exercise.

Gordon drew songs together from Nashville writers—good material. Some of the backing tracks were worked on in Nashville, by Nashville musicians—good musicians. But I was recording my vocals at Britannia Studios in LA. I was trying to sing country in a British-owned studio on Cahuenga Boulevard and then going home to a mansion in Bel-Air, and it sounded like it. I should have gone to Nashville, immersed myself in it, done it properly. Then gone out and promoted it properly. But that would have meant taking a proper chunk of time out from the live work and losing the revenue from those concerts, and Gordon wasn't about to let that happen.

Still, we got plays on country radio, nobody seemed too put-out about me muscling in, and *Darlin'* got onto the country charts. So did the follow-up album, called, plainly, *Country*. So I thought, okay, this is working. Of course, it meant nothing in Europe. You put on a Stetson and climb on a horse and you all but disappear outside the boundaries of America. These albums weren't even being released over there. No market for it. People from Europe were coming to the shows in America and saying, "What happened to the albums? Have you stopped?" As a recording artist, I might as well have been invisible at this point, as far as they were concerned. Which mattered to me.

Meantime, I was going out and doing my usual shows—not touring specifically to promote the records, but going back to the dinner theaters and casinos and performing as usual, with a short section for some of the country material thrown in.

Somebody rang the box office at Bally's, where I was playing in Vegas during this period, and said, "This Tom Jones show you're advertising: is that Tom Jones the pop singer or is it that other guy, the country act?"

To which I hope they said, "It depends which one you want to see."

But you could forgive people for becoming confused. I was becoming pretty confused myself. It was all disjointed and out of focus.

It got even more blurry, late in 1980, when an American producer called Burt Rosen got in Gordon's ear about doing a television show. I knew Rosen a bit from years before—he'd done a Raquel Welch special that I'd appeared on in the early seventies. I had no strong opinion about him, but what I did know was that the big items on Rosen's CV were at least a decade old at this point in time—not unlike the big items on mine, you would have to say. But the point is, some people on the money side of show business know about timing. They know when you're vulnerable— when you might be a soft touch. They know when your manager might be a soft touch, too.

"It'll get you back on television," Gordon told me. "Television always worked for you."

"Okay. And where are we meant to film it?"

"In Canada."

"Oh."

There was a new studio facility up in Vancouver which had just been built and was sitting empty and needed a production in it, and Rosen thought he could raise the money for twenty-four half-hour episodes of a music show hosted by me, and then syndicate them—sell them on to anyone who would have them.

Musical guests, a solo slot, duets. Just like *This Is Tom Jones*. Except ten years later. And done freelance, on the fly, rather than under commission from a major broadcaster. And no longer in Hollywood, but in Vancouver.

Gordon talked it up to me as hard as he could. But this project had all the hallmarks of what it so obviously was: one last, desperate shake of the dice.

But what else was there? So I checked into the Holiday Inn in Vancouver and went to work. My wardrobe for the show: sequined bolero jackets, tight synthetic pants in a variety of bright colors, giant belt buckle. For the more sober numbers, a velvet sports coat with a shirt and tie. In the title sequence, I stood, hands on hips, smile on face, while a shopped-in beam of light hit my belt buckle and exploded to all corners of the screen. In the seventies, this might have looked groundbreaking. In the eighties, it merely looked like something that might have looked groundbreaking in the seventies.

The budget for the set ran to some stairs for me to walk down, but not a lot else apart from the lights and a group of four women dancers, with whom I had to do some scripted flirting at the top of the show. The music was pre-recorded—a lot of synth, a lot of drum machine. Karaoke backing tracks, basically. Quality control had gone right out of the window.

Yet, in a detail that was typical of Gordon, the deal for the show included an arrangement with Umberto Menghi, the Italian chef who had a couple of renowned restaurants in Vancouver, and who would later go on to establish a vibrant restaurant scene at the new, up-and coming ski resort at Whistler. For a mention in the credits, Menghi would provide us with wonderful food while we were in town to film. We were making a shit television program but we were dining like kings.

Guests got booked. For a fee and the lure of a possible TV appearance, depending on syndication, why not? Tina Turner flew in. This was before her big mid-eighties comeback. We did Rod Stewart's "Hot Legs" together, and it came off okay. Gladys Knight came, too, and that was also fine by me. You knew you could sing with Gladys Knight, even to a cheap, canned backing track, and it would sound okay. We did the Bee Gees' song "Guilty." Chaka Khan, Teddy Pendergrass and Isaac Hayes appeared, all of whom I had a lot of respect for, although, in the context of the production it was next to impossible for anyone, however good they were, to come out looking sure of themselves. I sang Smokey Robinson's "The Way You Do the Things You Do" with Marie Osmond and I don't suppose either of us would chalk it up as a career highlight. Other guests were more famous for being actresses than they were for being singers: Marisa Berenson, Cybill Shepherd, Brooke Shields . . .

The show was simply titled *Tom Jones*. It was like the seventies show for ABC, except with none of the creativity, none of the skill, none of the energy, none of the things that made the ABC show work. You looked at it—at the costumes, and the production values, and the music—and thought: this is the work of an artist who is creatively bust.

I couldn't even tell you where it got screened. And this was potentially the saving grace about making a bad television show—a bad television show with your name all over it. In the days before catch-up TV and YouTube, a bad television show had less opportunity to follow you around. It went out—if it went out at all—perhaps late at night on some obscure channel that very few people had access to, and if you were lucky nobody watched it, and you walked away from it. No particular damage done.

But not in this case. Because in this case, after a period of time had gone by and the whole deadbeat project appeared to have been forgotten about, the huge success of *Reload* happened, and the bottom-feeders hit pay-dirt with terrible, low-quality CDs that began appearing everywhere. Some loophole in the contract which Gordon hadn't kept his eye on seemed to put the exploitation rights to the show's soundtrack in the hands of Burt Rosen. Rosen's company duly flooded the market with literally hundreds of shoddy, bargain basement compilations. *Tom Jones: Greatest Duets*, *Greatest Love Songs*, *Greatest Hits Live*—countless cut-price carve-ups of the thrown-together audio track from the show, with cobbled-together artwork, flogged off in duty-free outlets at airports and at the check-outs in petrol stations and discount supermarkets.

And after the CDs came the DVDs. All of this half-arsed stuff from the past emerged like a bad smell from a drain, returning to haunt me, cluttering the picture. It took a lengthy and expensive lawsuit in 2007, demonstrating breach of contract, to get that material off the market.

So much for the big comeback on TV. Like everything else at this point, it was a mess—for all that I was bravely pretending otherwise. A long, lingering mess. And the odds on ever climbing out of the mess seemed to be getting longer and longer.

MY GRANDMOTHER TAUGHT MY MOTHER how to lay out the dead. So by the time Mark and I had driven over to their house, in response to my mother's call, she had already bound my father's jaw closed with a bandage.

It was 1982. Mark had recently shown my father the invitations, back from the printers, to his wedding—the wedding of Mark Woodward to his American girlfriend, Donna Polom, in Westwood and afterward at the Bel-Air Hotel, where I'll get up to sing "With These Hands" for the couple's first dance. But my father didn't live to see his grandson wed.

"It's a pity," the doctor said, "about his lungs, because he has a strong heart."

My father died slowly, so we saw it coming, and so did he, falling to his prayers for the first time in his adult life. My mother died slowly, too, when her turn came, in 2003. Does that make it easier? It didn't feel like it to me.

They both lie buried in Forest Lawn cemetery, which sometimes seems a long way from Treforest to me and sometimes seems like no distance at all.

Low profile with Gordon in London.

33

Showbiz Graveyard

One day, in the early 1980s, I'm in the kitchen when the gate buzzer sounds. I check the video entry phone, and it's Michael Jackson.

The biggest pop star the world has ever known is outside my door in a baseball jacket and jeans, with La Toya, his sister, who's driving him. Apparently Michael is always coming past my house on his way up to Quincy Jones's place and he loves the way the house looks and has often talked about stopping and asking if he could see over it.

So I bring them both into the kitchen and offer them a drink, and Michael says he'd like some water. And then I show them round the house.

Michael is all breathless enthusiasm. "Childlike" is the word everybody uses about Michael Jackson, but there's no getting around it. There's a lot of "wow!" going on. When we get to the bar in the pool room, he spots the photo on the wall of me with Paul, Ringo and Dusty Springfield—that prized image I mentioned a few pages back, taken at the Melody Maker Awards in September 1966.

"Wow! There's Paul! Look, La Toya! Look at this!"

He's really taken with this picture and the various other souvenirs behind the bar—pictures of me with Elvis and Frank Sinatra—and he looks at them for a long time.

And then he turns to me and says, "Wow, Tom. You had a great career."

It feels important to me to correct him.

"Having," I say. "Not had. I'm *having* a great career."

I'M HAVING A GREAT CAREER but I'm also in a hotel room in the middle
of nowhere in America, watching my son beat up my manager.

Another of those nights. A show somewhere, then the restaurant, then
back to the hotel suite. Gordon is in town—one of his increasingly rare
visits, out on the road, flying in to check up on things. And we've drunk
and we've eaten, and now he and Mark and I are back in the hotel, in the
early hours, sitting around and drinking until the conversation starts.

Because, at this time of the night, and after this much drink, it's always
the same conversation. It's me saying to Gordon, Where's my song?
What's going on? What happened to my recording career? Specifically, in
this instance, why am I making these do-nothing country albums—one
per year, regular as clockwork? And it's Gordon replying, "What the fuck
do you know about it?" He's Gordon Mills. He doesn't need to defend
himself. And certainly not with a couple of bottles of red inside him.

It's me pointing out that my voice is getting shredded, out here on the
road. It's me, in my mid-forties, getting irked about the direction it's all
ended up going in, saying, "What have I turned into?" It's Gordon saying,
"What are you complaining about? You've got everything that you want."

It's the same old needle, the same old alpha-male shouting, the same
old "fuck yous."

Pretty soon Mark gets up and goes to bed in the suite's second bedroom. Nothing he hasn't heard before a thousand times. Nowadays these
elements are always ready to go between me and Gordon, just waiting for
the evening's drinking to trigger them, which it always will. And the ten-
sions never resolve, because nothing ever makes sense after midnight
when you're drunk. There's stuff here which needs talking about in the
cold light of day. But this is a conversation in which the cold light of day
never happens.

At some point Gordon says, "Mark in there—what's he doing for you?" Another theme. The closeness of Mark to me, and of me to Mark, is a constant source of anxiety and irritation for Gordon. It triggers something in him—the manager's instinctive fear of anyone who appears to have his artist's ear. And Mark's not shy about making his opinions known—including his opinions about Gordon and Gordon's handling of me, which aren't always flattering. For Gordon, there's suspicion and resentment of my son, asleep on the other side of the door.

Except my son isn't asleep. Mark hears Gordon's question through the door, resents the implication and comes barreling back into the room, where he pulls Gordon out of his chair, knocks him onto the floor and starts laying into him. My manager on the hotel carpet while my twenty-something son gives him a right seeing-to.

So this is new, at least.

Gordon shouting to me, between the kicks, "Aren't you going to do anything about this?"

It seems that what I'm going to do about this is stand and watch it, with a glass of champagne in my hand.

We are all drunk. We are seldom anything else at this hour of the night. Drunk while it all falls apart.

It's going wrong for Gordon, and it's going wrong for MAM. First Engelbert Humperdinck jumps ship—takes out an ad one week in *Variety*: "Gordon Mills no longer represents me." Which is news to Gordon. And news which makes him furious.

Some kind of fallout over payments, apparently, though I never get to the bottom of it. It's someone else's battle in a far-off country, as far as I'm concerned. The only thing in my mind when I hear the news is the memory of where Humperdinck was when Gordon took a hold of him: in a flat above a furniture shop in Hammersmith. And now he's in Jayne Mansfield's house north of Sunset Boulevard. So where's he getting off complaining about money? I'm looking at this and I'm just seeing disloyalty.

Then again, Humperdinck and I never were the closest of friends.

All that time as ex-pats and stable-mates in LA, for instance, and I have never been to his house, nor he to mine. But the way I see it, a separation from Gordon is equivalent to a separation from me—a betrayal by Humperdinck of the one thing we genuinely had in common, and I have no contact with him whatsoever after this, for a very long time. Our paths will cross again, but it won't work out happily.

Then Gordon comes to me one day in LA with Michael Balin, who's our lawyer, and says, "I have to ask you about management: are you satisfied with me being your manager?"

"Of course."

"Are you satisfied with being within MAM?"

"Yes. What's this about? A fucking survey?"

Gordon says it's because Gilbert has launched a lawsuit against him for money that he thinks he's due. I'm thinking: Jesus, Gilbert O'Sullivan? Gilbert O'Sullivan who hasn't had a hit since 1975 and who pitched up at Gordon's house on a bicycle?

But then, of course, in 1982, Gilbert sues Gordon in the High Court in London for £7 million in unpaid earnings and wins, getting the rights to his songs back as part of the settlement. And O'Sullivan v. Mills becomes a game-changing case within the record industry—a landmark ruling regarding management and agency and recording and publishing and conflicts of interest. The judgment was marginally modified on appeal, but even so it stinks for Gordon and costs him a shitload of money, while simultaneously blowing out his reputation and his chances of raising investment anywhere.

Humperdinck gone, O'Sullivan gone, money gone . . . stock price sinks to rock bottom, along with all the investment from my personal earnings. Death knell for MAM. End of the Empire.

(Or something like that.)

I see the impact on Gordon. A light goes out in him after this—Gordon, with his high-maintenance lifestyles on both sides of the Atlantic, his giant house in Holmby Hills, his mansion with its former zoo in Surrey. Gordon, with his exotic fishing trips with his aristocratic connections, his heavy-roller Vegas gambling habits. Gordon, this man I am totally dependent on. He's drinking a lot. He's less and less on the scene and more and more distracted when he is. If you can find him at home in LA, he'll be in a bathrobe with a glass of red wine on the go, any time of the day. Or you might be better off looking for him, in the evenings, at the Bel-Air Hotel. One night, leaving there, he puts his Mercedes in the hedge. When the patrol arrives, he tells them that the barriers marking the turning circle were out of line.

His marriage to Jo has come undone. He turns up in LA one time with his arm in a sling. He's gone back to England, apparently, and run into some fella who seemed a bit too interested in his wife, and he's had a sort-out with him on the lawn. He's damaged his arm falling over while they fought, he says.

And now he seems to be jettisoning some of the people who know him best—the people who know him well enough to have a word, people to whom he once might have listened when they told him to get in shape. There's Anne-Marie Brecker. She's been close to Gordon for years—a former Pan Am air hostess. (Her twin sister married Gilbert O'Sullivan.) She's a good, kind person—devoted to Gordon. She had his interests at heart. Gordon has set her aside, which worries me.

And then there's Gog Jones. Gog has been Gordon's PA for years—a lovely, humble, deeply loyal Welshman, funny, not a show business type at all. He followed Gordon to California, even though his family was back in the UK. But now Gordon has suddenly brought in an American guy called John Moran, a slick social operator, politically connected—knew Jimmy Carter, apparently, which Gordon would have enjoyed the thought of. Moran seems to be Gordon's new ears and eyes, and he and Gordon start hanging out together at Le Dome, Eddy Kerkhofs's "scene" restaurant in West Hollywood. It's there that Moran introduces Gordon to a raven-haired Tahitian called Annie Toomaru, whom Gordon now takes up with. And Moran's role leaves Gog wondering, "What's the point of me?"

Later, back in Surrey, having left his job and in the throes of depression, Gog goes out to his garage, feeds a pipe from the exhaust of his
car into its interior and takes his own life.

It's all unraveling, and Gordon is floundering. Where does he fit
in now, here in the eighties? The music industry has changed around him.
It's not just a bunch of sharp guys in London who all know each other,
like it was in the sixties. It's got so big, so international. He doesn't have
a handle on it anymore. Gordon has lost his touch, and the worst thing is
that, deep down, he knows it. And nothing's going to come to him on a
plate at this stage. People aren't crowding around him for a piece of Tom
Jones anymore. People aren't flinging songs Gordon's way in the hope
that I'll record them. It's going to take some ingenuity, some creativity.
But those things walked out the door some time ago and are showing no
sign of coming back.

I keep thinking of something I used to say to Gordon back in the
beginning, when we were casting around for direction, when things
were starting to take shape. I used to say to him, "If you try and white-
wash me, if you try and smooth me out, it won't fucking work."

And I was wrong. But I was also right.

Really the extent now of what Gordon can do for me is sign off on a
diary full of live shows and send me out on the road to earn money. And
then, in the gaps between the gigs, turn out those country albums for
Polygram. Those low-rent country albums—Gordon taking the production upon himself because he thinks he knows better than anyone
about producing Tom Jones, though I don't think that's true anymore,
and it's just another strain on our relationship.

Small-budget, corner-cutting country albums, produced in LA by a
former member of the Viscounts. I'm not going to be sounding like
Hank Williams here.

It's a bill-paying operation, at the end of the day. We do five of those
country albums in total, one per year, like clockwork, gently ticking over.
And each of those country albums takes me closer to the edge.

In 1985, Polygram offers to take up its option on a sixth album, and Gordon says we should sign. Why not? There's nothing else on the table at this point. But I tell him, "I can't." I have never stood up to Gordon on this kind of thing. Not once. I've trusted his calls and I've done what I've been told to do. But this time I simply can't face it. Can't face the half-arsedness of it. Can't be this lame anymore.

I say no.

And now there's nothing. No record deal at all.

It's all a mess, the whole Gordon thing. But I'm not always angry with him. Some of the time I'm sorry for him. And I'm certainly not about to go down the Gilbert O'Sullivan route. I'm not about to start questioning the man on royalties. Christ knows, I've never taken an interest in that stuff. Call me naive, but isn't that what you have a manager for? Royalties, management fees, executive producer credits . . . I'd rather not know. The only question I've ever had, really, is: can I afford it? And if the answer is yes, then good. If it turns out that he's been ripping me off these past twenty years, then I'd rather not know about that, too. Let's face it, without him, I might not have happened. If he hadn't come down to Wales in 1964 and pulled me out, I might still be there. I had the determination, but London was a long way away if you didn't know anybody. Gordon's attitude was that either he was going to make it happen for me or he was going to go broke in the attempt. He believed in me and he backed his belief. This is what I always come back to, when the arguments stop, when the storms pass, when the hangover clears. So, there's no question about it: I'm sticking with him.

But where we're going, stuck together, and where this all ends up, I have no idea.

ONE EVENING IN 1986, I was giving Gordon a lift home from Britannia Studios, and he began to complain about his stomach. He was clearly in some trouble, bending forward in his seat with his eyes closed tight against the pain. He got me to stop at the pharmacy on Beverly Glen Circle and he went in and bought a large bottle of Pepto-Bismol. Then he came back to the car, pulled the cap off it and drank the whole thing down.

I said, "Gordon, this doesn't look good to me."

He said, "No, no, it's my ulcer. This'll sort it out."

Ulcers. He's often mentioned ulcers—and always dismissively. "It's just my ulcer."

Gordon was too sick to work over the next couple of days, and then I had to go into Vegas for a two-week stint. Gordon always liked to make sure he was there on opening night, so along he came. But he looked terrible—far worse than in the car that evening. In the dressing room, he was wincing and holding himself. I realized how thin he had become. I told him he should go back to LA and see our doctor.

Later I called the doctor to find out what was what. He told me that Gordon had secondary cancer of the liver and extensive primary cancer of the colon. Apparently he had always refused to have colonoscopies when the doctor offered them. He was always instructing me to get myself checked over, absolutely insisting on it, and never doing it himself.

When I got back from Las Vegas, Gordon was in Cedars-Sinai hospital. I went to visit him. He was sitting up and seemed agitated. He said, "What time is it? Where are they with the morphine?"

He wanted to know what I thought his chances were. I said, "The doctor must have told you." He said, "No, I want you to tell me." So I told him what the doctor had told me, which was that he had a fifty-fifty chance if they removed the colon.

"Well, that's it," he said. "I'm a gambler. I know what fifty-fifty is. I'm fucked. And let it be a lesson to you. If you get any pain, get in and see about it right away. In fact, get in and see about it now."

I thought, fucking hell, he's still telling me what-for. Still dishing out the dogma. Still the Mule.

It was the last conversation we had. The next time I went in he was on a machine and unconscious. I held his hand and squeezed. His hand wasn't cold but it was . . . empty is the only word I can think of to describe it. I was distraught.

Not long after that, Gordon died. He was fifty-one.

There was a service in LA, and then Gordon's body was brought back to England. The night before the burial service, Mark and I got together with Anne-Marie Brecker at Shepherd's Market in London and drank and reminisced. The following day, Gordon was buried next to his father in Weybridge cemetery. His mother was still alive then and she was at the service with Jo. Troy Dante was there, Les Reed, Barry Mason, Larry Page, Annie Toomaru. Some of my cousins came up from Wales because they knew Gordon and respected him and were grateful to him.

I spoke during the service, as best I could, but I kept breaking down. I said that people in Wales were always telling me I was going to be a star. But Gordon put his money where his mouth was. He was the one that showed up for me.

I said that Gordon wasn't a manager, he was a friend.

I said that, actually, it was more than that: I'd never had a brother, but I felt as though I had.

Back in LA after the funeral, I was in Adriano's, a restaurant up on Mulholland Drive where Gordon and I regularly ate, and I was reminiscing with the owner about Gordon and recalling how opinionated and dogmatic the man could be. The owner said, "You couldn't tell him anything. He once asked me where I got the restaurant's salt and pepper cellars from. I said, 'Robinson's.' And Gordon said, 'Impossible!'"

It was the first time I had laughed properly since Gordon died.

A FEW WEEKS AFTER GORDON'S DEATH, Engelbert Humperdinck was playing at the Hilton in Vegas, and I was at Bally's, and he rang me and said he hadn't seen me in ages and could we hook up.

Now, quite apart from my feelings about his split from Gordon, I'd been hearing bits and pieces that Humperdinck had been saying about me down the years—stuff from drivers that we shared, and the managers of venues that we both played at. Stuff about how he took any opportunity to run me down and basically wouldn't let people mention my name in his hearing. So I wasn't exactly raging to meet up with him again. But he insisted that all that stuff wasn't true—that it was just people trying to stir something up. So I decided to give him the benefit of the doubt, and we arranged to have a meal at Antonio's in the Rio Hotel, in the early evening before Humperdinck's show.

My mother and sister were in Vegas at the time, my father having passed away. My mother didn't want to come. She still hadn't forgiven Humperdinck for that episode over the use of his real name, that Christmas back in the sixties.

"I like him as a singer, but not as a person."

I said, "Well, he did apologize for that, about twenty years ago, so we could forget it . . ." But she wouldn't. So Mark and his wife Donna came.

And the moment I sat down at the table, I realized that I had made a mistake. Humperdinck was full of it, straightaway. "You have to have this because this is what I always have when I come to Antonio's . . ."

Like I'd never ordered anything in an Italian restaurant before.

I'm looking at him and thinking, yes, you're still a cunt.

I was keen to know why he wasn't at Gordon's funeral. He said, "Why didn't you call me and tell me it was all right for me to come?"

After the meal, we went over and saw his show at the Hilton, and then we went back to his dressing room. He continued to be full of it. He was now wearing sunglasses and cranking on about karate. He was saying, "I really think you should take it up, Tom. I think it would do you the world of good."

I said, "I'm not interested, really."

"Oh, but you will be when I introduce you to this new instructor I've found. He's the master of what he does. When he walks into the room, his presence is unignorable. When you speak to him, you have to call him 'the Master' . . ."

And then he made us watch this new video he had made—something he had done in Germany, this really cheesy thing with girls all over it. I was thinking, "Who are you trying to impress here? Remember me?"

It was time to go, really. But before I could, Humperdinck said one more thing.

"Before you leave, I want you to know something. Gordon Mills was an arsehole."

He knew how I felt about Gordon. It was like he was begging me to chin him. I don't think I've ever wanted to hit anyone quite as much as I wanted to hit this man then. It was all flashing before my eyes. I could already see his teeth flying across the room. But I got hold of myself, said good night and walked out. I was trembling. And from then on I decided my only option was to avoid him.

I had a letter from him a couple of days later, delivered to Bally's, saying sorry and that he was drunk and that he thought the world of me. Well, fine. But I still thought it was better, all in all, to draw a line. From time to time people who knew us both would try to get us to make up.

"Life's too short, Tom."

But I'd only get bullish about that.

"Too right. Life's too short to be fucking about with Engelbert Humperdinck."

In Florida once, a promoter came at me: "Think about how great it would be if the two of you made it up and did a tour together. Think of the money . . ."

I had to say, "That would be just about the most painful thing I could imagine."

That notion has come up a few times—that and the idea of a "reunion" single. But it won't happen. It's best left alone.

With Mark on the road.

34

You Never Know (Ever)

When Gordon died, Michael Balin, my lawyer, warned me, "People are going to be coming at you right, left and center because you don't have a manager." Sure enough, even at Gordon's funeral, a couple of people took the trouble to pull me aside.

"Tom, if there's anything . . . You just call me. I'm here for you."

"Right."

And after that, the phone was soon ringing. A lot of these calls were from people I knew and respected in the industry—people like Larry Page, who managed the Kinks. And some of it was perhaps the noise of vultures circling.

Which is why you need a manager. I needed a manager to manage the calls from people who wanted to be my manager.

Which, in fact, is why it all fell into place perfectly naturally. The person fielding these calls from managers was Mark.

It seemed the obvious step to me.

"Why don't you do it? You know more about me than anyone."

Mark was thirty. He'd been on the road with me for fourteen years, looking on, taking it in. He'd done the apprenticeship and then some.

Maybe he hadn't yet had to operate on the business side, but there was nothing he didn't know about the way life on tour worked, and that was a good place to start. He'd been right alongside me through it all, seen the whole thing shift with his own eyes, from the peaks of 1973 to the troughs of 1986.

Way before that, too. When Mark was a kid and we went out to dinner in restaurants and at people's houses, Linda and I were always taking Mark with us. I didn't even bother asking in advance. I remember turning up for a meal one night with Burt Bacharach and Angie Dickinson at a restaurant and bringing Mark with us, and though it was a bit unusual, they were absolutely fine about it. It never occurred to us not to take him.

So he'd been around, absorbing stuff. We certainly wouldn't have to get used to each other, me and him—wouldn't have to spend any time finding out what made each other tick: that job was done. And he was smart. Mark was always analyzing and commenting: "Why are you doing that?" "Why don't you do this?" He was always throwing things at me. "Are you sure that's right for you?" Always ready with a view about the direction things were going in. He could be a pain in the arse with it sometimes, to be perfectly honest—all the questions. He was the grit in the oyster a lot of the time, as if he felt that was his duty. But he knew a lot about music, too—never stopped playing it, finding songs, getting me to listen to stuff that I didn't know, opening my ears. Once it was me who brought the records home from America that he listened to; now, more often than not, it was him bringing music to me.

The music in the dressing room before the show; the music in the hotel suite after the show: that was always Mark's doing. The boom box on the flight to Japan as long ago as the early seventies, playing the Average White Band's "Pick Up the Pieces," the backing singers that were with us, dancing in the aisles—Mark's doing.

And he was married to Donna, a classically trained pianist who knew both music and the entertainment industry—they could do the job together, help each other with it and help me. We could bring it into the family. And trust was there, naturally. If you can't trust your own son, who are you going to trust?

And if it didn't work out? Well, I figured that I still had the performing side to fall back on, in some form or other. I still had the voice. If nothing else came of it after Gordon, if Mark and Donna couldn't handle it and we didn't manage to get a toehold back in the recording industry, which certainly wasn't going to be easy from the point I had dropped back to, I still had the voice to sing with. I knew enough to keep that side ticking over, even if it meant going back to being a club singer.

So my son and my daughter-in-law became my managers, and if it hadn't happened so naturally, I would be claiming credit for the canniest decision in relation to my career that I ever made.

SOON AFTER MARK AND DONNA take over, I play a venue where a gift is left in the dressing room for me and the members of the band. It's a box containing a whole batch of Filofaxes—the "personal organizers" that are a big deal with professional people at this point in the eighties, until mobile phones come along and pretty much wipe them out. All the Yuppies have them. You turn up at meetings and out they come: whump.

I have never properly looked at one before. Leather case, ring binder, thick clumps of fresh paper, dividers with tabs: "Diary," "Phone Numbers," "Agenda."

"What's this? 'Agenda.'"

Mark says, "It's a space for you to write your . . . agenda."

"Oh."

I set the Filofax aside.

The point being, there was no agenda. There was no sitting down with pieces of paper and charts and graphs and carefully plotting a comeback. There was just doing the next thing that felt right, and seeing where it led. And sometimes the next thing that felt right would send you further up the road in the right direction and sometimes it would take you off on a long and inglorious detour. And there were more than a few moments where the next thing that felt right seemed to put the whole journey into reverse. But there were points, too, where something clicked, and the car accelerated forward so rapidly and so unexpectedly that it caught us all off guard.

Like with "A Boy from Nowhere." Not long before he died, Gordon had passed me a cassette he'd been sent by Muff Winwood at CBS Records. Two writers, Mike Leander (who produced, among other things, those seventies hits for Gary Glitter, back when that was still a more or less acceptable thing to mention) and Edward Seago, were trying to get a musical together, titled *Matador*, about El Cordobés, the Spanish superstar bullfighter from the sixties who became a legend. The subject immediately meant something to me: I remembered seeing posters of El Cordobés all over walls while I was in Spain back then and wondering about this guy and his fame. CBS was putting together a soundtrack version of the musical, as a precursor to the stage version, and was looking for singers. A lot of the orchestrations were already down, and Robert Powell, the British actor, had recorded the narration. I don't think Gordon rated the material that much. Plus it was a British-based project, and Gordon's inclination had for a long time been to turn away from UK things, where I was concerned, and concentrate on things that could be made to happen for me in America. The way Gordon saw it, the UK was over for me, and you could understand why he'd arrived at that view. Whole four- or five-year chunks had gone by when I hadn't even set foot there.

Still, Mark and I sat one night in a hotel room in Atlanta and played this *Matador* cassette through and found we were really moved by it—to the point of welling up in a couple of places. There was one number in particular that stood out—"A Boy from Nowhere." An old-school ballad, really, on a traditional rags-to-riches theme—a musical theater number, not naturally my favorite kind of thing. But I liked the story and I could hear some real drama in there and I could see how, with the right voice, it could be something that came across.

It was as good a place to start as any, after Gordon, so we pursued it with CBS, and told them I was interested in giving it a shot, and Leander and Seago came out to LA and I did the vocal for three of their songs: "A Boy from Nowhere," "I Was Born to Be Me" and "I'll Dress You in Mourning." It seemed to work really well, to the point that there was then talk of me maybe singing the El Cordobés role in *Matador* on the stage, which I might have been interested in doing. But that side of the project continued to struggle to come together, and the talk went away.

However, CBS decided to put out my version of "A Boy from Nowhere" as a one-off single on the Epic label in Britain in the summer of 1987— and, in many ways, there couldn't have been a better way for me to put my head above the parapet in the UK again. You were wondering what you were now worth to people, if anything, and here, by a stroke of fortune, was a relatively gentle way to find out—coming in as part of a project which wasn't some big, all-guns-blazing, solo comeback affair, but was first and foremost a trailer for a possible musical and therefore not really about me specifically. Epic sent over proofs of the sleeve, and I couldn't have been happier when I saw what they had done with it. The design was a plain red square, with, at the center, a small photograph of a boy in a sombrero. My photo was on the back. It was perfect—low-key. It wasn't saying, "Here's Tom Jones—he's back." It was saying, "Here's a song: see if you like it."

They wanted me to promote the record, and I readily agreed to do so. Promotion can be a chore, but for me, at this stage, after all this time, it felt great. I did a regional radio tour, jumping in a car and driving around all the local stations, talking up the single—something I hadn't done since the late sixties and which really took me back to those days. And suddenly I was on UK television again: on *Live at Her Majesty's* initially, a big variety show on ITV with my old friend Jimmy Tarbuck hosting and Shirley Bassey on the bill. Here, during rehearsals, one of the male backing singers stepped forward, with the score open in his hands, and politely asked me, "Are we pronouncing it 'Andalu-th-ia' or 'Andalu-s-ia'?"

It was a good question. I told him, "I'm going 'Andalu-s-ia' myself—but knock yourself out: whichever way you want to go with it."

After that, when the song began to sell, it was *Top of the Pops, Aspel and Company, Saturday Night at the London Palladium* . . . and each time I was getting the chance to put myself in front of people again, but in a restrained way. For a lot of Brits, I was now simply Mr. Las Vegas—and in many cases it would have been said with a sneer. A lot of people even assumed that I now lived there permanently, the term "a Vegas residency" creating some understandable confusions in that area. Yet here I was, entirely without those trappings. Because what "A Boy from Nowhere" definitely wasn't was sequins and mirrorballs. It was a simple, strong, storytelling ballad. There couldn't be any bumping and grinding while I delivered this number, because the song didn't lend itself to it, so some of those presumptions had to fall away. I just had to stand there and sing it from the heart and try to connect.

Back in Los Angeles, we sat up until the early hours of Wednesday morning to find out the midweek chart position, announced at lunchtime, UK time—the earliest indication of how well a single was selling, ahead of the formal announcement of the chart on the Sunday. And that, again, was a flashback for me to an earlier age—feeling that kind of excitement and anticipation for the first time in years, realizing that, as unlikely as it had come to seem, and when I'd almost got used to the idea of it never happening again, all the signs were that I was about to have a hit. Sure enough, that summer "A Boy from Nowhere" reached number 2, a height that I hadn't risen to since 1971, fully sixteen years earlier.

The success of that song felt fantastic. It was like clouds lifting. And part of the relief of it lay in the sense of being back on track, up and running again, not just with this one single but in the longer term. After all, the success of "A Boy from Nowhere" and the proof it offered that I could still appeal to people and sell records would be bound to tempt CBS into giving me a contract for an album, wouldn't it? Because, yes, the business had radically altered while I'd been sitting on the sidelines, but the fundamentals still had to apply, didn't they? It was just like 1965 and "It's Not Unusual." You just needed that one hit song, surely, and you'd be away into the skies. Liftoff.

Er, not quite. With the single riding high, we went to CBS with the idea of a brand-new album—and got precisely nowhere with it. They were looking at the idea of a Tom Jones CD, in the era of Michael Jackson, Whitney Houston and George Michael, and seeing a forty-seven-year-old singer who had just come out of the desert after a decade and a half, and they weren't buying it. Paul Russell at the record company was polite but evasive. Muff Winwood was more direct. "Everyone's a victim of their own success," he said, with a sigh of sympathy. "And the punters have all got the greatest hits."

Or in other words: congratulations on the single, and welcome back, Tom. But, at the same time, thanks but no thanks.

STILL, IT'S WHEN I'M DOING "A Boy from Nowhere" for *Saturday Night at the London Palladium* that a bloke called Jonathan Ross comes to see me, along with a TV producer, Graham Smith.

Ross is a young guy, in his twenties, in a glossy suit. He's where chatshow television is going at this point. Ironic. Getting it from Letterman in America. Sense of organized chaos. Not playing anything too straight. His show is called *The Last Resort*, in keeping with all that. It goes out late on a Friday night on Channel 4.

Ross has a running gag, apparently: "Next week on the show: Tom Jones and Michael Caine." And then we're never on. But what if one week I was actually there and I sang on the show?

"But they don't want you to do 'A Boy from Nowhere,'" Mark says. "They don't want it to be a record plug."

"Well, what's the point, then?"

342   +   TOM JONES

Mark says the show has a shit-hot house band, led by Steve Nieve, who had been the keyboard player with Elvis Costello. I could pick a song, have fun with it, maybe show another side. It could be good.

I'm thinking: Okay, I'll give them "Great Balls of Fire." When in doubt, "Great Balls of Fire"—that's always been my policy. But Ross's people don't sound made up about that.

"What else are you doing in your live show, Tom?"

I think about it for a bit.

"Well, I'm doing 'Kiss.'"

"What? *Prince*'s 'Kiss'?"

"Is there anybody else's 'Kiss'?"

It's true. Mark had suggested sticking Prince's "Kiss" in my live show, not long after the song was a hit in 1986. When I heard "Kiss," I was hearing an R&B song, but done in a Prince way—sparse instrumentation, falsetto. Some things Prince has done, like "Purple Rain," you think, forget it. There's nothing more you can do with that. But "Kiss" was so open, it left room for interpretation—taking it out of falsetto and hitting it full on, for starters. I was doing it live, and people were digging it.

So I play it on *The Last Resort*. Leather jacket and loose-fit leather trousers over a red T-shirt. ("You don't always have to wear trousers that show everything, you know," Mark says. He's right. I don't.) Even as Ross is introducing me, it's still on a knife edge. Am I someone it's okay to like? Or am I an old twat—back from the dead but not quite? How much is irony operating here? Where is irony drawing the line?

Steve Nieve's house band, who are just as shit-hot as Mark suggested, pile into the number hard, and I sing and dance in front of some giant, cheesy silver letters spelling "TOM JONES," taller than I am. Ironic again, I guess. Ross, on the side with enlarged hair and a gray designer suit, comes in to mop my brow at one point.

And then I leave the studio and fly home to LA and don't think much more about it.

Except that something in that performance gets through. People talk about it. "Did you see Tom Jones the other night, doing 'Kiss'?" There's a bit of a stir. It seems to have taken a few people by surprise. That guy, of all people, doing that song, of all songs—yet it was all right, wasn't it? It kind of worked. There are a couple of reviews in the papers—the gist of which is, basically, that rumors of my death during this last decade might have been exaggerated. I'd be pleased to find out they were right.

And then a letter comes from Clive Calder and Ralph Simon. Calder and Simon are a couple of South African guys who have founded the Zomba Music Group, a major management and publishing concern, and who then started their own label, Jive Records. Come 2002, by which time the roster has expanded to include Britney Spears and the Backstreet Boys, they will sell this label to Bertelsmann in Germany for £2.74 billion, which will no doubt be enough to keep them going for a while. At this point, though, Jive is mostly famous for picking up New York hip-hop acts and for having a massive international hit with Billy Ocean's "Caribbean Queen (No More Love on the Run)." I'm not sure exactly where I fit in, in the Jive scheme of things, but I'm not sure I care that much either. The key fact is, Calder and Simon have noticed the success I had with "A Boy from Nowhere," they've seen me do "Kiss" on *The Last Resort* and they're willing to take a gamble on a Tom Jones album from a standing start.

"Where are they based?" I ask Mark.

"Willesden," he says.

Hard not to reflect on the distance of all this from the polished splendor of MAM House, off Bond Street. But that was then and this is now. And what have fancy offices got to do with anything, anyway? We sign the deal in Jive's graffiti-strewn concrete building in northwest London, and at last I have a new album deal.

Meanwhile Anne Dudley gets in touch with Mark. Anne Dudley is a musician and composer from the band Art of Noise—an experimental pop outfit, making dance tracks with synths and samplers. Mark plays me some of their stuff, and I'm really intrigued by it. "How do they make that sound?" Anne has seen me on Jonathan Ross's show, and she's wondering if I've ever thought about recording "Kiss"—and, if so, would I like to record it with Art of Noise, as a new track to go on a greatest hits compilation that they're putting together?

Suddenly an avant-garde art-pop synth act wants to work with me. They're the first in quite a long time.

We talk to Jive: would they mind me doing this track as a featured vocalist with Derek Green of China Records, Art of Noise's label, before I put an album together for Jive? They don't have a problem with it.

However, I do have a problem: my throat. I'm due at the hospital in LA to have a polyp cut off my vocal cords—the legacy of thrashing my voice through all those multi-night appearances in the first half of the decade. That's going to take me out of action for a few weeks—or for good, if the surgeon's had a heavy night and slips up. And even now, on account of the polyp, my range is coming apart. I'm struggling to get into my higher register. It's clear that I'm going to have to say to the Art of Noise people, "Forget it. Bad timing, unfortunately. Don't have the voice. Some other time, maybe." But Mark says, "The song's in your mid-range. Just give it a go."

What's to lose, I guess.

JJ Jeczalik, is the Fairlight genius behind many of the early synth pop sounds, including the group Yes and much of Trevor Horn's work, and now he's one of Anne Dudley's partners in Art of Noise and responsible for their early avant-garde concepts. JJ sends a backing track over to LA, with almost nothing on it, really, apart from a drum machine and a guide keyboard, and I take the tape into a little studio in the Valley and record a vocal track onto it. I have three stabs at it, and I know that, in each case, I'm impeded, vocally, while I'm singing it. But, actually, maybe, that's a good thing. I'm not in a position to over-sing it and, in the end, maybe that keeps the performance clean and steady, firms it up. There are places

I might have gone off to with the melody, if I could—but I couldn't, so I didn't. Instead, I end up hitting it hard, down the middle.

Whatever, this is the version they're getting because I can't do anything else.

The tape goes back to London. And then, a little while later, Mark comes up to the house on Copa de Oro Road with a finished version of the track that Anne Dudley has sent him.

We take it into the pool room, where I have a sound system with giant speakers attached to the walls at one end. I put the recording on and twist the volume up loud—and, oh my. A synthesized swooshing noise whips from one speaker to the other and then—bam!—the vocal hits, and the drum machine and the bass drop in, and I'm standing there and thinking, fuck me. This thing is jumping clean out of the speakers. It's like being back at the Polya Glove factory and hearing "Rock Around the Clock" come over the radio—that break thing again, the hair on the back of the neck going up.

I'm reckoning this is as powerful as I get. If this isn't a hit, then I may as well pack up and leave. Seriously. Good night, God bless and thanks for everything. See you all on the other side.

But first there needs to be a video to go with the single—another new world that has opened up during my extended holiday from the recording industry. Because it's 1988, and MTV rules. No video on heavy rotation on music television, no international hit. So a production company gets involved—Propaganda Films. Some storyboards arrive in LA, which I'm excited to see—and less excited when I discover that they show me in a tuxedo, against a Las Vegas backdrop. Really? I'm singing Prince's "Kiss" on a track created by Art of Noise yet I'm still getting Caesars Palace hung around my neck like a giant glittering albatross. Still, they have another look at it when we ask them to, and the Vegas images go, replaced by an animated background of cartoon instruments and random figures and objects and words—busy, bright, fun. And I dance and sling a microphone around and fool about with a pair of shades, in a dark Issey Miyake suit over a black turtleneck. Hair off the ears, too. I've been ensuring that my hair covered at least the top part of my ears since the seventies—thirty years with hair-covered ears (another potential title for this book). So this in itself is pretty revolutionary. And MTV seems to love this video—plays it to death, opening up the global MTV network, inviting me into their studios in New York, Stockholm, Madrid.

Meanwhile, on American radio, a fella called Guy Zapoleon on KZZP in Phoenix, Arizona, has got hold of the record on import and won't stop playing it, and the news seems to spread out from there. Even so there's a debate in a few places about what, exactly, we're looking at here. Tom Jones doing "Kiss." Is it a novelty record? Not the first time this particular issue has surfaced in my career: it came up with "What's New Pussycat?," it came up with "Delilah." And now, to a lesser but still noticeable extent, it's coming up with "Kiss." Musicians I meet don't seem to feel this way about it, and young people, the MTV generation, who have never heard of Tom Jones until now, don't appear to be taking it that way either. For them, the novelty question doesn't really arise. But older people, in a position to bring some baggage with them, are wondering whether there's some kind of comic element here that it would be a shame to miss. So I'm experiencing a certain amount of low-level anxiety as I do the promotional rounds of the American Top 40 radio stations, talking the single up. I'm sitting in the waiting room outside the studio of a morning radio show in Minneapolis, for example, and I can hear the broadcast going out over the speakers and the DJ announcing that I'm due up, and I'm clenching slightly, waiting for the gag—something about panties, maybe, or Vegas. But it's great, because the gag doesn't come. And I realize that I don't have to worry this time, that I can relax and let the shoulders go down as I'm finally ushered into the studio, ready to go live on air.

Where the DJ's opening line is, "Tom Jones—congratulations! And we hear Engelbert Humperdinck's going to do 'Alphabet Street' next."

Nothing to do but suck it up. And here's the thing that makes sucking it up pretty easy—the thing that's not open to dispute: "Kiss" is a hit. A stonking great international hit—Top 10 in Australia and Norway and Spain and New Zealand and Holland and Sweden and Belgium and Austria. In the UK, it goes to number 5, higher than the Prince original. In addition to that, the Propaganda Films video wins the MTV Music Video Award for Breakthrough Video, beating the promo for Michael Jackson's "Leave Me Alone."

An MTV Award, a worldwide hit, a renewed presence on American Top 40 radio . . . there's the shape of a second coming here that would have seemed impossible as little as six months previously.

SOON AFTER "KISS" WAS A HIT, I went to a party at Tramp, the club in Jermyn Street in London, and at the bottom of the stairs I ran into Prince. He was dressed like some kind of eighteenth-century fop— braided coat, teetering heels, huge frilled sleeves, silk handkerchief waving. I may have imagined the handkerchief.

I paused to shake his hand and said, "Thanks for the song."

He replied, "Thanks for recording it"—surprising me with his voice, which was by no means falsetto. It turns out the guy has a fathoms-deep speaking voice.

And then I excused myself and walked on into the party as rapidly as I possibly could—not having anything at all against the thought of hanging out with Prince, but having in my mind a scene which has always haunted me from that Bette Midler movie *The Rose*. It's the bit where Midler, playing Mary Rose Foster, a big rock star, takes a helicopter out to Long Island to see Billy Ray, played by Harry Dean Stanton, a humble country singer and songwriter, one of whose songs Mary Rose Foster has recorded. And Mary Rose Foster is clearly desperate to know what Billy Ray thought of her version of the song and yearning to discover that he liked it because to find out that he didn't approve of it would be crushing to her. But Billy Ray isn't saying anything until Mary Rose is on her way out the door, when he finally says: "Before you go: don't you ever record one of my songs again." Utter humiliation for Mary Rose.

And that's why I moved quickly past Prince at the bottom of the stairs in Tramp that night. It would have devastated me to hear that he didn't like my version of "Kiss." The best approach in the circumstances seemed to be: right-turn and into the room. Don't give him the option.

ALSO AROUND THIS TIME, in 1988, I make a trip back to Wales and land up in the Treforest Arms with Dai Perry, drinking and winding back the years. On the pub jukebox are both "A Boy from Nowhere" and "Kiss," my two recent singles, both of which get a bit of a spinning, in honor of the fact that I'm there in the pub.

And when "A Boy from Nowhere," the big ballad, goes on, the older crowd in the pub start calling out to me, "Oh, yes. That's you, Tommy, that is. That's what you do best." And when "Kiss" goes on, the younger crowd say, "No, this is you, Tommy. This is where you need to be."

And time falls away, and it might as well be nearly thirty years ago, with the working men's club crowd over here, and the YMCA kids over there, and me in the middle, looking from one to the other and trying to work out a way to please both.

With EMF on The Right Time.

35

The NWCs

"Can we get six programs with Tom?"

Not really a question I was expecting to hear asked in 1992. I assumed television in that sense was over for me. I figured the gruesome shows in Vancouver, back at the start of the eighties, and their grisly afterlife had nailed down the lid on that particular coffin.

Yet here was Richard Holloway, the boss of Central TV, the regional ITV provider for the Midlands, wondering if I'd be interested in doing a series. Another of those calls that seemed to drop out of an empty sky. Richard had been a junior floor manager on *This Is Tom Jones* at the beginning of the seventies. Back then it had been his job to hold up the handwritten cue cards. Now he was running Central. And he wanted to commission a music show, presented by me.

There were no fixed ideas at this point, beyond the general notion of guests, conversation, performances, duets—the things that informed *This Is Tom Jones*. But maybe in this instance it could be purer, even more musical. The producer was going to be Graham Smith, who did *The Last Resort* and came to the London Palladium that night with Jonathan Ross, when I was promoting "A Boy from Nowhere." And the location was going to be Central Studios in Nottingham, which wasn't necessarily going to be on the itineraries of some of the guests that we would like to pitch for, but we would just have to get around that. We spent a long time discussing what the shows were going to be and do, and who we could involve within the budget, which was by no means large. Eventually we hit on the idea of splitting the programs by genre, hitting a different kind of music each week—country, blues, gospel, rock, soul—deconstructing those various styles and making the connections between them, so you'd see and hear how these seemingly different musics bled into one another.

It was going to take a flexible band, playing live in the studio, so we very carefully put one together, using some of the players from the Kurd concert at Wembley: Gary Wallis, the MD/drummer, guitarist Tim Renwick and percussionist Jody Linscott, who had toured with Pink Floyd. We got in Pete Adams on keys and Steve Pearce on bass, along with a pumping four-piece brass section led by Steve Sidwell, and, on vocals, a wonderful close harmony group from New York called True Image. At the helm was the excellent Irish director Declan Lowney, who went on to do great things with the TV comedy *Father Ted*. And then we shut ourselves away to work through it all.

It felt great. There was something really cleansing about it, in fact, from my point of view. I'm not taking anything away from the musicians I had been working with in Vegas, and around America. Those guys could really play, too, every single one of them. But, in those particular circumstances, the nature of it was that they were getting paid by me to do a job—a tough, repetitive job, a lot of the time, where you had to fight to keep the energy alive. (Drinking helped.) Whereas this setup was, by its very nature, fresh and adventurous and exploratory. (Drinking still helped.) Suddenly I was in a room again with players who had opinions and felt free to express them. "Why are you doing it like that?" "Let's try it this way." And I was just the singer in a band again. It's the simplest thing, really, but I'd been out of touch with all this for a very long time— making music in a group. There we all were: the doors of the rehearsal room were closed, the clock didn't seem to be running, the world had gone away. We were just having fun knocking songs around. And afterward we'd hit the Central Studio bar, where they had Bass ale on draft.

The whole experience served as a powerful reminder to me: *this* is what I do.

We managed to pull in some great guests from across the musical range, people who totally got what we were trying to do, which was simply to explore how music comes alive and how it gets fed: Sam Moore, from Sam and Dave, Daryl Hall, Al Jarreau, Lyle Lovett, David Gilmour, Cyndi Lauper, the Chieftains. EMF, a bunch of rabble-rousers from Gloucestershire, who were part of the pop-themed show, pitched up, and we got stuck into "Unbelievable" together, that thumping great hit of theirs which I really loved, taking the studio audience along with us, to the point where a kid suddenly jumped out and leaped right on my back. Which hadn't happened too often during the "Coast to Coast" shows.

Joe Cocker came on, too, and I was particularly pleased about that. Joe was on *This Is Tom Jones*, so it was nice to make the link back. I hadn't seen him since our paths had crossed on the road some years earlier—at the Pine Knob Music Theatre in Michigan, me on the way in, him on the way out. We'd had some drinks after his show and he'd come back to the Hilton with me and ended up in the suite in the middle of the night, telling stories and singing tunes. It wasn't like we were close and constant companions, but I always felt I had an affinity with Joe. Two working-class lads with big voices—non-writers, but people who loved blues and soul and did what they could with it. To see him in the room for this show in Nottingham meant a lot to me.

Same went for Stevie Wonder. When Stevie said he'd come on, we relaxed the "genres" theme and gave him a half-hour show to himself. Why not? By most people's definitions, Stevie Wonder *is* a genre. This being Stevie, there was no rehearsal and no word in advance about what he might want to play. The band just had to put together a batch of numbers from his catalog and hope not to get caught out. (Luckily they'd routined "Superstition" and "Higher Ground," which we ended up doing together.) Stevie then walked into the studio, sat down at the piano, the cameras rolled, and off we went—me talking to Stevie about the music he cared about, and him coloring in his replies by dropping at will into a breathtaking version of Ray Charles's "Drown in My Own Tears" and surprising me by suddenly singing a verse of "My Mother's Eyes," a song which had meant a lot to him in his childhood, as it had in mine.

But what brought him up to Nottingham in the first place? I wondered about it. When Stevie did *This Is Tom Jones*, back in 1969, he asked if he could play drums on a song. We did the take, and he wasn't happy with the way he'd played—thought he'd scuffed it up a bit and wanted to run it through again. But Jon Scoffield, the producer, was busy moving the show along and told him it was fine as it was. I saw Stevie was upset about that and I took Scoffield aside and told him Stevie should get another shot, which Scoffield reluctantly agreed to. I may be wrong but I don't think Stevie forgot that. Certainly here he was in Nottingham, giving his time to a show that nobody had seen yet and the destiny of which was uncertain.

We called it *The Right Time*, and it went out on ITV, where it was well received. And then VH1, the grown-up sister channel to MTV, spotted it and put the shows on multiple rotation, meaning it got some wide exposure on cable in the USA. VH1 also got me to promote the show around America, which I loved doing, taking True Image along so we could make some points with singing when necessary. That always seemed to go down well, although Howard Stern, inevitably, had his own take on it when we went in to do his show in New York.

"Smart move," said Stern. "You've got black people with you."

I can't really exaggerate how much nourishment I took from doing *The Right Time* at that point—from being involved in a creative, musical project like that. Respect from musicians had begun to show itself again, which was hugely reassuring to me. And I wasn't feeding the image, servicing the machine, promoting myself, selling a record. I was simply refueling, musically. And the result was that I got to put something in the

archive that I was really, unequivocally proud of. I was calmer and happier, making that simple set of six half-hour television shows, than I had
been in years.

And then, in the middle of making *The Right Time*, I was asked if I
wanted to play Glastonbury. I'd done state fairs in the US and various
other outdoor, multiple-bill festivals down the years. But Glastonbury had
grown and evolved until, by this point, in 1992, it was clearly now the
granddaddy of them all—no longer a countercultural event, out on the
fringes, but now actually something that was central to British culture. It
would put me in front of a huge audience of music lovers with a reputation
for being open-minded and appreciative. All in all, it was a thrilling invitation to get.

It was perfect timing, too. The band that we had assembled for *The
Right Time* was up and running and just right for the gig—a band, incidentally, which now seemed to be referring to itself as the NWCs (the Nowhere
Cunts. It was nothing to do with me). These crack musicians were sitting
there, waiting to go. At the time, we were doing Otis Redding, Solomon
Burke, Junior Walker, King Curtis, and it was solid. But we weren't doing
any of my hits. Was that going to be a problem? We'd find out in due
course. But with my recharged self and this band, maybe I could get a vibe
going where Glastonbury would get what we were doing and embrace it.

Someone in the band said, "It's going to be like Otis at Monterey."

Well, that would do.

We all drove over to Somerset from the house I had at this time at Welsh
St. Donats. Linda came, and Roslyn and Tony, her sister and brother-in-
law, with their kids. Mark and Donna, obviously. I was thinking the music
is solid, but how will it go? The other aspect of this deal was that I was
there in secret, as a surprise. On the poster, I was down as "a special guest
that we can't announce." Well, great. But that can work both ways, there
being such a thing as an unpleasant surprise. Was this going to be the right
kind of surprise? Or were they going to say, "Oh, for fuck's sake, not him?"

It wasn't raining, thank God. I'd seen pictures of what happens at

Glastonbury when it rains, and it didn't look pretty. The place seemed to turn into the Somme—people staggering around with trench foot, and mud where their clothes used to be. But fortunately it was sunny and warm, one of those magical British summer Sunday afternoons, heading into the evening.

Blur was on the bill. PJ Harvey. Morrissey. Primal Scream. The Levellers. The backstage area was very nice if you liked Portakabins. I talked to Peter Gabriel back there, whom I had never met before. We talked about Box—birthplace of my grandmother and the place where Gabriel has his studio. (It wouldn't have occurred to me at this point that I would one day end up recording in it.)

Then it was time to play. Van Morrison had just come off. I always got on well with him—liked what he was doing, right from the start. A proper blues singer, it seemed to me. Coming from the right place.

I said, "How is it out there?"

He said, "They need a kick up the arse."

This didn't sound encouraging.

I said, "Will I see you after?"

Van said, "No, I'm doing a runner."

He didn't seem too happy—hadn't connected with the audience, hadn't gone over that well.

Christ, if this crowd hadn't bought Van Morrison . . .

But I was thinking, fuck it. Let's have a pop at it and see what happens. Wasn't that the theme of the moment? I was out there doing things because I could. Doing things because it was amazing to be asked.

There were a lot of people wedged at the front who had been bedded down there all day, banking their places in the belief that the surprise guest was going to be Prince or U2. Those were the big rumors going around the site, apparently. Prince or U2. It couldn't be Sir Cliff, could it? It had to be Prince or U2. So potentially there was a battle to be fought right there, because when I walked out, I wasn't just going to be Tom Jones for these people; I was going to be Tom Jones who, in addition to that, wasn't U2.

I went on. Out onto the enormous floor area of the Pyramid Stage. It was unbelievable. A sea of faces seeming to stretch most of the way across western England and back to Welsh St. Donats. And mostly smiling, ready to go for it—not noticeably pissed off that I wasn't Bono and the Edge. So we exploded into it, and the horns were blaring, and right away the kids were jumping about the place, and it was all happening. Three numbers in, we took it down and did a ballad—an Otis Redding song, "I've Been Loving You Too Long." I looked out at this point and it was like something from a Hollywood Western. Away on the horizon, these kids seemed to be coming over the ridge in their thousands—flooding in from all corners, coming down to be a part of it.

We were absolutely steaming by this point, when, about halfway along the crowd, I noticed two young fellas who had picked up a banner on two poles and were waving it above the heads of the crowd. The banner read, "Tom Fucking Jones!"

Yeah!

We played for an hour and managed to put one hit of mine in there: "Kiss." The rest was pure soul and R&B. Lou Reed was in the wings, getting off on it. And that was great—and unexpected because Lou, bless his memory, wasn't exactly a pushover.

Afterward, in the hospitality area, John Peel, the DJ, came up. He said, "I really enjoyed what you were doing."

I said, "Thanks."

Peel said, "Yeah. But I realized I was standing in the middle of a field and wondering if you were going to sing 'Delilah.'"

I looked at him, trying to read his face. What did he mean by that? Would it have made his afternoon if I had done "Delilah"? Or would it have ruined his weekend, or possibly even his month? I had no idea.

Either way, thanks, again. And move on.

Young people were getting it. That was more the point. Young people at a festival. Tom Fucking Jones, indeed. Another turning point, right there.

With Robbie Williams: The Full Monty *at the Brits.*

36

Jimmy's Place

After *The Right Time*, things spin so quickly for a while that, within the space of a few months I find myself (a) on stage at Carnegie Hall with Sting and (b) signing a record deal with the same label as Dr. Dre and Snoop Dogg. Both of these experiences are, in their own separate ways, probably best filed under the category "how did *that* happen?"

The gig with Sting comes about when he calls to ask if I'd join the bill for his annual Rainforest benefit show in New York. This is 1993. Others performing: James Taylor, George Michael, Tina Turner, Bryan Adams, Herb Alpert and Dustin Hoffman, who is doing a reading. It's not a shabby collection. And it's not a shabby venue, either: a beautiful room, America's most gilded concert hall. I ask Sting if he could give me a month or two to think about it. . . .

. . . Actually, I sign straight up. Sting says, "Would you do me a favor and open with 'It's Not Unusual'?" I say, "Only if you do me a favor and play bass on it." Which he does, and it's a storm. I find I like Sting a lot. Proper musician. Sound pair of ears. Not inclined to give a fuck what people think. True Image, the singers from *The Right Time*, do backing vocals for my set, and we tear the place up. They then stay on the stage and do backing vocals for everyone else, too. After the show, there's a reception at the Tavern on the Green. When I walk in, the room stands up, and I'm so buoyed up by it that I don't quite know what to do with myself.

Not long after, Sting is playing at the Greek Theatre in LA and he asks me to go on and sing "Every Breath You Take" with him. Again, it's not something I need to think long about before accepting. And again, it's one of those pinch-yourself experiences, and an endorsement which means a lot to me at this point, coming from where it does.

Stewart Copeland, the drummer from the Police, is knocking about in the dressing room afterward. He says, "I thought you might have done 'What's New Pussycat?'"

I'm not sure whether this sneer is aimed at me, Sting, or both of us together. Fuck him, either way.

And then an opportunity opens up for me to become a recording artist at the home of the world's most notorious gangsta rap label. John McClain, the head of A&R at Interscope Records in Los Angeles, calls about a possible album deal. Interscope is the home of Death Row Records—Tupac Shakur, Dre, Snoop. Guns and gangstas. Death Row couldn't be hotter or wilder at this particular moment in history— nor more worried-about. Dan Quayle, who's trying to be US president, has gone after them on the whole "Parental Advisory," anti-American values thing. Their distributor, Warner Bros. Records, has got cold feet and abandoned the label, and now they're in with Universal.

Tom Jones at Interscope. It couldn't seem less likely. Of all the record companies in all the world, at this point in time.

We go for a meeting at the Interscope offices in Westwood, LA. A thoroughly unassuming area, if the truth be told, but I notice that the two guys on reception are packing heat. Again, it was never like this at MAM in Bond Street. The guys are former FBI, according to the rumor.

Upstairs is Jimmy Iovine, a noisy, enormously engaging Italian-American in his forties, permanently in a baseball cap. Iovine is an industry legend, doing very well for himself even before he co-founds

Under new management in the eighties.

Enjoying the company of a young Jonathan Ross.

Singing for Homer and Marge.

Reload: The Cardigans and Portishead, two class acts.

My Brits Lifetime Achievement Award performance.

Diamond, Brown, and Jones.

A proud day at Buckingham Palace.

The Queen's Diamond Jubilee, 2012.

The launch of *The Voice UK*, 2012.

Working with guitarists Ethan Johns and Dave Bronze and drummer Jeremy Stacey on *Praise & Blame* at Real World studios, 2010.

On stage with Ed Sheeran at the MCG in Melbourne.

Back with my friends the Stereophonics for the Teenage Cancer Trust, Royal Albert Hall, London.

Searching for
that moment
with Ethan.

A great night with Mark in LA
at the 2015 MusiCares Tribute to
Bob Dylan.

Beats Electronics and sells it to Apple for $3 billion. As a producer, he has worked on close to 100 platinum records: Springsteen's *Born to Run*, Meatloaf's *Bat out of Hell*, Patti Smith's *Easter*—you name it. He engineered for John Lennon on the *Walls and Bridges* album and he's got one of Lennon's old upright pianos sitting in his office. I'll get used to him shouting, despairingly, "You're all fucking nuts, you Scottish, or Welsh, or whatever it is." When we hook up in New York, he always hurries us off to Little Italy for the best imaginable Italian food.

So, suddenly my world is now Jimmy Iovine's phonebook. And Jimmy Iovine's phonebook is not short of numbers. Furthermore, during the making of the album that we happily sign up for, he seems ready to use every single one of them. Diane Warren, at this point America's leading supplier of radio-friendly pop and rock hits, gets a call. Teddy Riley from Blackstreet, the king of new jack swing, gets asked to produce some tracks. So does Jeff Lynne. So does Trevor Horn. So does Flood, who has worked with U2 and Nine Inch Nails. So does Youth, the techno and dub producer. So, for all I know, do any number of other people who aren't too fussy about having a surname in 1994. To be honest, it's pretty dizzying—the very definition of throwing enough shit at a wall. But it's also fantastically exciting and the most extraordinary educational opportunity for me—fifty-three, and suddenly finding myself flitting from one dynamic, Category A pop producer to the next.

As the album comes together, Jimmy gets in touch. "I've been listening to everything, and it's great," he says. "But I'm just trying to think of the track my mother is going to like."

Seriously? Even now, at Interscope, with lethal rap acts down the hall and armed guards on the door, with money flying around to bring in the hippest producers and writers known to man, we're still wondering how to please Jimmy Iovine's mother?

Nothing against Jimmy Iovine's mother, obviously.

But even so, it's a slightly deflating moment—the old assumptions about who I am and what I do resurfacing, proving impossible to shake.

Still, we push on. With Trevor Horn, I work on a song called "If I Only Knew," written by an American experimental hip-hop band that Iovine has got hold of, and who call themselves Rise Robots Rise. We work on the track at Trevor's house in Bel-Air and finish it off in his studio near Henley-on-Thames.

The number's a rap: it doesn't have a melody. Trevor says he'll get Lol Creme, who used to be in 10cc, to come down and write one. I hear myself saying, "Can I have a stab at it first?" I find a melody to sit with the backing track, and we record it, and it works.

Another first for me: some creative input in the songwriting. Thinking about a tune that I wrote completely on my own from very early on called "Looking out My Window," I realize the extent to which I've been excluded from that side of things up to now. When I took that song to Gordon and we recorded it, I looked at the label, and the songwriting credit read "Mills and Jones"! Gordon said it "sounded better that way." Well, not an understatement to say I was a little upset, and made him change it. But I was always a bit too unsure to push myself forward in that area, definitely. Too lazy, also. Certainly never even encouraged, back in the day. But controlled, as well, by a writer/manager who wasn't particularly keen on sharing writing credits. So now I'm thinking, great—all this new stuff in my life, and a writing credit on a possible hit single.

But Jimmy Iovine has a word with me. "Listen, Tom. These Rise Robots Rise guys are working out of a tiny basement apartment in New York. The money from this song is probably going to change their lives. Do you really want a slice of that?"

And I say, "Too fucking right I do."

Okay, no I don't. I allow Jimmy Iovine to guilt-trip me out of a credit. But I do get a hit out of it. "If I Only Knew" goes to number 11 in Britain in 1994. It's also a huge hit record in Australia, where Triple J, the main Top 40 station, decides to play it every hour for twenty-four hours. It brings me back in that country and sets me up for a tour, where I fill the Rod Laver Arena for four nights.

The album for Interscope comes out in 1994 and is called *The Lead and How to Swing It*. It's a Welsh thing: if you're swinging the lead, it means you're bullshitting. Probably too convoluted for a title. David LaChapelle takes the cover shot: me looking pretty muscly, if I may say so, in a string vest and some light blue trousers. It's certainly putting some distance between me and some of the old images but maybe it, too, like the title, is a bit confusing. Whatever, the album doesn't quite fly. It certainly doesn't earn out. In fact, given the amount they threw in, I'd be surprised if Interscope wasn't still paying for it now.

Still, despite this commercial setback, relations remain cordial and optimistic, and Jimmy seems open, in principle, to the idea of another album. Sometime after this, in the dressing room after a show at Bercy in Paris, the drummer Steve Jordan, whom I know from working with him in the Paul Shaffer band on *Late Show with David Letterman*, and the renowned bassist Pino Palladino, a Cardiff lad, stop by to say hello. They talk to me about doing an album of R&B and soul songs with them—not from the traditional catalog but with newly written material in that vein, with one or two less well-known covers thrown in. Wilson Pickett's "Engine Number 9" is one thought.

Sounds like a great idea to me. It takes a while to come together, but Jimmy Iovine eventually gives the project his blessing, and we go into the Hit Factory in New York in early 1996 and start work. Mavis Staples comes in and duets on a number called "Getting Too Big for Your Britches." Bernie Worrell from Parliament and Talking Heads is on keyboards, Cornell Dupree and Waddy Wachtel are on guitars, there's Steve and Pino, and we've got the Memphis Horns in there. Great players, great playing. Great dope smokers, too, but that's another matter. It's a huge and warming time for me. As a solo singer, back in the seventies and eighties, how often did I really care who was in the studio with me on sessions? I just went in and got it done. Selfish, really. But here, in this context, I'm looking around the room and taking it all in. Cornell Dupree played the intro on Brook Benton's "Rainy Night in Georgia" in 1970, which I always loved. And now, to my delight and amazement, he's in the corner of the studio—big pipe of tobacco on the go, sitting in a chair, legs crossed, giving a slow, gentle nod as he plays, cocktail to one side. Heaven.

We record twenty-six tracks in total, everything analog, onto good old-fashioned tape. (Irate call from Jimmy Iovine: "I can't believe the fucking tape costs on this thing! Nobody uses that much tape.") I'm pretty sure there's a great album in this. I'm also sure that some of the best work, vocally, that I have ever done is on these recordings.

In the end, though, that's not how Jimmy Iovine sees it. This time he doesn't say anything about worrying what his mother is going to get out of it. But he thinks there's no obvious single, which he may or may not be right about. His overall verdict is that it's all "too authentic." The album is shelved.

I don't get this and I'm maddened by it at the time. It sounds like bullshit to me. How can something be *too* authentic? It's authentic or it isn't. How could too much authenticity be a problem?

Then again, looking at it more dispassionately, this was 1996. It wasn't the album that Jimmy Iovine was waiting for, and it wasn't the album the world was waiting for, either. That live sound on records would come round again, of course. Authentic soul would come round again. Everything comes round again if you wait long enough. But it wasn't being heard much in 1996.

Even so, twenty-six tracks, all that great playing, some of my best vocals, all that authenticity . . . I was pretty sore about the waste. Still am. Maybe they'll release it when I'm dead.

MORE AND MORE DIFFERENT EXPERIENCES. More and more places I didn't expect to land up. More and more outcomes that would have seemed remote, to say the least, a decade ago.

Anne Dudley, who came to me with the suggestion for "Kiss," now asks me to record a version of Randy Newman's "You Can Leave Your

Hat On" for a low-budget British movie she's working on, about male strippers in Sheffield. Nobody's really talking big box office about this project, but there is a bit of a buzz happening around it, and I like Anne, so I do the song. The film is *The Full Monty*; the track gets used to accompany the movie's climactic stripping scene, and the project turns out to be the year's biggest release after *Titanic*.

Off the back of that, I then end up on stage at the Brits in early 1998, performing a *Full Monty* medley with Robbie Williams—me in a dark suit and tie, Robbie head-to-toe in leather. Nice kid, Robbie Williams—someone in whom I recognize myself at that age. I've met him once before—with Take That at *Top of the Pops* in Elstree. He separated himself from the band and came over and gave me a hug, which was nice of him and unexpected. And the Brits duet goes over great—a nice, cross-generational thing going on, mutual respect.

That knife-edge thing again, though—like on *The Last Resort* with Jonathan Ross in 1987. It's still there. Which way will the audience go with this? Old fool messing about? Or classic singer who has swung right round to the right side? That's not getting resolved in a hurry, and it's not something I'm complacent about. For example, I'm standing backstage, ready to go on and sing at the Capital Radio Party in the Park in 1997—a big outdoor event in Hyde Park in London—and Chris Tarrant, the DJ, is about to present me. And I'm bracing myself because I'm thinking, it's Chris Tarrant—he's bound to use a line here, isn't he? He's bound to do an underwear joke: "Get ready with your panties, ladies." Something like that. And why not, from his point of view? Tarrant's only on stage for a moment. If he can get a laugh in that time, job done.

But I would so rather he didn't, if it were at all possible, because I've got to follow that line on, walking out there, the underpants guy . . .

And he doesn't. He just brings me out, straight. So I'm thinking, maybe I'm getting there. Maybe the assumptions are shifting, and some of that baggage is falling away a little. There's evidence of that. But it's a constant, low-level anxiety at this point.

With Stereophonics: Stuart Cable RIP.

37

Everybody Loves a Train

The shelving of that lovingly nurtured soul album marked the end of my deal with Jimmy Iovine and Interscope, and once again I was out of contract. I had been in and out of the doors of more record companies than most artists release albums. But each time a deal ended, it was bound to be a worry—and increasingly so. For a singer closing in on sixty, recording contracts weren't necessarily going to be like busses. You could never be sure there would be another one along in a minute.

Thankfully, on this occasion, another one turned into the street. In 1999, we heard from Gut Records, an independent label based in Maida Vale in London and run by Guy Holmes, who used to work for Island Records. Gut had had a huge success with its first release, "I'm Too Sexy" by Right Said Fred, which went to number 1 virtually everywhere, including America. Now Guy was into making edgy records, but their approach to me came via his business partner, an Australian called Don Reedman, whose background was putting TV-promoted albums together for K-Tel records, the big compilations outfit. For Gut, Don Reedman had just brought in Jayne McDonald, the cruise ship singer who got lucky with an appearance on a BBC docusoap. And now he was trying to bring in me.

I decided not to think about that too hard.

The pitch was for an album of duets. My old hits, the plan seemed to be, but reworked in the company of people like Rod Stewart, Elton John, Shania Twain, Cher, maybe Sting—all subject to availability, obviously. Availability, and willingness on their part.

This was shaping up to be something of a golden age for the duet— or certainly a busy age. Surprise hook-ups, people playing stylistic mix-and-match. Frank Sinatra singing with Gloria Estefan. Pavarotti singing with Jon Bon Jovi. The technology was playing into the hands of projects like these. ISDN lines (lines attached to the Integrated Services Digital Network, to give it its full name) had come in, meaning you could be in another studio altogether, in another country, possibly even on another planet, and phone your part in, without any loss of sound quality, although perhaps with the loss of plenty of other qualities, such as soul, feeling, interaction, etc. Natalie Cole had had a massive hit singing along with a recording of her father, Nat King Cole—dead since 1965. Even the inconvenience of no longer being alive wasn't necessarily a hindrance to cracking the charts wide open with a duet.

The troubling thing, from my point of view—whichever way it would eventually be put together—was how solidly mainstream Reedman's duets project looked. There wasn't much thinking out of the box going on there, with the concept they'd come up with; with all due respect, it wasn't anything I hadn't done before.

Mark and Donna and I set about drawing up our own wish-list, trying to think a bit more imaginatively about the combinations. And we came up with a slightly different overall concept: instead of everyone coming to me, which is the standard way around in these duet projects— the guests dropping by and appearing on the featured artist's terms—I would go to them. We would get the guest in each case to suggest the song they wanted to do and then, if they were up for it, I would go into their environment—into their studio, with their producer, and their musicians, and we would record the tracks that way. And then, with any luck, we would end up with a collection of genuine and different-sounding collaborations—and have a nice, exploratory time of it along the way.

I'm not sure how excited Gut Records was at the prospect of this. Looked at on paper, it wasn't quite the plumb-down-the-middle, stack-'em-high, sell-'em-low idea that Don Reedman had run past them. But all credit to Guy Holmes: he eased Reedman aside, took the project on personally, backed it and told us to get on with it. In fact, a bit further down the line, Guy ended up remortgaging his house in Hampstead in order to pay to finish the recording. That's how persuaded he was by what he was hearing.

And it didn't turn out to be a bad gamble.

Van Morrison, an old friend, was a solid start—certainly not mainstream, and quality all the way. The Stereophonics were an early name to go down on our list. They had invited me to go and see them at Wembley, where they were supporting James, and I found I totally related to them. They were a Welsh band, for one thing—from the Cynon Valley: Kelly Jones, Richard Jones, Stuart Cable. A set of very solid individuals. They'd cut their teeth in the south Wales working men's clubs, the same as I did. It turned out they had even rehearsed in the same pub that I'd rehearsed in with the Senators—the Thorn Hotel in Abercynon. They reminded me a lot of how I was, in my twenties. And when we hung out, they treated me like one of their own. They loved the idea of coming in on a duet and they chose "Mama Told Me Not to Come," the Randy Newman song. Perfect.

We were thinking about young Welsh talent, and that took us to Cerys Matthews. Cerys was the singer and writer in the band Catatonia, but she had also sung vocals on a track called "The Ballad of Tom Jones" by Space, a band from Liverpool—a single released by Gut Records, coincidentally. (Oddly enough, Space's own singer was called Tommy Scott, as I had once been.) Cerys, too, loved the concept. She had always wanted to do a big band swing number, so we did Frank Loesser's "Baby It's Cold Outside" with full orchestra and the works.

Then the Cardigans, from Sweden, came on board. That was probably the game changer from Guy Holmes's point of view, because the Cardigans were a massive international item at this point. We asked them what they were interested in doing, and they put up the Talking Heads song "Burning Down the House." Fine by me. I flew out to Malmo, and we recorded it with producer Tore Johansson in their Tambourine studios—me, Nina Persson and the band feeling right at home.

The setup really seemed to work, wherever we were, actually. Nobody got intimidated or felt restrained, everyone was comfortable—the sessions were more like jams than anything else, and all the more pleasurable for that. And, as a result, the whole project began to open up and out. James Dean Bradfield from Manic Street Preachers—more young Welsh talent—did "I'm Left, You're Right, She's Gone," one of Elvis's steals from country music. Robbie Williams, continuing our friendship from the Brits, picked out Lenny Kravitz's "Are You Gonna Go My Way," which was a blast. Neil Hannon of Divine Comedy, who's an extremely smart guy, chose Portishead's "All Mine"; and then Portishead found out about it and asked, "Why haven't *we* been invited?" So I ended up in a studio in Bristol with them, doing their magnificently arranged version of the spiritual "Motherless Child."

We already had more than enough for an album when Tracey Fox, our invaluable product manager, brought in a demo of a song by a guy called Mousse T, a German DJ. The song was called "Sex Bomb" and, on the demo, it was being sung by a girl. But it was jumping out—an instant hit song, it seemed to me. It reminded me of one of those tongue-in-cheek, filthy, innuendo-laden blues classics—a late twentieth-century Howlin' Wolf number, you could almost say.

The only problem was the lyric. The way the girl was doing it, the chorus went, "Sex bomb, sex bomb, I'm your sex bomb." Back to that again. Did I really want to be going around saying "I'm your sex bomb," knocking on sixty?

Strong song, though . . .

So Donna thought, what if we flip it to "You're my sex bomb." Address it to someone else rather than swagger around making a boast out of it. Right away it sat more comfortably. I worked out the middle breakdown section myself, which everyone was happy with. But Gut wasn't sure at first whether it ought to be on the album. "The cast of the album is fantastic, we've got plenty already, and we're not sure it fits," they said. But it seemed like the wrong question to be asking. What did fit, in the context of this record? The record was deliberately, gloriously all over the place. "Sex Bomb" duly took its place on the running order for the album we were now calling *Reload*.

"Burning Down the House" was the first single. I can still remember Mark ringing up for the midweek chart position and telling me, "It's number four." And me saying, "You're fucking joking." Because even when the record was finished we were still thinking that it could go either way, commercially.

So that meant heading over to the BBC and hooking up with Nina Persson for a *Top of the Pops* pre-record. I was really looking forward to it—showing this new side. It wasn't me and a female artist singing a love song into each other's eyes, in the old style. It was me singing a David Byrne song with just about the coolest and most self-possessed singer on the planet at that moment. It was new ground, a new platform. I wasn't harking back to any of the old ways here.

So Nina and I got up on the soundstage, with the studio audience standing in front of us, and went for the take. The track kicked off, and we were only a handful of bars in when I noticed something fly out of the audience. Something soft and white. It passed across me and narrowly missed Nina and dropped to the floor behind her.

A pair of panties—the first of a small barrage.

I looked across at Nina, the ice queen of Swedish rock, who was clearly thinking, "So this is what I've signed up for."

It wasn't fans, though. The *TOTP* floor manager, of all people, in the interests of "staging," had handed out underwear to the audience and told them to lob it up during the number.

Incredible. Even now . . .

We weren't having it. We halted the performance. Mark explained to the floor manager that we weren't looking for that kind of audience participation on this particular number. (He might have been less polite about it than that.) And then we started again from the top, and got through to the end in the absence of panties. Really, though, I had to wonder what direction I would have to run in, and for how long, before the underpants thing was in no danger of applying.

Shortly after this, I was asked if I wanted to do the ITV show *An Audience With* . . . Celebrity-studded crowd, lobbing up questions between songs. A major honor, really, in TV terms. And huge mainstream exposure. But what kind of exposure? I think I would have been slightly wary of this in any case, but the incident with the panties at *Top of the Pops* had made me even more so. The approach came from Nigel Lythgoe, who had been a dancer on one of my TV shows back in the day, but was now head of entertainment and comedy at LWT. A year later he would become a bit of an item as "Nasty Nigel," the most waspish judge on the panel of the talent show *Pop Idol*.

I like Nigel well enough, but he can be a prick, and I don't think he'd mind me saying so. He'd got these writers working on the show who were looking for a comedy element. One of the suggestions was, "What if we had a massive ball of underpants and the audience had to guess how much it weighed?"

Yeah, right. And what if I shot myself in the head right now?

They were going for the whole Tom "Vegas" Jones thing, as they saw it. A staircase. A thrust stage. "Tom's *got* to have a thrust," Lythgoe kept saying.

It seemed pretty clear that the show was going to be first and foremost a piss-take. Well, fair enough. But I'd just made a record that I was really proud of. And in any case I didn't really need the help of the LWT people to turn me into a caricature. I'm more than capable of doing that myself, thank you very much.

We got Graham Smith back in, from *The Last Resort* and *The Right Time*, to sort out some of the writing and the design. No balls of panties. Equally importantly, no staircase and no thrust stage. We wanted it plain and simple: a rectangular stage with the band on it. To our delight and relief, ITV agreed to it all.

The show got written, the band was rehearsed, the guests got invited, and everything was set for a Saturday evening recording session at the LWT studios in London. Coincidentally, that morning I happened to be in the building for an appearance on *CDUK*, the ITV chart show with Ant and Dec, which went out live. When I was done, Mark and I decided to pop next door and put our heads into the *An Audience With . . .* studio, just to see how things were shaping up.

And fuck me if there wasn't a plexiglass, underlit staircase descending to the floor, and a full thrust stage poking out deep into the auditorium.

We collared the stage builder and told him the whole lot had to go. We had an agreement, after all. We weren't about to argue. "Either the staircase comes down and the thrust stage goes, or this thing doesn't happen."

The show went very well in the end, a hugely successful broadcast, and it did the business for the record.

And fair play to Nigel Lythgoe. He said nothing whatsoever about the last-minute rebuild of the set—until the point right at the end of the evening when I was leaving the aftershow party and saying good-bye to him.

"Oh, by the way," Lythgoe said. "Let me know if you ever need a thrust stage and a staircase, because I've got one in my garden."

So that was how we spread the word about *Reload*. Guy Holmes had been telling everyone at Gut that if this album didn't sell more than a

million he would fly every single one of them to Ibiza and treat them to a
holiday. The staff really enjoyed their trip to Ibiza, and at the age of fifty-
nine I had recorded the most commercially successful album of my career.
Six million copies. Plus a giant international hit single with "Sex Bomb."
And those album sales were without America. Guy Holmes couldn't get
a deal to release *Reload* there. American labels wanted to put a couple of
American acts on there before they would think about it—which would
have been perfectly okay with me, and no problem to manage, I'm sure.
I'd already run into the Dixie Chicks, out on the road, who'd had a go at
me for not inviting them to be a part of it. But Gut's deal with the Americans didn't work out, in the end. Which was a shame, given that I was
living and performing there during all this. If I could have had the success with that album in America that I'd had elsewhere in the world . . .

It's never perfect. There's always going to be something nagging
at you.

IT IS DECEMBER 31, 1999, and the world is about to end. According to
the rumors, anyway. The twentieth century is about to become the
twenty-first century, and nobody is quite sure whether the computers
are going to be able to take it, or whether we are about to witness a cat-
astrophic bug-led meltdown in which the power fails, nuclear missiles
begin launching themselves from one side of the earth to the other and
the clocks start running backward to the dawn of time.

But at the exact moment when a century ends and a new one begins,
I'm standing next to Bono. So that's all right. He's got the connections,
surely. If the world ends, he'll be able to phone someone, won't he?

To be more specific, I'm standing next to Bono on the steps of the
Lincoln Memorial in Washington, DC, at the Millennium Gala. President
and Mrs. Clinton's big New Year do for the nation. Performances by Kenny
Rogers and Will Smith. A film from Steven Spielberg. Fireworks, smoke
and tickertape. Half a million people stretching away ahead of us into the

night. It's been my duty and privilege to sing "It's Not Unusual" backed by a band containing Greg Phillinganes, Steve Ferrone, Nathan East—Michael Jackson's guys, essentially. And then the whole cast has gathered for a finale of "Midnight Hour"—routined at the piano during the afternoon by Quincy Jones, with Slash from Guns'n'Roses, in his top hat, strumming away.

A couple of things. We're outdoors in Washington, DC, on December 31. So it's freezing. Secondly, it's been a long and completely dry day. Not a glass to be seen. However, after the show it's all back to Bill Clinton's place for mingling and, finally, a drink.

So, the twentieth century has become the twenty-first century, and, as I stand in the White House, at fifty-nine years of age, warming up around a glass of champagne, I can reflect that the world has not ended. Indeed, the world is as alive to me and as full of possibilities as it has ever felt.

McLaren F1.

38

Flippy Doors

There should have been a *Reload 2*. That would have been a good next move, in my opinion. The first one had sold, and it seemed to me that there was still plenty of life in that way of going about things. I was in my sixties and having hit singles, which people seemed to think was pretty remarkable, and I was getting a kick out of working with other artists and was more than willing to see if I could carry it on for longer. But Gut Records wasn't interested in another duets record for contractual reasons. So I was out of a deal, yet again, and back in the trenches.

Well, okay. By now I was getting pretty used to the pattern.

And then I met Wyclef Jean. This was at a *Top of the Pops* awards show at the Manchester Evening News Arena on November 30, 2001. It took place just after news had come through of the death of George Harrison, which put a huge damper on it from my point of view. Didn't seem possible or fair.

Still, there among the guests was Wyclef, a tall, charismatic Haitian guy in his early thirties, with long dreadlocks and a beard, who had made it big in the nineties as a member of the Fugees, and then as a solo artist and producer. His second solo album, *The Ecleftic*, showed the range of people he was interested in working with: Kenny Rogers, Mary J. Blige, Kid Rock, Youssou N'Dour, Earth Wind and Fire. And in 2000 he'd had a massive crossover Latin/hip-hop hit with Carlos Santana, "Maria Maria." There didn't really seem to be any boundaries with him.

We talked a bit at that Manchester event and hit it off. He was accompanied then (and nearly always thereafter, as I was to find out) by his cousin and musical collaborator, Jerry "Wonder" Duplessis, and by a mountain of a bodyguard—a bearded 300-pound former American footballer who never said a word and was referred to as Beast. Lovely eyes, Beast had—though you might not have mentioned that to his face.

It felt natural to me to ask Wyclef if he would be interested in recording an album with me, and I was delighted when he said he would. There were no record companies involved, but there was money around after *Reload* and "Sex Bomb," so we decided to fund the recording ourselves and worry about selling it later. So then we had to strike a deal with Wyclef, who turned out to have an interesting approach to that end of the business.

"We don't like necessarily to be paid," he explained, sitting opposite me and Mark. "But we do like *things*."

"Like, what things?"

"Well, there's a new car . . . What's it called? You know the one . . . The new car with the flippy doors."

"You mean a gullwing Mercedes?"

"No, no, not that."

"Er . . . a McLaren F1?"

"That's it! A McLaren F1. One of them."

"Right."

"And there's another one, too. Because Jerry's going to need a car as well, you understand."

"Is he?"

"Yeah. There's that other new one. Is it a Zomba?"

"A Pagani Zonda, maybe?"

"Yeah, that's the one! A Paganini Zonda!"

Beast, it seemed, would not be needing a car, which was good news for the budget. Still, we had to source these two models for Wyclef. Which didn't come cheap. And later we got a further phone call.

"You know the cars?" said Wyclef. "We're having trouble getting them out of customs. Can you pay the taxes?"

We drew the line at paying the taxes.

Anyway, with the deal struck, and some studio time in the diary, Wyclef was keen to hang out with me a bit. I think he was wondering, what's it like to be out and about with Tom Jones? What goes on? So the next time we were both in London, I took him to the Metropolitan Hotel in Park Lane, home of the Met Bar and Nobu and a regular stop-off for me. The place was crowded, as it often is, and we sat out in the foyer, having drinks—Wyclef, Jerry, Beast and me.

Pretty soon, a girl came over, said she wanted to introduce herself and say hello.

"It's very nice to meet you," I said.

And then, without further ado, right there at the table, she whipped up her dress and showed me the piercing on her clitoris.

"Well, thank you very much for that," I said. And then she went away.

That was it. My legend with Wyclef was sealed. "Man, you go out with Tom Jones, girls show you their pussy!" He told everybody he knew, meaning that my reputation preceded me, wherever I went with him. Whole weeks later, he'd introduce me to friends at his studio or out in bars or clubs, and the reaction was always, "Tom Jones! We know about you, man! Yeah!"

At the appointed time to start recording, late 2001, I flew out to New York and checked into the Rihga Royal Hotel. This wasn't all that long after the devastation of 9/11, and the city was actually an extraordinarily peaceful place to be. New York had been through a trauma and was trying to come through and be civilized and get on with things, and there was something just a little bit softer about it at that time.

I spent a few days in the hotel suite waiting for the call from Wyclef which would summon me downtown to his Platinum Studios—a delay occurring because, like a bad holiday hotel, Platinum Studios didn't appear to be quite finished yet. Eventually, though, we got going, and, for a few very entertaining weeks, Wyclef's world was my world. There was a constant drift through the studio of guys in do-rags and bandanas and trousers with one leg rolled up, called things like Teflon. The engineer operating ProTools, Serge "Surgical" Tsai, was from Surinam, and I've got to confess I barely understood a word he said. At the same time, I had my assistant, Don Archell, with me a lot of the time, and he's from Bermondsey and I don't think "Surgical" understood Don too clearly, either. It was, altogether, an interesting cultural melting pot.

A joyful musical adventure, too. We made "Tom Jones International," a dance track which was the single, and threw in a version of "Black Betty," the old Ram Jam number, and a take on Bob Seger's "We've Got Tonight." It was fun to be involved in. Back in London, we sold the album to Richard Branson and V2 records for slightly more than the price of a McLaren F1 and a Pagani Zonda. And the album, which came out in 2002, did a bit, albeit without setting fire to anywhere.

At this stage, though, that wasn't really the point. The point was, very simply, that I was sixty-two and hanging out with Wyclef Jean and his crew. And really, when I think about it, that's the thread here: from London in the sixties, through *This Is Tom Jones*, to Vegas and all the way on up to *The Right Time* and *Reload* and beyond. The thing that I was looking for, over and above anything else—the thing that I was getting, that was making me happiest—was the chance to be around talented and colorful characters. And I got more than blessed with it.

The Queen's Diamond Jubilee concert at Buckingham Palace.

39

Rock'n'Roll Queen

I'm not in the Rock and Roll Hall of Fame. I've not been inducted. Even though there's more rock'n'roll in me than there is in 90 percent of those fucks that are in there. But maybe it's because of some of the records I've made. I've thrown people off the scent a bit in that regard and I'll admit to that.

So, I'm not in the Rock and Roll Hall of Fame in Cleveland. But I am, since 2006, a Knight of the British Empire. I guess you take your consolations where you can find them.

I had the Officer of the Order of the British Empire first, in 1999, and I thought that was unbelievable. Other people in entertainment that I knew had had it already. But I was living in the States and I didn't know whether that would affect my chances. Once, on a receiving line after a Royal Command Performance, the Queen said to me, "Are you still living in America?" And straight out of my mouth it shot: "Yes, but only for convenience sake, Your Majesty." I thought: please don't hold it against me.

But she didn't. I went to collect the OBE with Mark and my grandchildren. Roger Moore was there, receiving his Commander of the Order of the British Empire, but he didn't rub it in.

And I figured that was that. But then, in 2006, while I was on tour in the UK, Mark told me there had been a letter about a knighthood. A knighthood for my services to music. What a fantastic feeling. But it shook me up a bit, I don't mind saying. Don Archell, my assistant, said, "This has got to you, hasn't it?" He could see I was worried about it. I was thinking, "What do I have to do now? Do I have to be any different? Do I need to change in any way? If somebody is going to be calling me Sir Tom, I'd better straighten up." I wasn't thinking of turning it down, but it worried me. Would everybody be calling me Sir Tom? I always thought "Mr." was pretty formal.

"Should I call you Mr. Jones or Tom?"

"Tom."

But Sir Tom—that would be taking it up another level. I was shaken by it. And I stayed shaken by it until I actually received it.

Alexander was out of the country, so this time it was Mark, Donna and Emma who came to the Palace. A big day. You leave your guests and go to the waiting room with the other recipients. Most of the people seemed to be academics. They walk you through the procedure: stand up and back off; take a few paces backward before you turn your back on the Queen.

I remember her smiling, very warmly, as I kneeled down. When I stood up, after she had laid the sword on me, she said, "You've brought so much enjoyment to so many people."

I said, "Well, I've enjoyed it too, Your Majesty."

Cliff Richard was the first pop singer to be knighted. And then there was Paul McCartney, Mick Jagger and Elton John and then me. And since then Van Morrison. I just thought it was flattering to be included with this group of great musical artists.

Then outside for pictures. And then off for lunch in the Marcus Wareing restaurant in the Berkeley Hotel in Knightsbridge, where Phil Bowdery, my good friend and long-time concert agent, joined us, and Jools Holland and his wife Christabel. Jools and I had become good friends when I first appeared on his television show, *Later*, in 1999, and we made a very successful album together in 2004—some traditional R&B and boogie-woogie, music we both love. Jools came along with his OBE proudly pinned to his lapel.

So now I was Sir Tom Jones. I don't ask people to use the title. They tend to get it wrong anyway: Sir Jones, Sir Woodward. But I don't stand on it. I met Sir Ben Kingsley at a Prince's Trust do. It had been in the paper that he insisted on being called Sir Ben—wanted that title used. But he told me that the story wasn't quite straight: he didn't insist on it, he said. He was just so proud of the fact that he liked people to use the title if they could and liked to let them know.

I said, "That's all right with me, Ben."

My medal is in a drawer in my house in LA. Not on display, because I'm modest about it. But what I do have on display is the picture taken after the ceremony. So I'm not that modest about it.

I don't think about it every day, but when I do I get a thrill out of it because it's something I never dreamed was possible for me. When I was knighted, I thought about my blind Uncle Albert, who was an ardent royalist, which wasn't always the case with people in south Wales. I thought about my grandfather's war medals, which Albert had mounted up and framed as a wedding present for my parents. I thought about how I used to look at that collection of medals and how I would never expect to get a medal from my country. And now I had two. And I wished that my mother and father could have lived to see it.

I WENT BACK TO BUCKINGHAM PALACE in 2012. I was asked by the Palace to play at the Queen's Diamond Jubilee Concert. Paul McCartney, Elton John, Stevie Wonder, Grace Jones, Robbie Williams, Ed Sheeran, Will.i.am, Annie Lennox. Huge canopied stage right in front of Buckingham Palace, built around the Victoria memorial. It was the most surreal, fantastic setting. Late summer evening sun. Box jammed with royalty.

Packed crowd stretching away up the Mall. Hundreds of thousands of Union Jacks on sticks. Seventeen million people watching on British television. I came on after the wonderful Renee Fleming, the American soprano who'd sung an aria from Puccini—beautiful, but rather taking the party mood somewhere else, I thought. I opened with "Mama Told Me Not to Come"—thinking it would be a good gear change. And then we did a new arrangement of "Delilah"—pair of acoustic guitars, playing it as a blazing Flamenco.

I was flashing back to 1967: my first Royal Command Performance, at the London Palladium, doing "I Can't Stop Loving You." When I was backstage, I thought I was all right with it, but everyone else was in a panic, so I started to twitch too. Tommy Cooper was running around shouting, "I can't find my fucking trousers." Everyone was so nervous, because it was royalty. I was young, and it got me nervous.

It's different now. It's been a lot of years since I first sang for Her Majesty. As I left the stage I felt what a great day it was, and it made me very proud.

At the end of the night, all the performers gathered on the stage for the big finale. McCartney was playing "Ob-La-Di Ob-La-Da" and we were all really enjoying ourselves—Shirley Bassey, Cliff, Elton John, an almost full set of rock knights, give or take a Jagger. It was bizarre, really. And then the Queen came on the stage, escorted by Gary Barlow, which was another sight you hadn't particularly banked on seeing, and she ended up standing right in front of me. So there we were, on a stage rammed with international pop stars, and with an audience of hundreds of thousands of flag wavers disappearing away to the horizon, and the Queen turned around and said to me, "It's cold, isn't it?"

After the show we went into this purpose-built gathering area at the back of the stage, and the Queen suddenly came in, seemingly on her own, and was just standing there, with nobody particularly near her, really, except me. It was flashing through my mind, all the protocol stuff: first of all you address her as "Your Majesty" and after that,

"Ma'am." But you don't ask her questions. She talks to you. You answer if she asks. Don't go making conversation. I was up on it.

The thing was, Prince Philip had been taken ill that night and hadn't made it to the show. He was in hospital, and nobody knew what the problem was or quite what was going on. So it seemed wrong to me not to say something.

So I said, "How's your husband?"

She didn't get stormy and say, "You talkin' to me?" She said, "I won't know until after the show."

I got away with it. So maybe the rules aren't as tight as all that.

And I'm glad I asked.

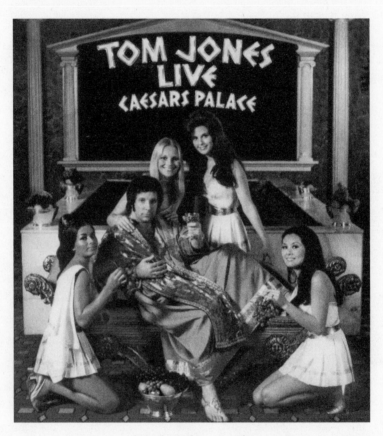

A subtle album cover from my time in Las Vegas.

40

Why Don't You Love Me Like You Used to Do?

I loved Las Vegas, but I ended up paying a price for it. Gordon always said, "You make a name for yourself in Vegas, it will last you for the rest of your life." And I believed him. And he was wrong.

Gordon took the conservative view: get it right in Vegas and it will see you out. Like it was a pension plan or something. But, of course, it wasn't hurting Gordon to keep me there. In Vegas, Gordon got to live the life—the private plane at the airport, the comped hotel suites, the comped meals, the comped high-end brandy. He got to live the Vegas life that I couldn't live because I was doing the shows. That used to piss Linda off. She would go to dinner with Gordon and Bill Smith, our financial adviser, sometimes, while I was stuck back in the dressing room between performances, eating chicken in a pot and matzoh balls to try and get some moisture into my throat. (Get an ear, nose and throat specialist to make a list of places not to sing, and I can guarantee you that Vegas will be number two on that list after the Moon. Your choice: air conditioning indoors, or parched desert air outside. Neither are working wonders for your vocal cords.) Linda hated seeing Gordon and Bill wining and dining high while I was working my bollocks off. And

Gordon loved the gambling. This was a man who thought nothing of sticking $60,000 on the tables at baccarat. This was the man who once bet Paul Anka $25,000 that he could beat him at tennis—and this is in the 1970s, don't forget—and paid up when he lost. Jo Mills loved the gambling, too. Jo came back one night with a pit boss, or a casino manager or some guy, and asked if I would sign a marker, to vouch for her, because they wouldn't give her credit. "And please don't tell Gordon."

Not my problem. What *was* my problem in those years? Vegas was pretty convenient for me, too—I'm not going to deny it. Just up the road from home. Good money guaranteed. I could take the family across with me—a fun place to invite people to. And I had my fun there, too, no question. My home in Bel-Air with Linda, my son always along with me . . . I could sit in the steam room in Vegas and think to myself, Everything in my life is just fine, thank you very much.

But meanwhile the recording side was quickly drying up, and, in the absence of anything else, I was getting royally stuck with the "Vegas" label. And people rarely mean anything complimentary when they put that one on you. They rarely mean anything straightforwardly nice when they call you an "entertainer" either, though, fuck me, maybe they should when you consider what's involved in entertaining people—and not least in Vegas. A Vegas crowd isn't an easy crowd, for all the reputation it has for being one. The Vegas crowd hasn't necessarily come out to see you, like fans might. These aren't necessarily your people, already onside. The Vegas crowd are mostly holidaymakers or conventioneers who are simply in town that week, and you happen to be on. So they're sitting there, saying, "Okay, then: entertain me, like you're supposed to." And then they're gone and, a couple of hours later, another crowd is in their place, saying the same thing. That's not an easy gig, whatever anyone tells you. Every night the slate gets wiped, and you're having to prove yourself again and again.

In any case, it seemed unfair to me, that "Vegas" label. Listen now to that *Live at the Flamingo* album I did in 1969. That's not a "Vegas" show:

that's not what people thought of at the time as typically Vegas. I have never done a Vegas show, is the truth of it. I have never had the dancing girls, never had the fireworks, never left the stage in a fountain of shiny tickertape. I've never glitzed it up. I might have worn a tuxedo. But so what? So did Sinatra. And Sinatra, in Vegas, went on in front of a band and sang. So did Dean Martin. So did Sammy Davis. They walked out, they stood in front of a shit-hot band, and they sang. And that's what I did—my own version of that, with a rock/soul attitude. Just me, standing in front of a band, like I've always done.

But when you've done Vegas, you get stamped with that. "Tom Jones is bringing his Vegas show to . . ." What Vegas show? Christ, that irritated me. It made me want to shout back, "I don't have a fucking Vegas show. I've played Vegas, but that doesn't make me the owner of a Vegas show." There were rock bands that were more Vegas than me, with huge production, stagecraft, explosions and whatever other kind of spectacular. The Rolling Stones, U2 and many other big rock acts were riding around on inflatable cocks, for fuck's sake. That's when they weren't being chased by mechanical dinosaurs. What's not Vegas about that?"

But that's Vegas, and if Vegas itself doesn't eat you up, then what people think about Vegas will do the job. Doing Vegas, I may have over-sung and over-entertained, to make up for a lack of production that the audience expected. It took a heavy toll on my voice, and I ruined my chances for a long time of being taken seriously as a singer. I didn't know it but I was digging my own grave.

And Vegas, like everything else, got smaller for me. I stepped down a bit, from Caesars Palace to Bally's. Then down again. By the end, I was playing a small room at the MGM. It came to that: 700 seats. They were always saying they were going to make it bigger, but they never did.

One night, at the MGM, Burt Bacharach came backstage after the show. It was great to see him. We laughed about "What's New Pussycat?"

"I know you didn't like it at first," he said. "But it paid off, though, right?"

And I said, "It really did."

And then he looked me in the eye and said, "I wish we could have done more for you. I regret that."

Nice of him. But Christ, that was a mournful moment. Like that was then, and this is now, and what went wrong along the way?

At the MGM, they used to keep the Brown Derby restaurant open for me so I could go in there after a show—and they'd keep the pianist on, too. I landed up in there one night with Shirley Bassey after she had been to see the show. Two Welsh battlers for whom, whatever you wanted to say, life hadn't worked out too bad. We sang some songs. I did "Kansas City." Shirley decided to sing "Summertime." The pianist wanted to know what key she would like to sing it in. Shirley said, "No idea, love. I sing in the cracks." I hadn't heard anyone use that expression since I was in the clubs in Wales. Then she sang it, unaccompanied. Shook the walls. Brilliant.

But that kind of night was increasingly rare. The big branded production shows had come to town. Family entertainment. When I went into Bally's, so did the show "Jubilee": burlesque, showgirls, animals, visual effects. That's where the town was headed. Soon it would be Cirque du Soleil spectaculars, people climbing the walls, and the Cher show. Cher's spectacular at Caesars lasted ninety minutes, but how much of that was she on the stage and how much of it was she out the back, getting the next costume zipped up? I mean, I'm not knocking it. But it was a different scene, and no question. The things that I had loved about Vegas in the beginning were no longer there. Elvis was long dead, and the place had moved on, and I hadn't.

I scaled right back on it, but I still carried on going there because it was work. It was a reliable earner, and I was reluctant to cut the strings completely, because if those last couple of decades had taught me anything it was that the winds change fast and often, and you never know when you might have nothing else. But Mark had often said, "You don't belong here now." And eventually I said, "I know what you mean."

I knew what he meant, but I needed telling. I needed Mark to say, "This is not meaning anything. I think this has had its day. Would it bother you if you didn't sing in Las Vegas?"

I stopped altogether in 2010. I had diehard fans who moved from the East Coast to Vegas just because I played there so much. Moved there to live. I was sorry for letting them down. But it was an important thing for me to do—and a break I should have made a lot earlier, if I'd had the courage. But I finally faced up to it. I needed to be elsewhere.

Working with Ethan Johns, Andy Fairweather Low, Dave Bronze, and Jeremy Stacey (out of shot) at Distiller Studios.

41

What Good Am I?

I gave up dyeing my hair in 2009. I'd been getting it blackened up for years, but it wasn't fooling anyone, so I thought, fuck it: I'll go gray.

Also, I think it looks good. I mean, don't get me wrong: if I didn't think the gray looked better, I'd still be dyeing my hair. Vanity doesn't just vanish.

So I stopped dyeing my hair and I started working with Ethan Johns. And these facts may not be unrelated. Someone casually asked Ethan why the producer of Kings of Leon and Ray LaMontagne and Ryan Adams and Laura Marling wanted to make records with Tom Jones, and he answered, "Because he stopped dyeing his hair."

It was a sign of something, I guess. Maybe a sign that I might be ready and able to be a bit more exposed, honest and truthful, which is what Ethan Johns is all about in the recording studio.

We'd had an approach from Island Records—another label riding in out of nowhere to offer an album deal. Specifically they were wondering if I'd be interested in recording an album of hymns for the Christmas season in 2009. They were thinking of calling it *Hymn*. Better, I guess, than *Oh No, It's Hymn Again*. But it was still sounding a bit Woolworths to me. And as Woolworths had just gone bust, that wasn't such a great thing.

Even when we'd batted aside the *Hymn* idea, Island still seemed interested in doing something. I went into the studio and worked on a couple of tracks with Dan Gillespie Sells and Richard Jones from the Feeling, really nice guys. But it wasn't quite clicking, so that got set aside. And then Island's head of A&R, Louis Bloom, mentioned my name to Ethan Johns. They were desperate to get Ethan to produce something for them, and they'd run a whole crop of top names past him, without him biting. And then they got to me, and apparently he said, "Oh, that sounds interesting."

I didn't know Ethan. I knew of Glyn Johns, his father, the legend who recorded the Beatles, the Rolling Stones, the Who, the Faces, the Eagles, you name it. Ethan was working on something at Abbey Road, so we arranged to go over there and meet him at 10:30 one night. (That's the shank of the evening as far as I'm concerned. I'm very rarely in bed before 4:00 a.m. unless I really have to be. Sleep until midday, rise for lunch: I'm a nocturnal creature, really.)

We sat in the studio cafeteria and talked. Ethan had a lot of hair at the time, and a thick beard. A very cool guy. A lot of people seem to find him mysterious, but I didn't at all. I found him refreshingly straightforward— not least sitting there in the context of Abbey Road, where people have built all those myths.

He mentioned Peter Gabriel's Real World studio in Box, where he said there was a great-sounding, bare-walled room where you can record live. He talked about working up some songs—some blues stuff, some gospel, some things from the rock catalog that I might be able to get to the heart of. And then it would be about going into this room with some players, explore some songs and record them. And then we would see what we'd got.

Nobody had talked to me so simply about the recording process in a very long time.

Ethan looked me in the eye and said, "So, do you want to try and do something?" And by then I really did.

At the first meeting in Wiltshire, nobody had signed up to anything, and we were just seeing how it went, feeling our way. The Wood Room at Real World turned out to be a stone-built outbuilding with rough, white-painted walls. There was no separate control room, just a rectangular, high-ceilinged space. More like a rehearsal room, then, than a studio—and an encouraging, unintimidating place in which to sing, in that sense.

At the center of the space was a big, old, square microphone—an RCA ribbon mic. I said to Dom Monks, the recording engineer (a man of very few words and a lot of talent), "Wow, that's an old one."

He said, "Yeah, ancient."

I said, "Well, like, how old do you think?"

He said, "Ooh, about 1939, 1940."

I said, "Oh, you mean the same age as me?"

Jeremy Stacey, a great drummer who regularly plays with Noel Gallagher, had flown in from New York. Dave Bronze, formerly with Dr. Feelgood, was on bass, Richard Causon, who's Rufus Wainright's regular, was on vintage keys, and Ethan on guitars. (Ethan claims not to be a guitarist but he's one of the best accompanists I've ever sung with. Our timings just seem to match.) We played the tremendous, anxious spiritual by Susan Werner, "Did Trouble Me." After a few runs at it, Ethan said, "Shall we listen to that?" I hadn't even realized we were recording.

We went over "Did Trouble Me" this way for four or five hours, until it became our version, in that room, on that day. And that, I realized, was what Ethan was looking for and would continue to look for, until we had an album: not a cover—you can always do covers—but a version, which is a different thing, a different level of ownership, a different level of interpretation and investment in the song. Your version, not your cover. A moment in time, caught on tape.

The process was so unmannered, so matter-of-fact, so gloriously without bullshit. At times we could basically have been a bunch of blokes in a garage fixing a car, frankly. This was by no means about me, the singing star, going into the studio to put a vocal on a track, in the way that I was used to. In fact, it was everything that that wasn't. No headphones, no glass walls, no separation, and Dom the engineer sitting right in the room with us. This was a natural process, all the elements coming together at the same time—no overdubs or drop-ins, a matter of getting people to play and sing the right thing at the right time. And what the right thing is, and the right time, you discover as you go.

We did the *Praise & Blame* album in this way, with Bob Dylan's "What Good Am I?," Sister Rosetta Tharpe's "Strange Things," John Lee Hooker and Bernard Besman's "Burning Hell."

Praise and Blame changed my life. The reaction was beyond anyone's hope or expectations. For the first time in my career, I was getting incredible reviews for my recorded work, from writers and publications that matter, both in the UK and the US. My road took a hairpin turn, and I soon realized I was finally freed up to do the stuff I was born to do. But it was risky, and in my heart I hoped the public would feel the same, and thank God they did.

Two years later, in 2012, we did the *Spirit in the Room* album, with Leonard Cohen's "Tower of Song," Blind Willie Johnson's "Soul of a Man," Tom Waits's "Bad As Me." We've been assembling a third album through 2015, while I've been in the process of writing this book. And this time we've had the pleasure of being joined by Andy Fairweather Low. And through all of this, Ethan's message has essentially been simple and the same: just sing. And it might seem strange that a singer needs to hear that, but it's a fact. Everyone who has had success is asking themselves: what's my next success? What do I do next? It eats at you like that, until it's actually eating into your voice. And Ethan is essentially saying, "Don't worry about that. Just sing."

These are albums of which I'm extremely proud—albums, too,

which have met with critical acclaim, which is not always where I've been headed. In fact, mine is a career in reverse, in that respect. Most people travel from critical acclaim to cabaret. I seem to have traveled from cabaret to critical acclaim. I've done the journey backward.

Critical acclaim—and also acclaim from musicians, which is always going to feel good. The night before the 2015 Grammy Awards in Los Angeles, Bob Dylan finally accepted a long-standing invitation to be honored by MusiCares, the music industry charity who regularly organizes an eve-of-the-Grammys tribute concert. Dylan accepted the award, but only on the grounds that (a) he wouldn't perform at the concert himself and (b) that he would be allowed personally to curate the performers and the songs from his catalog that would be sung on the night. He told the organizers that they had to secure twelve specific artists, and if they couldn't get them then he'd have to back down. In a few days, the organizers had secured everyone—and fuck me if I didn't have the honor of being asked to sing "What Good Am I." In the event, they ended up with over twenty performers that night, because everyone wanted to be there for Bob. Bruce Springsteen played, Neil Young, Bonnie Raitt, Crosby, Stills & Nash, Willie Nelson, Jackson Browne, Aaron Neville, John Mellencamp, Jack White, Norah Jones, Sheryl Crow . . . If a bomb had gone off in the room that night, most of the greats of the music industry would have gone up in smoke, there were so many illustrious names and faces.

Eventually, with artist after artist having delivered wonderful performances, Dylan, who hadn't been seen all night, sparking rumors that he might not even be in the house, abruptly appeared on the stage to accept his award from ex-President Jimmy Carter and, with a sheaf of paper, walked up to the lectern and gave a forty-minute acceptance speech which was the most remarkable piece of oratory I've ever heard from a musician—a gripping recap of his career, studded with accounts of the writing of some of his songs. I sat at the table enthralled—enthralled and also amazed to have played a humble part in that evening.

People often talk, in relation to my story, about the distance from the Valleys to Vegas. The distance from Vegas to the stage of the Los Angeles Convention Hall on that night in honor of Dylan was, in many ways, just as far, if not farther.

But that's the deal. If you're lucky and you stick around for long enough, you eventually get the chance to sound like yourself. I went all over the place, in my career, and there's no question I made mistakes, recording-wise. And I played some wrong places—Vegas too long, overstayed my welcome in others, for sure. But somehow I came out the other end. And when I get the right thing, I can still come through real. And when I come through real, I'm quite hard to ignore.

IN 2012, I GET A GIG as a coach on *The Voice*. I have lunch with Alan Yentob and Danny Cohen from the BBC and Yentob says, "In order to do *The Voice*, we need The Voice."

Do you see what he did there?

I've seen the American version—liked the idea of the blind auditions and the spinning chairs. Liked the way the show talked about "coaches" and "coaching" rather than "judges" and "judging." Liked the way the show was about singing, in a pretty pure way, and wasn't in the game of humiliating people for pleasure, as on some other talent shows.

But the first thing I want to know before I sign up is, who else is going to be on the show? I don't want to be up there with just anyone.

The producers organize a dinner for the potential coaches, just to check we're going to get along. The dinner is in a small private room at Soho House in London. Around the table are Will.i.am, Jessie J, Danny O'Donoghue from the Script, and me. None of us have met before, so there's a bit of corner-of-the-eye stuff going on. We're shown a clip from the American version, and then Danny Cohen, the controller of BBC1, gets up and says a few words about the show—designed to reassure, I guess. But at one point he says something about how "the script will tell you when to move on." And at that point a voice cuts in loudly to interrupt him.

"Well, no one's going to tell *me* what to say."

It's Jessie J. Brilliant—laying it on the line, as Danny Cohen flushes slightly. Right away, I'm looking at Jessie and thinking: *you're* going to be okay. And Will and Danny don't seem like they're going to be anybody's puppets, either. So I'm in.

Later there's a press launch for the first series at a hotel in London. Will and Jessie are huge pop stars at this point. Danny's the unknown Irish guy. And me . . . well, I'm Nelson's Column, or something. A monument of some kind. I haven't quite worked it out yet. Anyway, Danny Cohen introduces everyone, and then there are questions from the floor.

Somebody asks Will, "Why did you agree to do the show?"

Will says: "Because Tom Jones is on it."

Laughter here from the press. But Will, bless him, looks surprised by the reaction and carries on speaking.

"Somebody who has been around this long and done so much over so many years—if he's on it, it makes sense to me."

I'm touched by that, and nobody seems to be laughing anymore.

So, off we go on series one, and I start to enjoy it really quickly. I find I like the people I'm with. Will.i.am reminds me a little of Wyclef Jean. Bright. Out there. Brings that producer's approach: it's all about sound for him. Big fan of Sergio Mendes and Little Richard, both of whom he asks me about working with. Also a lover of Walt Disney. Can't help him there. He's got the innocence of a twelve-year-old child when he speaks, uses all sorts of expressions of his own, but he speaks with enormous clarity, in fact. Jessie J, as she quickly established round the dinner table, is a ballsy kid—talented, driven. Questions herself all the time, though. Jessie will watch the videos back after every show, analyzing them, looking for things that she could have done and said better. And then there's Danny who, because he has the lowest profile of the four of us, will have to put up with being called Danny I Dunno

Who when the series kicks off. But he's smart and funny and properly knowledgeable about music.

Because the hours of filming are so long, and even though it takes a lot of concentration and mental energy, you almost can't help relaxing and becoming yourself. And you're not talking about yourself, which is a relief. You're not selling an album or trying to get people to part with their money. You're just conversing and interacting and offering a view on some singers, which, as a singer, I don't struggle to have. And, yes, this is a strange and unlikely job to have dropped into my lap, in many ways, at the age of seventy-two. But I pretty quickly figure out that the best answer to the question "What am I doing here?" is: "I'm being me." There's no other reason to be on the show, is there? So therefore, I try not to work too hard at it. I just go out there and be myself.

Lesson learned, in that regard. Over the top and back.

Ricky Wilson from the Kaiser Chiefs replaces Danny in the third series, and Ricky becomes the fella I'm closest to on the show. Regular guy. No bullshit. On his first day at the blind auditions, the producers are coming at him with stuff, and he's getting a bit overwhelmed and starting to doubt himself, and I get involved and calm him down a bit, and we're cemented after that. Kylie Minogue comes in for Jessie. Kylie's a pro. She has a professional veneer which is there, on camera and off, which it's hard to feel you're getting behind. But it's a really nice professional veneer, she's been at it a long time. And then, for series four, Kylie goes, and Rita Ora comes. Rita's driven like Jessie, but less hard on herself. She's having fun with it. Although, after one series of stealing both the show and the nation's hearts, she decides to sod off to *The X Factor*, which is a pity.

All of these combinations rubbed along. Nobody was getting on anybody's nerves that I was aware of. We were in and out of each other's dressing rooms. And there was a team thing going on when we were standing there, waiting to go out for the live shows. Because live television will make you twitchy, no question about that. So we could all be looking at each other as if to say, "Don't think you're on your own. We're all here."

The idea of scripting the show might have bitten the dust very fast, but they still give you a book with some suggestions for lines in it—things you might plausibly say at certain points in the show. It's television after all: there's no value in anybody getting lost for words. But we were all very dismissive of the book—and ready to call each other out for using it. You caught someone using a line from the book, you shot them a look: "I know where you got that from."

People snipe at the fact the show hasn't yet produced a recording star. I thought I'd got one with a girl I had in the first series, as good as or better than anyone else out there, I thought. Huge, open, round, full voice. But it didn't happen. It's beside the point, though. To make it as a recording artist, you don't just need a voice, you need great material, self-confidence and steely determination. If anyone's in a position to know that, it's me. And in any case, it's a singing contest. If you win it, you win it. Congratulations, you just won *The Voice*. For those who don't "win," many recognize the value of the experience and go out successfully to start a career or better the career they already have going. And each of those artists delivers something that means something to their fans. Isn't that enough? Nobody says about the guy who won *Mastermind*, "Ah, yes, but he never really went on to do anything else, did he?"

We finished the fourth season at the beginning of April 2015. Everyone seemed pleased with how it had gone and we all happily said good-bye and went off to do our various things. I assumed I'd be back to start filming in the autumn. There was no particular reason to think otherwise—even when the summer wore on without anyone from the BBC getting in touch. My contract with the show was always season by season, with an option to renew at each stage, and the BBC was never very quick about confirming that they wanted you back. It was always a struggle to get that particular piece of information out of them. It's not the best way to be handled, but that's the way this part of the BBC seemed to work, so what could you do? We went ahead and made our plans for 2015 and into 2016—planning a long way ahead, as you have to in the music industry—and made sure to leave holes in there for season five of *The Voice*. The more time that went by, the more I reckoned *The Voice* would be filling those holes. After four seasons and all that mutual loyalty and goodwill, they wouldn't just cut you off without notice, would they?

So, in August 2015, with a month to go before the show went into production, when the call from the BBC eventually came, I assumed it was going to be about who was joining the show. Rita, obviously, was going to need replacing and the word was they had been talking to Paloma Faith, which I was really pleased to hear about because I had already worked with her and I think she's great.

In fact, what the BBC told Mark was, "We've made our choices and there will be two changes and Tom won't be invited back." The replacements were already signed up—Paloma Faith in for Rita, Boy George in for me—meaning the BBC had been working on this for some time. What's more, they were going public with the news the next day. They said, "We'd like to know what you want to say."

So they were getting rid of me and asking me to say something nice about it for the press release. I think they were hoping that I would suggest that I'd left the show because I was too busy to do it. I declined the opportunity to do that.

To say I was shocked is to put it mildly. But my shock wasn't about the fact that they replaced me. My shock was about the way they did it. The show was always changing coaches and moving on—I knew that. Nobody had the right to think of themselves as a permanent fixture. The BBC could have said, at the end of the fourth season, or any time after, "Thanks for what you did, but we're having a cast change." We could have gone for dinner, or had a drink. There could have been a conversation of some kind. Four seasons, after all: you feel you've earned some warmth.

But no.

Charlotte Moore, the current controller of BBC 1, used a press state-ment to say that she "personally thanked me." Can you "personally" thank someone in a press statement? It seems you can at the BBC. The basic thing that Mark Lindsey, the commissioning editor, had to say to my management was, bottom line, I was out of contract. Indisputable as a bald statement of fact, I guess. But what a cold place the BBC is. Sometimes you wonder whether it's run by humans or a machine in a basement.

It's a shame because I always treasured the BBC—always had this strong, British attachment to it. Christ knows, I go back to when Bill Cotton was the man in charge. He was funny, he was witty. He was someone who understood creative people. He was a creative person himself—knew intuitively what makes entertainment work for the Brit-ish public. Sadly, there's not so much of that at the BBC today.

When season four closed, the BBC got me to pose for a photo, hold-ing a card with details about how to apply to take part in *The Voice*, season five. The shot was still hanging about on their website in the days after they had got rid of me. It looked kind of funny at that point. Maybe I should have held onto the card and used the phone number.

But I guess the story is, once again, that you never know. Ten years in the business, twenty years, fifty years. You simply never know.

Ah, well. I like the show. I think it's good telly and I still wish it well and always will. I like the idea that it's one of those vanishingly rare programs that whole families sit down and watch together. And I liked being part of it. I liked the moment of silence when our backs were turned and the singer walked out. If they walked heavy, you could hear them arrive at the mic. And you're thinking, what's this going to be like? What's about to go down here?

Plus, I liked being the old guy—the elder statesman. A figure of authority. A man whose unrivaled experience the room deferred to.

Finally.

That was all right with me.

Melinda Rose Woodward.

42

Tomorrow Night

I catch myself sometimes, driving down Benedict Canyon Road in Los Angeles, getting behind a slow car that I can't overtake and starting to boil up a bit, feeling the frustration. And then I'll think, hang on: what am I driving here? A Bentley with the top down. Or is it the Rolls today? And where am I heading? To Beverly Hills? And is there any real hurry? Probably not.

For fuck's sake. I used to walk in the rain because I couldn't afford the bus. Sometimes you've got to check yourself.

This story could have ended with Gordon, in 1986. And I'd have had no option but to say: well, okay, rocky finish, but I had a good run. Plenty to be thankful for. Plenty to be amazed with gratitude about, actually.

But then for it all to turn around and begin again and grow again— these adventures since, these experiences, this whole, extraordinary second wave . . . well, how lucky is that?

Sometimes you've got to check yourself.

The luck that I found myself with this voice in the first place. The luck that when I lost my manager, my son and my daughter-in-law were there. Mark and Donna, with their creativity and clarity. The sheer luck of that. A Godsend.

A lot of sons don't want to be associated with what their fathers do. Fortunately mine does. And I know that he's doing what he wants to do and that he's happy, which is what you want for your kids as a parent.

He's in the wings with me before I go on.

"You okay? Everything all right?"

"Yeah."

LINDA WANTED TO MOVE from Bel-Air, and I could see what she meant. It was a big house, and we'd been in there a long time. The one thing that Dean Martin's place didn't have was a view. We'd had a view in Wales, we'd had an amazing view in St. George's Hill. So we sold the house on Copa de Oro Road to Nicolas Cage and bought a house on Mulholland Estates, where you can see out into the valley.

We downsized, I suppose you could say. To a slightly smaller house in a gated community. Linda's happy because of the view and she doesn't feel as vulnerable. There were robberies going on in Bel-Air that were freaking her out. And we're off the Homes of the Stars bus tour, so I can go down to the mailbox wearing whatever I like, including nothing.

Charlie Sheen lives across the street, and Paris Hilton a bit further along. Robbie Williams's house isn't far away. Kids feel free to play in the street, and it feels like a neighborhood. Brian Wilson of the Beach Boys lives here. I don't know how much he knows this is where he lives, but it is.

And I can walk around the estate, in a way that you can't walk around Bel-Air, because there are no pavements and nobody walks anywhere down there and somebody will probably call the cops on you if you try it. Not up here. So most days I'll find something I want to listen to, and I'll put on my CD Walkman (being about the only person in the world who still uses a CD Walkman) and set off round the estate. Where, on occasion, I'll pass Brian Wilson, walking the other way. And I'll say "Hello, Brian." And, on a good day, he'll say, "Hello, Tom," and on another day he won't.

And Shaquille O'Neal, the basketball player, is up the road. He's seven foot one, so he's not easy to miss. Shaquille has had a basketball court put in, obviously. I remember walking by one day and, from a distance, seeing some people out on that court and thinking, "Ah, that's nice—a father playing basketball with his kids." But actually, when I got closer, I realized it was Shaquille playing with some grown-ups. When I went by, one of them spotted me and called out, "Hey, there's that Elvis guy." Well, thanks.

Sheila, my sister, lives nearby, and on Sundays I'll collect her, and we'll go off for lunch at an Italian restaurant that we both like. It's what we do on Sundays. And if I'm away, I'll phone her up instead and make sure she's okay. I have some friends in LA but mostly, though, when I'm there I don't really want to be out much. I want to be at home with Linda. And home is where Linda wants to be, too. She didn't want to come out and do what I do. And that's okay. It's not for everyone. I got famous, and she felt the best way to cope was by staying right out of it. We were young friends together and each other's first loves. We were also destined to live in very different ways from one another. Linda has always known exactly who she is—always been powerfully sure of herself. It was a huge part of what attracted me to her in the first place—that certainty, that self-knowledge. Even as a child, it was there. And nothing was ever going to change about Linda's character just because musical success eventually came along and swept me up. She carried on being Linda. She carried on being herself. She keeps her world small and chooses not to come out of that world very often. But I can go into that world, and be central to that world, and that world is where I'm happiest.

Linda was ill a while ago and needed surgery. And she got through it. But it was a major operation, and I had to wonder whether I was going to lose her. I was as worried as I have ever been. It came home to me how she's been part of me through my whole adult life. Even though I've toured for years and been away for months, she has always been there. And if she weren't . . . well, surely that's it for me. I'm finished, aren't I? I find it hard to see myself getting on stage and singing after that. If she dies, that's a huge part of me gone, and I'm not sure I'm going to make it.

It was a billion-to-one shot that our marriage would survive. And our marriage survived. From the age of seventeen until now. Fifty-eight years at the time of writing. This is what it means to "go back" with someone. And we go back, almost to the very beginning; back to Pontypridd and playing on the streets and Marney's shop; back to the phone box and the dance halls and the fields and living together for eight years in Cliff Terrace, raising our son. Back to the man I was then, before everything took off and all the show business happened, which is just layers on top of that, really. And she knows how to peel those layers back and when I'm with her, I'm me, like with no one else.

And we sit together, like any other married couple, and we eat and we watch the television and we talk and we talk, and we talk. It's very simple: we love one another. That's the bottom line. We love one another, and that's why we're still together.

That question that Elvis Presley asked me, all those years ago: "What do you take to stay sane?" It only occurs to me now how I should have answered that question. I should have said, "It's easy. I have Linda."

She holds the connection to who I am. Not just Tom Jones, but also, far more importantly, that other guy, Tommy Woodward from Laura Street.

But I already told you about him.

ACKNOWLEDGMENTS

Thank you to Giles Smith, who helped me with the words and whose gentlemanly presence helped ease the path of these stories.

To my family, with love and gratitude.

To all those in the musical world who did even the smallest thing to help me along the way, thank you.

And to all who have appreciated what I do, I tip my hat.

PHOTO CREDITS

All photos copyright © Tom Jones and family, except where otherwise stated.

INDEX